WE WERE NEVER SAINTS

CHEYANN LARUE

we were never saints

CHEYANN LARUE

IN THE END, what damage did I have? What was left with? Some nightmares? A scar on my shoulder that woke me in the middle of the night, flaring up with minimal anxiety? For all that plagued me, it was nothing compared to the damage that had been done to *them,* to the Kingsleys.

Even now, with the back of my thighs rubbed raw against the rough grain of the old wooden chair, sitting in this abandoned barn with its ceiling slats rotted and falling through, I can see the stars. I have a view. *They* didn't have a view. They watched their books crisp, their photos glow red and disappear. They watched their life slip away.

It's been a constant circular wonder of mine, what *they* thought about as they took their last breath. Morbid, I know, but perhaps more reasonable now that I am likely to die myself. They were afraid if my thoughts were any clues into their final moments.

I'm afraid. I'm scared this is all that's left of my life, and no one will ever know what became of Allyson Parrish.

"Where are they *now,* Ally?" The Man With the Torn Smile questions.

Like all the previous times he has asked, and I have answered, I know he will not be satisfied. The Kingsleys are dead. If all my hopes and prayers could not bring them back, then his torture certainly won't.

then, june

"PINECONES ARE LIKE POISON TO PIRATES," I said over the low babble of the song on the radio.

Pulling my gaze from the stars outside the window, I turned it to Grey. He didn't jump into our game leaving me to feel silly, immature even, in the quiet. Had he outgrown the game? No, he seemed off. His eyes remained fixed on the pavement ahead as if he hadn't heard me. The vehicle made a right, steering down a dirt road. *My* dirt road. *Was he taking me home?*

Confused, I waited for him to tell me why we were there. The seventies-style brick rancher didn't feel like home. Not when I had spent my middle school nights studying in my bedroom overlooking the oak in the back-yard, and not as Grey placed the Jeep into park out front, still saying nothing. It felt like my mother's house. It was a place I'd go when required, much like school, but not *home*. Home was the Kingsley's.

"Sorry—what did you say?" Grey asked. His voice came

flat, absent like he had been since we left for our date earlier in the afternoon.

"What are you thinking?" I pried.

Normally, I didn't need to ask. We grew out of the habit once we'd learned each other well enough to simply *know*. I basked in my apprehension in the growing space between us that was usually filled with his chatter, with philosophy quotes, or ideas for a new novel he was working on.

"Oh, God. You're not breaking up with me, are you?" My mind scrambled to find a basis for my unease. With the exception of this moment, the four years I'd spent loving Grey Kingsley had been next to none. He was the only boy I'd ever loved, really. The only one I'd ever cared to.

When we started dating, I thought I had jipped the system somehow. Most people never find their soulmate or have to wait their whole lives. It seemed unfair to the rest of the world that I found mine on the first try. I feared he was starting to doubt that I was his.

College was just around the corner, and with it would come a vast new world. Grey would encounter a sea of women far more outgoing, self-confident, and self-assured than I was. Perhaps he was feeling the weight of my attachment. Maybe I was an anchor, and he was nervous about telling me so. I prayed that wasn't true, that it was just my left shoulder, just the devil whispering into my ear.

His dark curls, as full of volume as if he had spent the day on the Spanish coast, compressed as his head tilted back into the seat. He howled in a fit of laughter. "Are you— are you serious?" He managed to get out in between breaths. "You think I would break up with you? Al, do you not remember how long I had to convince you that you even *liked* me?"

My worry subsided as my scrambled thoughts snapped

back into place. The world had tilted for no reason at all other than futile teenage insecurity.

His apple eyes, granny smith green, held mine for a split second before he broke the distance. Pressing his lips to mine, he held my chin steady between his thumb and index finger. I'd always loved how he kissed as if our lips alone were not enough to secure us together.

His figure was strong and solid beneath his hoodie, my favorite of his. I'd liked it even before he'd cut the sleeves last summer, making it what he called 'year-round fashion.' The porch light cast out, refracting off the pale scar on his chin. On instinct, I ran my fingers across the indentation as I often did when it caught my attention. He grabbed my hand, bringing my fingers to his lips.

"If I ever broke up with you, I'd be at your door begging you to take me back five minutes later. That'd be my limit. Five minutes of not knowing what you would say next before I couldn't bear it." He said before exiting to hold open the passenger's side door. I took the hand he extended, wrapping my pale fingers around his tanned ones, and stepped out into grass coated in early summer dew.

"Is that why you've brought me to my house instead of yours? So you could have a door to beg at?" I joked half-heartedly. He smirked, finding my quips clever, even the ones I used against him.

"I'm just stressed about this whole college thing. My *dad* really wants me to take the scholarship to Brown but *I* want to go to Berkeley with you."

Looping my arm through his elbow, he guided me up the steps to the porch. I should have let my mother know before showing up. I was seventeen, and technically, I lived there. As if I was an intruder standing on my mother's

WELCOME mat, I felt anything but welcome. I debated using the doorbell to announce my arrival. I hadn't slept in my own bed in months. Outside of the weekly dinner, I barely set foot in this house. I fumbled with my keys while Grey continued.

"Before you say anything— it's not *just* you guiding my decision. I've always wanted to live in California. Go to the beach anytime I want. Maybe learn to surf from some beach rat named Jacob or something."

"Jacob?" I laughed. "That is the least stereotypical surfer name I can imagine. Not Kai, or Ken, or Johnny?"

"Like Johnny Tsunami?" He teased. "Alright, Al. What-ever the dude's name is!" I glared playfully, and he held his hands up in defense. "I guess it's why I've been in a mood. I'm sorry for not saying anything sooner; I didn't want it to weigh down the night. I thought I could hide it better." Grey hung his head in shame while I giggled at his absurdity.

"Grey, it's funny that you're apologizing because it is so unnecessary." My features gave way to the concern I felt beneath my giddiness. "You don't have to hide what you feel from me." A strange look flitted across his face. "If you want to talk or need some time alone to sort things out right now— that's okay."

His hand moved to cover mine from where I had placed it on his arm in reassurance. It was rare to see Grey emotional. Contrary to our night so far, his mood was predominantly cheerful, happy, even cocky. If he cried, it would be a first for us and not a milestone I ever cared to reach. I'd never wanted to be responsible for hurting him or to see the result of him being hurt by something else. Grey was beyond capable of caring for himself, but it didn't change how protective I felt. I couldn't protect him from making this decision, though. No matter what he chose, he was going to disappoint someone. I hoped it wasn't himself.

"Thank you for understanding. I love you, Ally. Always." He kissed me once more before departing. He didn't promise to see me in the morning or promise to call when he arrived home. I contributed his behavior to the decision he had to make.

My mother and Michael were asleep when I came in around ten, and I didn't bother to wake them. I brushed my teeth, keeping my phone on the counter for Grey's 'Made it.' text. Climbing into bed, I switched on the TV to something mindless. After an episode, I rechecked my phone. The five minutes he couldn't go without talking to me had ticked up to another thirty after he should have been home.

I tried his sister when he didn't answer my third phone call. When Charlie Kingsley, my best friend, who picked up even when she was showering, did not answer, I felt I had reason enough to take my keys off the hook and drive over. I didn't want to be the overbearing girlfriend, so I resigned myself to ensuring his car was parked safely in the drive. I needed confirmation that this something-terrible-has-happened feeling was all in my head.

In the car, I played through worst-case scenarios. The closer I crept to their street, I'd almost entirely convinced myself that I was being overly paranoid. There had been no swerve marks in the road, no tire tracks going into the ditch, and no jeeps overturned on the highway.

In the distance, smoke billowed up through the trees, and I felt relief. The Kingsleys were always ones to celebrate with a bonfire. Charlie and Grey would take the stage alongside me later that month to accept their diplomas. They had gotten into all their choice schools. It was a pretty good reason to celebrate. I had been silly to worry.

As much as I had come to feel a part of their family, they still deserved to have moments alone, independent of me. We had the rest of our lives to be intertwined. I would not intrude.

I'd planned to turn around in their driveway when relief froze like ice beneath my skin. Dread stole the comfort from the air. As their house came into view, I realized the smoke had not been made from a backyard bonfire but from the house itself, which sat before me engulfed in flames.

Horrorstruck, I noticed Grey's Jeep parked in the open garage bay. With shaky hands, I dialed 911 and provided them with the address while my tires kicked up stones from the gravel until my car sat in the yard, only a few feet from their porch steps. The operator warned me to wait for authorities, but her breath was wasted. I let my phone fall to the floorboards, already sprinting towards the door. If there was even a chance, I had to take it.

The doorknob wasn't hot like I expected it to be, not like the movies. It was unlocked, as it always was, and I immediately choked on smoke. I fought the idea that I had just opened the door to an oven and that everything and everyone inside was already baked. Stepping in, I called out their names.

Ahead in the living room, fire consumed the sizeable white sectional where we had sprawled out for Tom Hanks nights, for trivia, for sleepovers with our friends. To the left were the stairs, and if I could make it up, then maybe I could throw something through a window. Give the space enough air until the firefighters arrived to save us all. I knew I wouldn't be able to drag them out myself but if I could buy them time, that would be enough to make this risk worthy.

I called their names again, but I was only met by the crackle of fire. The fire had become its own storm, wreaking havoc on the house and everything inside it.

Marilyn, my honorary mother, was probably face down in the kitchen where she'd gone for a glass of wine before bed. Charlie was likely passed out atop her blush comforter from smoke inhalation, her nose tucked between the pages of the latest issue of Vogue. I pictured it catching fire, leaving scars on her perfect face where there should be none.

She was the only person I knew who still bought magazines, and at that moment, I hated her for it. I hated the flammable stacks she kept piled around her room, which had become so much more dangerous than their digital counterparts. I hated the books Grey kept lined across his shelves, providing fuel to the enemy.

I imagined Grey walking to clear his head, wandering around the woods surrounding the outlying fields behind the property. I imagined him down by the beaver dam, his headlamp bouncing across the landscape, the leaves crunching under his Redwings. I wished for him to be anywhere but here, anywhere safe.

I believed I could save them. Before the sickening crack came from the ceiling above me. Before the plaster fell gently like snow into my hair, and the beam came crashing down, pinning me in place on the oriental rug in the foyer. My lungs compressed beneath the wood, deeming me incapable of calling out any longer. The burning was absolute agony as the skin melted from my shoulder, but it was them that hurt me the most. The thought that I had failed them, had failed us all, when I lost consciousness.

TWO

now, june

"PINECONES ARE LIKE POISON TO PIRATES." *I echo, staring out at the road. Grey smiles warmly back from the corner of my eye.*

"House fires hurt like hell." He retorts. My head snaps in his direction in time to see his skin melt off his body and the car swerve off the road.

I wake up from the nightmare and recognize nothing but books. For a moment, I think I'm in Grey's room surrounded by literature until the text seems too close, the spines threatening to fall over on me. The colors are all wrong. The teal walls and burgundy shelves that had been painted to match the front door are no longer where they should be. I'm ripped from the past to the present in seconds, only fragments of me feeling like they returned at all. It's disorienting.

Oh, right. It all comes flooding back, and I remember where I am.

I've been here a week and no longer understand why people think relocating will allow them to outrun their problems. I've brought all mine with me. England is no different than home. It's just another place where they don't exist.

The entire plane ride from Virginia, I was riddled with anxiety. Unexcited to be heading somewhere new, I felt only panicked. I was getting further away from all I had left of them. At least at home, I could be sure they had been real. Here, sometimes, it feels like I've made them up.

My therapist tells me I have an adjustment disorder. I don't like when she's right, but I can't deny she was onto something. Everything is changing again, and I hate it. Everyone seems to think *this* change will be good for me. I've been going along with it, not because they think it will be good, but because they haven't given me a choice.

After the fire, I rescinded my acceptance to Berkeley. How could I go? I didn't want to be a songwriter anymore. I didn't want to be anything. When fall came, my classmates moved into their dorms while I stayed at home. More specifically, I stayed in my room.

I never wandered into communal spaces, careful not to be seen or heard. Still, my stepfather felt my presence as if I somehow had the power to drag the rest of the house into my depression. I did everything he asked. When he had me committed, I worked the program. When he sent me to therapy, I showed up every week, and although I was never on time, I never missed a session. It wasn't enough. He wanted me out.

"You're going to live with your aunt." My mother said when she broke the news. I waited for her to finish the sentence. *You're going to live with your aunt and uncle in Bel-Air.* She didn't. Nothing was funny anymore. I couldn't remember to laugh at even the rare jokes that occurred in my mind.

With no response, my mother sighed in exhaustion.

"You've barely left this room in a year, Allyson. You were supposed to get a summer job. Go to college. Ever since..." she trailed off. "Listen, you used to love it when Libby came for the summer. She's very excited to have you stay for a while."

My mother made it sound all sweet like maybe it was a decision I got to make on my own. Like I could say no. So, I did. I said no when I was packing. Or rather, she was packing around me. I said no even as she and my stepdad, Michael, were putting me on the plane to England. I kept saying no, but they didn't listen. It was easier, I suppose, to get rid of me.

It isn't that I didn't like my aunt. I loved Libby. I loved her alternative lifestyle with her fridge full of organic vegan shit, free of nut oils and colored dye, and her lack of modern amenities. I loved that she was always covered in dust and clay from whatever sculpture she had been commissioned to create.

In fact, before the fire, Libby was the only family member I had been close to. So, it wasn't that I didn't want to be around her; I didn't want her to be around *me*, not like this.

I wanted to preserve her image of my innocence, bared in denim overalls, tripping through the sprinklers in the Virginia summers. I wanted her to still see me as the little girl who dropped a sparkler on her toe that Fourth of July but didn't stop smiling. One Band-Aid and I was up and running again.

But a Band-Aid can't fix this, and I don't want her perception to morph into the crumbling girl I see looking back at me from the mirror. The girl I'm staring at now in the gold frame Libby has perched on a shelf across from my bed. I need to turn it down. I don't like the reflection when I jolt awake. My haunted eyes are frozen inside the face of a stranger. I don't even recognize myself anymore.

"Ally! Did you drink all the soy milk?" Libby yells from the kitchen, interrupting my self-assessment.

Libby has a flat in Brixton. It's two stories high and has a small yard, or rather, "garden," as it's more commonly known in London. She's built a greenhouse in the back to act as her studio. The only bathroom and bedroom are upstairs. This was her only reservation for my moving in, where I would stay.

The building was old, Victorian-era old, and had been constructed with a wide staircase to accommodate the travel of larger luxurious pieces of furniture up to the top floor for the original owners. This was before the building was split to accommodate three apartments instead of one home. Libby's portion housed the original entry and the original staircase.

The old foyer, now her living room, is packed tightly with a small sofa placed before a TV that still had an antenna. The space should feel claustrophobic, but I've taken to it, finding the closeness of its comforts cozy rather than crowded.

With the gap under the stairs not being utilized, Libby added a small library where she could store all the flipbooks she'd collected over the years showcasing her favorite art exhibitions. It's where my twin-sized bed has been implanted, with less than three feet of space at the end.

The two arches sustaining the structure of the stairs have been flocked with curtains, allowing me to employ privacy when I wished for it, which was more often than not. Unfortunately, the thin fabric helped little with sound blocking. I roll over and cover my face with my duvet, hoping she'll assume I'm still asleep if I don't answer.

"Ally!" Libby yells again. "We don't sleep until noon in this flat!" She chirps like a parakeet, no doubt peeking around the curtains by the closeness of her voice.

"You don't ever sleep." I retort, adding my pillow to the comforter already over my head.

"Coffee is in the kitchen. Black like your soul with a sprinkle of cream and half a pound of sugar. Just the way you like, Al."

I hear the swoosh of the curtain falling back closed and picture her returning to the kitchen in her velvet kimono and yoga pants like some art student. I warm slightly to the idea of leaving my cocoon to join her. A broken girl isn't everyone's ideal houseguest, but Libby has been sweet.

She's always had a soft spot for me. When I lost my father, she lost her brother. We experienced that grief together when I was only twelve, and she was twenty-five. I'm nineteen now, and we seem to be the only two still grappling with that loss. I think that's why she's been so kind as to let me crash here until university starts in a couple of months. I feel like I'll never move on, but I've been too harsh. I've been the closest to happiness here.

At home, my mother avoided big, heavy, unpleasant subjects. Instead, she preferred little ones. Who had slighted her at work, what rude thing her boss had done, how someone had cut her off in traffic. These were the events she liked to sit at the foot of my bed and recount while I tried to numb myself from the world. Whenever I'd mention *them*, she'd mention my next therapy appointment as if to redirect the conversation to a more appropriate time and place. Libby isn't like my mother. She listens.

On my first night here, the night terrors hit with double their usual harshness—the distance stirring my separation anxiety into overdrive. Libby brought me a glass of milk and talked me through my bad dreams and memories. She read to me from Grey's favorite book. She played with my hair until I fell back asleep.

I smile when I hear the fridge open and contents being shuffled around as she searches frantically for her bullshit soy milk. I would never touch that crap. No matter how desperate I was.

The smell of coffee infiltrates the layers over my nose, and my stomach churns. My mouth anticipates the taste of it. I follow the sound of the radio station playing 80s hits and stumble into the kitchen. Turning the volume down on the old machine, I grasp for my coffee like a knight reaching for the holy grail.

"Whoa, hot momma," Libby says, wiggling her eyebrows.

I realize I am still wearing the lace jumpsuit from my outing last night. I groan at how my skin must look underneath it, at how the lace would have imprinted into my flesh like pink and pale tattoos, like scars— or burns. Absentmindedly, I reach for the mark on my shoulder left by the beam and feel relief as my cool fingertips trail across it.

"Why do you insist on getting up so fucking early?" I ask her incredulously.

"We can't all sleep until noon Ally. Or curse like a sailor. You never used to curse like this." She remarks more to herself than me.

"Well. I used to be a different person, L." I retort, using her least favorite nickname.

"Please don't call me that." She gripes from her spot at the table. Her strawberry-blonde hair is disheveled and sticks out in all directions. Her messy bun is secured together loosely by a pair of chopsticks. A strand springs free, falling to her face. She makes no move to push it away.

Libby is thirty-two now and still in her prime. She's flawless: no crow's feet, no hint of a wrinkle line forming around her lips. She's utterly untouched by the tells of age. Tells most women start to show in their late twenties. I wonder vainly if it's her passion that has allowed her to outrun time and if I, too, will be so lucky.

While I admire her, she sips her coffee using her left hand despite being right-handed. Her dominant hand languidly holds a copy of today's press, stopping every few sentences to peer up at me from over her glasses. Her legs are crossed, always the same leg over the other. Being my father's sister, she shares these mannerisms of his that I had long forgotten. I wonder if the movements were something they picked up from their father or if they even picked up on it at all.

"I didn't drink your crappy ass milk, but I can pick up more from the market. Just make me a list."

"Mmmm. Deal." She mutters. She alternates from sipping her coffee to chugging orange juice from a half-gallon container. "How's it coming on the job front?"

I nod, hoping she will drop the subject.

Truthfully, I haven't looked too much into jobs. I try to make it through the day without too much pain; if I do that successfully, it's a win. I also have yet to find a new therapist in London, thinking if I let enough time pass, I'll get away without having to at all. Libby's gone easy on me since my mother spends every second of our daily five-minute conversations talking about nothing but my "health."

Speaking with her is nauseating; she talks *at* me but never *to* me. She asks questions and then tunes out the answers. Like a mirage of a mother, she pretends she is here for me. Like a mirage of a daughter, I pretend I'm not here at all. Every night, I hang up the phone, leaving out that I've found my own form of therapy, which has proven more effective than any they've subjected me to.

As for the job, it's only been a week. I don't know why Libby's so gung-ho about this, but I attempt to placate her.

"Don't give me the nod along, Al. How's it coming?" Libby asks, turning the entirety of her focus onto me.

Fuck.

"Fine." I keep nodding.

Libby sighs. "Why don't you do something with music, Al? You're so talented, and you have almost two months before you start university. Wouldn't you like to have some money to take with you?"

"I have plenty of money."

It's true. Between what Michael-the-stepdad sends me and the trust my father set up, I'm able to pay half of Libby's rent and cover university costs without issue. I also have *their* money, but I have refused to touch it. I haven't even looked at the account since a lawyer stopped by and informed me of it.

"Have you even set up the account they left you?" She inquires as if she can see into my mind. I decide something in my expression must have given me away. I've always been too easy to read.

The Kingsleys were like family to me for four years, but I had never expected they would leave me anything, let alone a small inheritance. I also never expected they'd die, so what do I know? I don't *want* their money. I wanted a future for them. Now, one reminds me of the other, and I try not to think about it too much.

"That's really none of your business." I snap at her.

"Kind is different than nice," something Grey used to say replays in my head. *So much for kind, Grey.* We have another one-sided conversation. I talk to him, but he doesn't answer.

"How do you even know about that?"

"Michael." She says simply. She migrates from the table to the sink to clear the dishes that have begun filling it.

Fucking Michael.

I make a note to call him later and share how I feel about him telling everyone my business. If he wants me to heal, he needs to butt out of my life and go back to digging in my mom's pants or whatever it is that he does. Okay, bad thought. Maybe not that.

"What are you going to do today?" She questions as she stacks mismatched plates in the green cabinetry.

Flashes of Charlie laughing and loading the dishwasher flip through my mind. Her blonde hair falling in a satin curtain between us as she would chatter on about one crush or another. I flinch, standing up abruptly from where I had been seated at the island.

"A shower seems like a good place to start," I say quietly, leaving her behind. Though my behavior doesn't escape her notice, she doesn't try to stop me. I feel at war with my better nature. As much as I want to let her in, I'd rather be alone. The war ends when the warm water hits my skin and washes away some of the pain.

then, july

I WAS BORN with a degenerative bone disease. When I was eight, I went into remission. My body became resilient. My bones began to offer a sturdy frame to my structure. It felt like my wishes had finally been granted, and I was able to return to a normal life.

After spending so much time alone in the hospital, I was excited to attend school. It thrilled me to be around kids my age, to figure out what kind of clique I would fit into, and to wonder if I would have those adolescent experiences like the ones I had grown up reading about in books. I was disappointed to discover that I was mostly alone, even in health.

Word spread around my middle school once my former condition had gotten out. I was forever branded as the 'sick girl.' Kids were mean, and the few who weren't were afraid to befriend me, afraid they'd be spun into the rumor mill themselves. "Be careful around that one. You don't want to catch it." was carried through the whispers in the hall. I had lab partners and acquaintances with whom I shared school projects, but *friends* didn't come easy to me.

It wasn't until the summer before freshman year that my luck began to change. The first weeks of July were the turning point of my life. I never knew how much she would impact me, how one person could influence every moment, the butterfly effect that was Charlie Kingsley.

A traffic sign forever altered whatever path I may have gone down. The crushing of metal, the scraping of glass, and the carelessness of a girl applying make-up instead of paying attention to the road. She'd stepped out of the KIA that had slammed into the back of my vehicle, marched over to me in a fit of rage, and threw out accusations of how I had come to a sudden stop in front of her. *At a stop sign.*

"You were driving irresponsibly, and quite frankly, I'm disappointed in you," She snarked, snatching my ID card from my hand. "*Allyson.*" She finished, an air of superiority around her now that she knew my name. I already knew hers from the photos I'd taken of her ID and insurance card.

"Okay, Charles." I joked, hoping to provoke her. It worked.

"*Charles*?!" She yelled. "That's just rude. It says 'Charlie' right there!" She corrected, pulling out her ID to prove her point.

I saw that Charlie was fifteen, a year older than me. Her ID was from Illinois, where driver's licenses could be obtained a year and three months earlier than they could here. I stared at the plastic, entirely jealous, prepared to disguise it beneath layers of sarcasm.

"Does it? Because Charles is a dad name, and you kind of sound like a dad right now. One that is *really* bad at drag. Let me guess— you were doing your makeup when you rear-ended me?"

Amidst all the chaos, she'd forgotten to put her mascara tube away. As she ranted, it swung about still in her hand.

The narrative behind our accident was clear, and she looked ridiculous as she stood before me. She huffed, a black streak running down her cheek, perfectly unable to find an excuse.

"I'm pretty sure your state-issued ID said you were only fourteen, so who's really going to get in trouble here?" she asked, crossing her arms in front of her as she recovered.

"Well, my stepdad is a cop. This is a private road that we own. And he asked me to drive down and pick up the mail. I think I'll be just fine, thank you. What were you even doing down here? No trespassing signs excite you or something?"

Her eyes went wide.

"I was exploring, okay? We just moved here, and it's quite a bit different than Chicago...a lot less to do." She sighed, sitting beside me on the dirt road comprised mostly of dust and broken oyster shells. I couldn't find fault with that. Matthew's was basically a peninsula. There was one way in and one way out. No matter what direction you drove, you would end up at the water, at another dead end.

Considering her car was practically totaled, and my dad's old Ford pickup had merely a dented bumper, we compromised. With minimal damage on my end, I'd agreed to skip filing a police report and called a tow truck instead. As we waited, she had the nerve to ask if I wanted coffee. For reasons I still don't understand, I said yes.

Maybe it was how straight she stood for a teenager. Her shoulders weren't slumped from hours bent over a phone looking at social media. Or that she had poise somehow, even with her cheek vandalized. I was drawn to her as I would become drawn to all the Kingsleys.

From that day forward, we became inseparable. My somber July nights were transformed by energetic dance parties in Charlie's bedroom with her younger sister, Gigi. During the day, we would spend our time at thrift stores, where she would search for a particular fabric or a garment with a specific color and sheen.

Charlie was a designer. All the clothes she wore were her creations, and I was her stand-in model while she fitted them to size. Most of what was created in modern times was a copy—a collage of many things that had already been. Every song is influenced by another, and someone else's words inspire every book. I thought it impossible to create anything new, but Charlie found a way. In a world of replicas, she had originality.

She used plastics, wrappers, and bottles to design dresses, including one made of bottle caps. Her latest project involved creating a dress liner from recycled pesticide labels and stringing tiny butterflies from a vintage Chanel wedding gown found in a trash pile. The final product was the most beautiful dress I had ever seen. It was stunning from a distance, and it was a warning up close. Pesticides had been killing the monarchs, and Charlie never shied away when there was a statement to be made.

For a fifteen-year-old, she made more money than most adults I knew. Marilyn, her mother, suggested she post the dresses for sale online. I'd model them in her TikTok videos, and she'd attach a link where people could purchase the one-of-a-kind garment.

The butterfly dress was sold to an art enthusiast and activist in New York City for three thousand dollars. He appreciated the message and found her level of skill impressive. They insisted the man was overpaying while he insisted he was getting a bargain. He had written back, "I'm offering what I feel the piece is worth now, but you see, I'm stealing from you. In ten years, your designs will sell for ten times what I've paid, and I will have one of the originals."

While Charlie designed, I wrote. I'd scribble lyrics in my journal while she sketched silhouettes in hers. As time went on, she began to subtly encourage me to pick up my neglected guitar. She strategically placed it around the room so I'd have to move it to grab her a pin or take a seat. Finally, I gave in and picked it up. It felt so right in my hands, so safe to sing in her room, that I never put it back down.

Every time I created a new song, Libby would be on the phone while Marilyn, Charlie, and Gigi gathered around with excitement to listen. Marilyn crafted a banner labeled "The Sunset Sessions" that she would proudly display whenever I performed in one of Charlie's latest designs. She would capture the moments on her phone, and Charlie would urge me to allow her to share the videos, believing it would be an incredible marketing opportunity. Although I was comfortable being featured in her videos, I preferred to remain behind the scenes. Having experienced a lot of attention in middle school, I was not keen on being in the spotlight again.

With all their support and encouragement, these girls became my family. Mine hadn't been all that present in my life. My mom drifted in and out, switched from doting to distant. She had been increasingly vacant ever since I switched hospitals as a kid. When I moved to the new facility, she stayed with me every night at first. Then, her visits became less frequent. They turned to one night a week, then once a month, and finally, once every few months.

After I got better, my father quit, and we moved back home. But even there, it still felt like visiting; only now I was visiting *her*. The divide grew after he died. While I expected us to find each other in the loss, we fell further out of touch. She blamed me, I think, for his death.

Marilyn had become more my mother than my own. She owed me nothing, certainly not her time or money. Yet she took me on every weekend trip to the Outer Banks. She let me tag along to their mother-daughter spa days and every homemade meal around their kitchen table.

She worked from home as a marketing consultant for a big firm, and though she wasn't hurting financially, I felt indebted to all she had spent on me. When I'd protest, she'd insist. She told me it was my cut for helping Charlie to ease my guilt. She didn't know it was payment enough just to be included in their world. But, it was Marilyn's nature to give. She had an understated elegance and a genuine kindness. I wanted to be just like her. Like all of them, really. These women were my role models.

As our first summer came to a close, I was faced with another event that would alter my life forever—the arrival of Charlie's brother, Grey Kingsley.

Grey had spent the summer months backpacking with his father, James, across coastal towns in the northeastern United States. I had seen glimpses of his face in photographs around the house and heard endless stories about him from the girls. How he had climbed El Capitan when he was only thirteen. How involved he was with the local volunteers in Chicago, from where they had moved earlier in the year. How he wrote like Charlie designed, without merit, without reserve— words pouring from him like sketches poured from her. Marilyn assumed he probably had three or more completed novels sitting on his shelves waiting to be published, though he was too modest to ever let anyone read them.

I was curious about this boy. So much so that he became like a legend; I'd quiet down when they mentioned his name like I was eavesdropping on celebrity gossip. He wasn't a person to me but a character from my favorite stories, like Robin Hood or Peter Pan. He was good, interesting, and familiar. I felt like I knew him the way people felt like they knew their favorite band.

It hadn't occurred to me that he'd come home one day. The legend would be personified. In physical form, I knew, like most things, the shine would tarnish as he became human. I thought I was prepared.

In rural Virginia, everyone has a yard or a field pretending to be a yard. The Kingsleys' home was no exception to the rule. Their house was an old Civil War-era property built to house soldiers. The white siding was aged and antiqued, framed by its wide wrap-around front porch. The home reminded me of a dollhouse that had been scaled to size. Marilyn always left the door open. She liked the natural light that filtered through the screen, brightening even the darkest corners of the foyer. She was the only person I knew who enjoyed the summer humidity and the heavy breeze of the country nights as they intermingled with the air conditioning.

It was one of these sticky nights that I awoke in Charlie's bed and peeled myself off the sheets. The moonlight cascaded through the open window onto the floor, highlighting the undisturbed dust particles where they rested. The curtains rustled in the wind as I tiptoed out of the room towards the kitchen, wearing nothing but my satin pajama set.

Pulling open the fridge, I searched for the milk. I liked

how it cooled and soothed my stomach like lavender for the soul. I shut the door with more force than required, flustered that the object of my desire seemed to have disappeared. I sighed, realizing I'd have to settle for water.

I was opening the cabinet to find a glass when the hair on the back of my neck began to stand up, and I knew I wasn't alone. Charlie was where I left her in bed; the old floorboards would have given her away if she had followed me. Marilyn's sleep apnea machine was actively whirring as I padded down the hall, telling me she was still soundly sleeping. Gigi was at a friend's, and Grey and James weren't due home until Sunday. It was Friday.

I mapped out where the knife block would be on the counter and estimated how quickly I could reach it. Five seconds. That's all I needed. Not that a knife would be any match to this intruder if they had a gun. Still, I had to try. I was fourteen. I knew nothing about self-defense, but I was small and could use that to my advantage.

I moved as fast as I could. Not even a breath had passed before the handle of the blade was in my palm. It did me little good. The intruder was already there, pinning me against the granite as my only defense was knocked out of my grasp.

"Who are you, and why are you in my home?" A man's voice growled in my ear.

His home? I tried to get a look at his face, but he held me still, so I could not move. This must be James, Marilyn's husband. They must have come home early. Had she failed to tell him I'd be here?

"My name is Ally, and I was invited; thank you." I spat out the words, not caring if I offended him.

He released me at once, stepping back. I rubbed my wrists, spinning to get a better look. My scowl was fixed in place, ready to confront him. To ask if this was how he treated all his house guests.

It was not the figure of a man but a boy that met my gaze. The most beautiful boy I'd ever seen. The pictures didn't do him justice. He appeared almost grown. His face still held to adolescence while his body had begun to take the shape of a man's. It was easy to see why I thought this was Charlie's father and not her brother.

"Oh, you're that girl. Charlie's friend? Ally, right?" He said casually, like he didn't just assault me. Leaning back against the island, he crossed his arms over his chest. It was upsetting that I found him cute. I was angry he hadn't yet apologized. I noticed the milk jug on the counter behind him next to his glass, and my annoyance grew—*the milk thief.*

"Yup. I believe that's what I literally just said." I managed to sputter out bitterly.

I returned my attention to hunting down where I had left my cup. Retrieving it, I stepped into the moonlight that poured in from the window. In the pale glow, we could distinguish each other's faces clearly. We took on a precision that had been lost in the shadows.

He stopped breathing as I leaned around him, invading his personal space the way he'd invaded mine. Our eyes locked as the bare skin of my arm brushed against his. My fingers wrapped around the carton sat atop the counter behind him and moved away as I filled my glass. As I lost proximity, he regained composure.

"You're not the least bit curious about who I am?" He smiled. It was too much of a contrast. Compared to the guy who had just slammed me into the cabinetry, this version was a different person. I decided then I didn't like him. The stories the girls had told offered nothing about his mood swings.

"You're that guy. Charlie's brother? Grey, right?" I glared.

Amusement played across his features as his lips twitched into an even bigger smile.

"Yup." He answered confidently.

I finished with my glass and placed it in the sink before I restored the milk to its rightful place in the refrigerator.

"So," I let the word hang in the air. "you're back now? You'll be here from now on?" I asked, unsure of what answer would satisfy me most.

"I kind of live here, Ally. So yeah, I'll be around." His smile hadn't left, increasing my desire to smack it off him.

"Great." I huffed, starting for the stairs. I was eager to retreat to the safety of Charlie's room full of magazines and scraps of fabric.

"And you?" He turned his head, waiting for an answer. "You'll be around?"

"Are you kidding me? You've been gone all summer, and instead of coming home and introducing yourself, which would be the polite thing, the decent thing, you practically body slam me and accuse me of being an intruder. I'm five foot two. I'm fourteen. You look like more of an intruder than I do, you man-child! And now, what? You're ignoring that even happened?" I hissed. My fists balled at my sides as anger surged inside of me.

"Polite and decent? Are you fourteen or forty, Ally?" He joked at my expense.

"Ugh!" I groaned, starting to walk away again. Charlie's door was just a flight of stairs away. In moments, I'd be inside, free to forget about her hot jerk-wad of a brother. *No, no, Ally. Not hot. Only a jerk-wad.*

"Ally, wait." His voice pleaded genuinely, and I did what he asked despite my better judgment. "I am sorry. About before. I shouldn't have accosted you like that. Please forgive me."

"Why should I?" I was the one acting like a child now. Completely intolerant. And accosted? Now, who was acting like the forty-year-old?

"Because you're Charlie's friend. Her *best* friend, from what she tells me, and I can't have you hating me." He sighed at the end of his sentence, sounding remorseful. Even after his apology, I couldn't shake how he had gotten on my nerves.

"Charles and I can relocate our sleepovers to my house and solve that issue entirely. If you'll excuse me, I'd like to get back to bed."

"Charles? Please tell me you don't actually call her that." He laughed.

"Only when I'm especially angry with her, like right now, for misleading me. She said her brother *wasn't* one of the assholes."

"Ally, you can't relocate." He objected. "If you're never here, you'll never get to know what a nice guy I am. That would be massively inconvenient for me." He retorted, looking away. He'd returned to his chair at the island, sipping the rest of his milk like this was a normal conversation and not a showdown.

I forgot about going to bed. *Massively inconvenient?* That was doubtful. It seemed best for us to see each other as little as possible from here on out. I got the feeling that a destructive relationship with Grey could put a strain on my friendship with Charlie. I refused to let that happen. And I didn't know how to make nice with the guy when he aggravated me every five seconds. I'd known him for less than 10 minutes, and he was already the most maddening person I'd ever met.

"*Inconvenient? Really?* Being in the same house sounds inconvenient for *me*, not you." I was appalled and unable to conceal it.

"Maybe. But I can't get to know you if you're never here, and I get the feeling that I'd like to. This short exchange has really stirred my interest." He said, smiling even wider than before. He stood to leave the kitchen. Passing me, he paused. "You wouldn't want to break my heart already, would you, Ally?" He joked before mounting the stairs to his room.

I stood stunned, not understanding what had just happened. Understanding even less why I had liked it.

now, june

I WAS RUNNING LATE. It was 9:05. I preferred to be seated by 9, already on my first drink. I had made a schedule, and I was a creature of habit. It was funny, really, how I was never early to anything anymore. Before, I was always early. Early to class, early to my dates with Grey, early to the Kingsley house. It was one of many things that had changed about me after the accident. In fact, now I was perpetually late. Late to therapy, late for dinner with my parents, late for the damn flight to England, but I was never late to the bar. These five minutes were beginning to make me sweat as I waited to cross the street to my usual dive.

It was there, at the corner of Cross and Kingly, where I saw him again. He stood casually, leaning against the aged brick of a pub across the street, lifting the beer every so often from the ledge and raising it to his lips. His stance was one I had seen so many times before: legs crossed, shoulders slumped, but never enough that it could be considered a hunch. It hadn't occurred to me that I had the gesture memorized. I had been programmed to recognize it anywhere in our four years together. To pick it out of a crowd. It was so distinctly *him. Grey.*

The rich, chestnut brown of his hair catches the light under the pub's lamppost, glimmering. The street is clear to walk, but I am not. I have lost all motor function. Frozen, my feet have cemented to the ground, making me power-less to do anything other than watch him.

I wait for him to notice me here. I wonder if he feels the same pull to me that I've always felt to him. If he does, then he'll turn. He'll cross to where I'm standing and say some-thing ridiculous like, "It took you long enough to get here. Twelve months is too long, Al."

But of course, he doesn't.

Instead, his back contorts, his spine lurching forward in laughter. I don't let myself crumple under the disappoint-ment when the sound finally travels to me, and it's the wrong laugh. It wasn't real, just like the 405 times this has happened before. I've learned to shoulder that disappoint-ment. Imagination is a sultry bitch. It is so cruel, yet capti-vating all the same.

Not Grey 406 is simply the latest reverie. I can't recall when I started counting. I guess when it became enough of an issue to take notice. Not Grey 10 was a guy at a bus stop who wore the same colored chucks he did, Not Grey 27 had his dimple, Not Grey 100 held a door in the same fashion, and the list goes on and on. His ghost never lives with me in whole. Like me, he exists only in fragments now.

The enchantment breaks, allowing me to move again.

At last, I cross the street, making my way to the door of the wrong bar, unable to look away from the wrong boy. Every raise of his arm, sway of his hips, and shift of his body weight is unfamiliar. I struggle to remember what had made me so transfixed in the first place.

Like a Master of Ceremonies, the hinges creak loudly, announcing my arrival. My flinch is violent. Luckily, it goes unnoticed by the other patrons, too drunk on conversation and pints to stir their attention towards my noisy intrusion. The bustle is drowning, and exactly what I had wanted. The noise is calming. It is step one in Ally's Do-It-Yourself Program. *This* is my therapy.

The bar is old; the floorboards are knotted to match its age. Little has been done in the way of renovation; instead, the owners chose to preserve, highlighting the building's original candor. I'm no historian, but if I had to guess, I'd date it back to the early seventeenth century. If it weren't for the plants potted in every corner and boughs of ivy climbing the cracks of the ceiling, the room would have appeared more suitable to a ship's hull than a city side street. I like that narrative better: a tavern built for pirates. I imagine Captain Hook drunk, waltzing in to order a drink, and smile lazily to myself.

The same material, the same knotted boards frame all sides. For a moment, I lose my sense of direction and can't tell which way is up. If not for the furniture, I wonder if flipping the room would make everything look the same. Instead of the ceiling, the floor would be overgrown, as if it had been forgotten. I feel more at home here than my usual drinking hole. Well suited in my analogies. Overgrown, forgotten, upside-down. For me, everything's been upside down since I lost them. Or maybe it's always been just me —the upside-down girl.

Step two in my program is whiskey. Moving on from my hesitation, I quickly regain purpose and find my way to a seat in the corner. I'm still trying to adjust to the difference in culture. In America, taking a seat without being asked to sit down is rude. Overseas, it is disrespectful to wait as if someone should have to tell you to take a damn seat already. I think this over and wonder why both make sense.

I make sure to choose a barstool that is far enough from the crowd so that I can keep to myself. I focus on tiny details to maintain my distractions. This is important to me - it's a necessary evil so I don't revert to thinking of him, or any of them. Honestly, it's not that I've taken to drinking; I've taken comfort in finding these small windows. These 'Mirror People' as I've come to refer to them in my head. Examining my neighbors, I spot the similarities in our outward reflections.

The man at the end of the counter is unaccompanied, clutching his glass of amber like it can save him—as if it's a crystal ball that will soon provide him with answers. The haunted look in his eyes has its own gravitational pull, weighing down the room. Our gazes lock briefly, and we both nod in recognition as he spies the same ghoulishness in my own stare.

Wandering on, I become further sustained by an older lady sitting in a booth by the window. She and her girl-friends share the same hair, grayed with age. She projects back their laughter but catches a break from pretending as the conversation shifts. Her face cracks as she turns away from them to stare out the window. I know she isn't seeing the road or the passing cars. Her pupils dilate and flick around, tracing the path of something that isn't there. In this second, she only exists in whatever memory plays out in her head. She's living a half-life. Half of her is here and now, and half of her will forever be then. Whatever then is. Her friend giggles and whispers something in her ear. The half-woman transforms back to the here. Her past self suddenly forgotten.

My earlier antsy behavior has dwindled, and I'm

starting to feel more relaxed. These strangers somehow offer me glimpses into myself. They become familiar. This is step three: Recognition. It's an important part of the process—the most important, even. This is the step that makes me feel less alone.

I'm irritated that step two hasn't been met yet, and as if on cue, the bartender materializes in front of me, throwing a towel over his shoulder as he quirks one daunting dark eyebrow. I know the universal cue for "What do you want?" and I want to tell him, *I do*. Opening my mouth and reciting the simple "whiskey" that generally falls from my lips with ease should be natural. But I've grown tongue-tied, and it has impaired my ability to speak.

For the second time tonight, I'm under a spell. He's not just striking; he's devastating. Of all the people in the bar, the face of the man in front of me is what I look for the most. The complete and utter tragedy of his dull irises, glazed over, as if incapable of feeling anymore. When he leans forward to assess me more fully, the lights hit them, and sadly, they do not glint; they do not sparkle. This boy has lost his sparkle.

The bartender is tall. He's too tall, really. I imagine there's rarely a doorway he doesn't have to stoop to pass through. Guessing at his height, I'd say six-three, maybe? I wonder if he has brothers and how tall they are. He towers over me while he waits for me to order, and I feel safer somehow, in his shadow. The first sign of his irritation breaks through as he takes a deep breath. More accurately, a huff. Impatiently, he shifts from one foot to the other.

"Are you going to order?" The dark angel asks, his voice as velvety and toxic as I could have imagined if I had gotten that far in my assessment.

I want to beg him to say something else when the last

word leaves his mouth. I want to hear his accent catch on certain words so I can psychoanalyze what each catch means. So I can suppose if those words meant more to him than the others. If the way he says "order" with such disdain has a reason. Does he despise taking people's orders? Is he ex-military, and does the idea of taking another order bothers him? Or maybe it's something to do with his father? My last guess surprises me because it has such a lack of basis. It also surprises me because I know it's the correct guess.

Why am I so fascinated by him? No, *enthralled*. Enthralled seems a better fit.

"Like today?" He pressures, wanting me to crack beneath it. I debate not answering to spite him, but what would that do? My desire for alcohol is more significant than my desire to see what would come of a pointless experiment. If I did not answer, he'd likely walk off and not return, leaving me to focus on far less exciting subjects.

"Water and whiskey," I say, surprised at how sure and confident it sounds.

After my exaggerated pause, I expected my words to come out unsteady. I expected to look away in embarrassment that I had been caught ogling so fiercely. But my voice did not waver, and I did not look away. I can tell he expected a similar reaction. His eyes widen enough for me almost to make out their color, and a smirk turns up the corner of his lips.

"I take it you'd like those separate?" He steps away, not bothering to wait for my response, and I can't fight my smile. He's a smart ass too.

He leans against the counter, balancing his weight against his hip as he pours my drink. He steadies himself with a hand on the bar's edge as he fills my water. He keeps finding support holds like the air is too dense without them. It's another trait I recognize—the weight of expectation.

It's how I know I was right about his father because I got my instability from my mother. After the accident, after losing *him*, she would appear in my doorway. At first, she was full of motherly concern. As the months passed, the concern faded to anxiety. The anxiety transformed into resentment as I continued not to move on, not to meet her expectations of what grieving should look like. Her empathy faded as her new husband began to toss around his input. Her maternal demeanor dissolved as time inched forward. I sunk deeper into my bed with each passing day. The same expectational weight forced me down; my bones fossilized in the foam of my mattress.

I roll my eyes when the bartender returns and places the water in front of me without ice.

"Not up to par?" He asks, his voice laced with judgment.

"I forget you guys don't serve shit with ice here," I say more to myself than him.

I miss American food. I miss my drinks coming to me cold with condensation on the glass, not lukewarm from the tap. I miss ordering a Coke with the fizz bubbling around the floating cubes. Another round of homesickness spins in my stomach, and I grow nauseous. I shoot the whiskey like medicine, wiping my mouth as I place the empty glass back on the counter.

"Another." I request. I hope it comes out like that—a request, not an *order*. I try to soften the word to make it sound flowery, like it's blossoming from my lips. Instead, it just sounds raw.

He snickers, seemingly out of character for him, and goes to retrieve another.

I'm already brainstorming a list of nicknames for him. "Eyebrows" is at the top. His face is separated into straight planes, and his cheekbones, his jaw are perfectly angular. Really, it's those demanding eyebrows that set off his looks. They're too big for his forehead, too big for his dark eyes. They shouldn't work on his face, but they do. They add to it the way a masterpiece adds to a museum. Making everything else a compliment to their authority. Like his face arranged itself to appease those brows, his features all tilted to meet them like weeds growing towards the sun. The imbalance is alluring, interesting.

Other girls at the bar are giggling and stealing glances in his direction. I try to see what they see with untrained eyes. He's got that tall, dark, and handsome thing going on. His look is unnatural, unparalleled. More like a person who should be in an ad selling liquor, not in a bar pouring it. To them, he's a one-night stand, a James Dean kind of good time. To them, he's a project: a bad boy they want to turn good or a torrid two-week love affair. Their version of him is boring to me. Less compelling than my own.

He sets my second drink down without pause and goes about his work. There's an authenticity about the way he moves. Everything is purposeful. He never takes a break, never stops to stare off into the crowd. When all the orders have been taken, the drinks have been served, and the counter has been wiped down, he finds another thing to busy himself with. Things I would never think of, like changing the dimmer light bulbs or dusting the glasses stored further back on the shelf behind the bar. He has his own distractions, each charming me more than the last.

Maintained by his work ethic, I find it admirable. Somehow, I know him already by these minuscule actions. He's lost like me, like the lady by the window. But he isn't stuck. His perpetual motion propels him forward. What is the thing he's outrunning? So close to his coattails that he's unable to stop or slow down for fear that it might catch up. I'm making more heavy assumptions, but again, I'm sure of their accuracy.

I pull a pen from my purse and scribble lyrics on a napkin. I try to verbalize the way the world would see the man.

Please forgive my face.
Sharp is terrifying; sharp is safe.
Sharp means nobody gets too close to the blade.

It comes out sounding like how I see myself. More about me than the subject I was trying to capture. I crumple up the napkin and shove it into my jacket pocket. I self-reflect enough all the hours I spend in bed.

I notice how the other bartenders also appear to be too aware of his presence. He doesn't seem conscious of how they leave him a wide berth, as if intimidated that they might end up in his path.

His nose replaces his brows as the most interesting part of his face. I look for inclinations that it's been broken before, a bump, a dent, any sign that he's been in a fight. It's perfectly straight. His eyes harbor dark rings underneath them, perhaps from lack of sleep, but there is no purple bruising. I can't locate any evidence to match a violent personality. His only warning is the sharpness I had written about. Outside of his attitude, I can't find a reason why he would be intimidating, let alone feared. Yet, I, too, feel afraid in that inexplicable way.

The fear triggers something inside of me. What am I afraid of? I have nothing left to lose.

Grey and the scar on his chin reappear when I close my eyes. On the side of my glass in the condensation, I trace the pink and white drag across his chin left from a childhood dog bite. It feels like a curse how my thoughts always lead me back. Today marks a year—the anniversary of their death.

The world blurs. The whiskey catches up with me moments after I shoot my second glass, which was a double this time. I didn't order a double, but I suppose the bartender is as perceptive as I am. Step two is accomplished. I like the blur. I like the slow-moving nature the crowd takes on. I like how all the voices flatline into one collective babble. Again, I feel like I'm in the hull of a ship. All of us are underwater. Unclear. Indecipherable.

I trace his scar for the fifth time. I pray to a God I stopped believing in that the glass will transform, and it will be him. Grey, here in London. Nestled into this nook beside me. In an instant, I see the room differently; everything would have a new tint to it, a glow. The energy would affect me differently. I'd pick different people to focus on— different stories to share with him. The laughter would be set apart, individualized. It was the smiles that would fuel me then. Smiles that only seem to mock me now.

I can't lose myself in the what-ifs. They are a false hope. I've given up on false hopes. It's too dangerous a game. The better part of this year was spent living in my mind, creating an alternate reality where Grey was still alive. Still mine. It was my therapist who pointed out how damaging this was to my mental health. I was giving sustenance to an impossible dream that could never be. No amount of effort or trying would change what had happened. So, I started to tear down that fantastical world instead. It took bits of the real one with it. Blocks of my memory are gone or fuzzy. Now, I can't picture it the same. I can't fully imagine how different things would be if he *were* here.

Still, I hear his voice in my head, ranting about how this place would have looked a century ago, how horses and carriages would have been stopped along the street. There'd be a beating of hooves instead of the modern wind of cars whirring past. I've kept his voice preserved in old voicemails and saved videos, but I can't bring myself to listen to them, and my recall alone is beginning to fail. It doesn't carry his tone right.

At the thought of forgetting him, a pit in my stomach opens, swallowing my earlier comforts. Loss creeps up like a shiver before it consumes me. I pull the whiskey glass back to my lips and sip, trying to replace the unpleasant feeling with the swirling heat in my chest.

I turn my head and take in the pack of people. I hunt for a better state of mind, a different story to get wrapped up in. A couple of older gentlemen smack their glasses together. The men have white hair, their faces freckled with moles like trees are freckled with knots to show their age.

When their glasses clink together, the fizzy liquid slops over the edge and lands with a wave on the dark wooden table. A nagging feeling tells me the tables are always sticky, even after a hard scrubbing. I touch the countertop, which seems to be made of the same material as the tables. My suspicions are confirmed. It is sticky. It sits like a film lingering on my finger. I cringe.

"Something else wrong?" The barkeep reappears, pressing both hands to the counter in front of me. I have this image where he'll try to pull his hands off and won't be able to. For the first time, I take in his hands, which are scarred and calloused just like mine. I notice a familiar white line and realize he's a musician. I've had enough guitar strings pop on me to recognize the small lines they leave. I rub my fingers across my marks.

He leans closer to hear my answer. I have to remind myself what he asked. Oh, right. *Is something wrong?*

"No." I lie.

"Sure." His eyes crinkle at the corners. I try to make out what shade they are again but can't. I'm squinting like that will help magically improve my vision, add magnifying spectacles where there are none.

"If you want a picture, get on and ask already." He says, as full of exhaustion as he seems to be of himself.

"Why would I want a picture of you?" I ask, taken aback and disgusted that he would suggest such a thing. Do the other girls think he should be in ads for liquor? Do *they* ask him for photos?

He stares back for a moment, then shakes his head, his body rippling in laughter. It's a rich sound, somehow the right laugh, and I don't let myself stop to think about what that means.

"Okay, well...well, that's just great." He raises his arm to scratch the back of his head, still amused but now with a dash of refreshing humility. "I sound like an arse."

"You do." I confirm with a nod, finding humor in his own, then more seriously: "But no, I don't want a photo of you. I don't know why anyone would."

"Uh, wow. Okay." He says, holding his hands up, pleading for me to stop talking.

"No, I don't mean— I just— What color are your eyes?" It comes out of my mouth before I can stop. Impulse control has not been my strong suit lately.

"Shit brown. And yours?" I jump at the harsh language,

even with his proper English accent wrapped around the words, cushioning them as they exit his mouth. A low rumble makes its way through his body. He is laughing at me again. It's a marvelous sound. Clear yet graveled.

"Blue," I mumble. "My eyes are blue."

He leans over the counter for a better look. I can feel his breath on my nose.

"So, they are." He says, lingering for a moment before returning to work. The whole exchange has been awkward and confusing, though not uncomfortable, and I'm cursed to watch him carry on, following his movements and how his arms flex when he presses the rag onto the surface of the back bar top.

"Are you purposefully flexing?" I inquire while silently cursing my lack of filter. His shoulders are straining against the material of his shirt. The cotton doesn't seem built to stretch and clings to his body in unholy ways.

"Are you getting a good look, then? " he asks, not bothering to face me. His smirk is evident in his tone.

"No," I state in one hard syllable.

"Shame."

Fascinating as he is, I'm unsettled, thinking he might want something from me. Unnerved that he may think *I* want something from *him*. It isn't interest I feel, well, not like *that*.

This guy has become my new source of entertainment since I've stopped watching television. I've been avoiding anything that could resurrect a memory. Everything on TV is filled with love stories and people with supportive best friends, which only serves as a painful reminder of what I've lost. I already have enough reminders on my own.

This boy has quickly become a mystery—a riddle for me to solve with hardly any clues. I appreciate the fun of it without any complications. However, if he starts thinking I want to sleep with him, that would definitely be a big complication.

The conversations carrying on behind me all seem louder than before. The room is shrinking. As the walls close in, my heart speeds up—the boy with the curly hair steps inside, letting the summer breeze trail in behind him. A few ashes from his friend's cigarettes have found their way into his hair and drift in the wind, dancing around like a halo before falling to his shoulders. He catches my stare, lingering. I dart to something else, feeling annoyed with the hoax.

How did I ever think he even remotely looked like Grey? He is shorter by quite a bit. His face is broad, and his nose is a button in the middle of it. In my comparison, I have begun to stare again. Noticing my attention, he smiles and makes his way across the room. *Fuck. Fuck. Fuck.*

I consider turning my body and gaze away to send a message, screaming, *I'm not interested!* I debate too long, and when I blink, he is standing in front of me with an expectant look. He's said something to me, and I've missed it.

"What?" I ask blankly.

"I said hi!" He yells over the chatter.

"Oh, hi," I mumble, unable to sugarcoat my annoyance. This is precisely what I meant about complications. I feel myself flush in irritation. All I had to do was break eye contact, and I could have avoided this interaction.

"You're very beautiful." He says, my blush having different implications in his mind.

My first thought would be rude to say: that I don't want to talk to him. I say nothing instead and nod as if agreeing that, yes, I am very beautiful. *Like that's better, Al.* A disgruntled groan escapes my lips. It's frustrating that I have lost the ability to communicate. He misconstrues the sound as disagreement and jumps on the opportunity.

"You are!" He exclaims. "Now, you say something nice about me. Come on, then!" He's chipper. It's the kind of bubbly demeanor I would have been attracted to at one point in my life. Now, the sing-song of his tone rings like nails on a chalkboard. The moment is further ruined by his breath, which has been soured by beer. The smell stains my nostrils as it hangs in the air.

I close my eyes and will him to go away. I shouldn't be in this situation. After a second, I try to re-engage. I'm being weird and rude again.

"You don't have to think so hard." He laughs lightly. It grates in my ears—the wrong laugh.

"You reminded me of someone I knew, that's all." I surprise myself by spitting out an honest answer. I assess my empty glass, wondering what kind of serum has made me spill my thoughts. This place does have an age to it. Maybe they practice witchcraft instead of intoxication. Perhaps the bartender gave me a truth potion instead of the whiskey I ordered.

"Handsome bloke, then?" *Not Grey 406* takes the cue to sit beside me on the empty bar stool. He taps his fingers against the sticky countertop, and I swear I can see their pads stick before he pulls them away.

Two beers appear in front of us. The room is fuzzy, and I don't recall if Not Grey ordered them or if Eyebrows sensed I needed another drink. Something lighter this time. I trickle down a few sips before responding to Not Grey's question.

"He's dead," I say flatly and take a bigger sip. That should do it.

The guy laughs. Taking in my lack of humor, his face falls. I meet his stare and hold it. Now, I wait.

"I better get off, then. I'm pissed." He chokes out nervously and pushes away from the bar. I don't stop him as he leaves. They always leave. It always works. Looks like a dead ex is good for something.

"Heartbreaker, much?" I snap to attention, coming face to face with brown eyes.

There is only a foot of counter between us, and from this close, they aren't shit brown at all. They're more like coffee beans. He leans forward. No, wrong again. There are flecks of green in each iris. The outer iris is a dark green, almost juniper. It fades to a golden amber in the center. His eyes remind me of the pine trees that grew in my yard back home. The dark lashes around them flutter as he blinks but when he opens them again, his gaze is steady with mine. I look from eye to eye. I can't decide which description I like more: coffee beans or pine trees.

"Last call." He says after a moment, but it comes out quieter than either of us expect. He straightens and heads off beyond some doorway. A buzz I didn't realize was there slowly dissipates in his absence.

I left some bills on the counter, not bothering to count them before I went. I'm sure I overpaid, but I'm at my limit for interactions tonight.

I pause at the door. It rattles me that I missed it before, but a small stage is hidden amongst the Friday night chaos in the center of the tables. On it sits a piano. The sparkle of the lettering glimmers from across the room. It is a C. Bechstein, one of the oldest brands in the world. While I can't be sure of the year, this one has age to it. The wood is discolored and chipped. It has been well-loved. Every fiber in me pulls to go to it. To play. Even stronger is the pull to sing again.

I can't.

With a fleeting look, I force myself out the door.

* * *

When I return, Libby's is quiet. I stumble through the foyer, cursing myself as I make my way to the kitchen. The green tile floor catches what little streetlight filters through the window, helping to guide me. The color is putrid, a stale green—the green of school cafeterias or my grandmother's ancient Tupperware.

When I moved in, I hated the tile. Like most of England, it was old. Newer flats were overpriced, and being a struggling artist, my aunt couldn't afford it. I'm not sure she could afford me without my parents' money, but at least she wanted me, which brings me back to the tile. Tonight, I don't hate it. Tonight, I think it's nice that it has history. I think it's nice that its owners wanted it, even with all its ugly green flaws.

I shift the fridge's contents to find my real milk, hoping the dairy calms the bile building in my stomach. I shuffle through too many green leafy things that taste even worse than they smell.

My phone chimes on cue with another message from my mother asking how I am. She's been asking for two weeks since I finally reached my limit and stopped answering her calls. Maybe I'm still saying no. She didn't hear me then, but perhaps the silence would finally make it clear. I chug the milk and set the glass in the sink for washing. My head pounds in a cry for sleep, so I head for the bathroom to brush my teeth before bed.

The French doors off the kitchen reflect my movement and cause me to jump. I flip the switch to cut on the lights outside. They stall before flickering awake. A face stares back at me through the glass, wearing an awful grimace. I fight a scream.

A clay statue stares back at me. A sigh of relief falls from my lips. Thank God. I stroll into the glass room, Libby's greenhouse-converted studio, taking in her latest creation. My relief turns to pain, and a whimper replaces the sigh as I examine her work.

A boy my height is standing, his mouth open as if shrieking, eyes wide. His face captures one emotion: panic. But his body is perfectly still. The veins in his arms are not straining. His hands fall relaxed at his sides. His clothes are on fire, the skin underneath melting away to exposed muscle, mangled flesh, and bone. A smooth surface is met by searing decay. Like a napkin getting wet, the skin is wrinkled with burns. Despite the damage, his posture shows no stress. Only his face. It is catastrophic. She's titled it "Pompeii."

That night I dream of the statue, only his features are replaced with Grey's. He cannot move, but he feels all the pain. As he burns, I'm back in his house. I'm trying to save him, to save all of them, but I can't move either. I can only watch as he burns, as my future burns around us.

then, august

I'D VISITED MORE states in three months than I had in all sixteen years of existence. I was surprised my mother signed off to let me go, but I never should have underestimated Marilyn Kingsley's gift of persuasion. A few margaritas deep, my mom had agreed to let me tour the country with the Kingsleys in their camper. Grey and I trailed behind the fifth-wheeler in his Jeep, heading to a national park in Maine.

I'd been lost in my mind, looking out over the constant fields of rural Pennsylvania. We'd been driving for over five hours, and the light outside had shifted, darkness creeping over the horse pastures in the distance. Charlie was passed out in the back seat, while Gigi remained in the truck with James and Marilyn.

There was something so enchanting about living inside my inner world in the presence of others. Like I was in another time or looped in a thought. It reminded me of the end of a really good movie, how the credits would roll, and I'd still be hanging on the last scene, reveling in the storyline. I felt comfortable not making sense. I was okay losing myself around Grey.

He gave me a twice-over, and I threw him a lazy smile, answering his unspoken question: "What do you think when you don't think?"

His mouth fell open in laughter.

"What? What does that even mean?" He croaked out. The rasp was heavier in his voice, an effect of the drowsiness. We had all stayed up too late playing cards. Marilyn warned us we'd be tired, but we worried not; we were young and resilient. We were stupid. She had been right, as mothers so often are, and we were all exhausted. I was determined not to sleep until Grey did. I didn't want him to bear the responsibility of staying awake alone, to risk falling asleep at the wheel.

"I think peanuts are really pineapples," I said with confidence, pursing my lips as if it further proved my point.

"What? What are you talking about?" He let go of the wheel to grab his head on both sides as if it were to explode. "You are venturing down some looney paths here." Grey chuckled, filling me with happiness. He tilted his head back, chugging from his can of Mountain Dew.

"Your turn." I taunted.

"Oh no, you're not pulling me into this."

Nodding, I mumbled: "Makes sense. You're less creative than me."

His mouth fell open at the accusation.

"People have strings." He said moments later.

"That was dark as fuck."

"Brightened by your colorful word choice." He notated goofily before he grew serious. "You know, there are philosophies out there that say our free will is just a cognitive lie. We tell ourselves we're getting to make our own choices because, like computers, that's how we were programmed. We don't know anything else." He ranted, staring out the windshield. I considered this for a long time.

"This city used to be a dollhouse. Now we think we operate on our own." I added to his storyline once I'd had time to process.

"We look into the windows of each other's lives. There's always love and laundry." He played along, his seriousness evaporating. I giggled, loving our newest game. Nonsensical as it was, it was so us to drop poetry like bars. We never planned for our talks to go deep, but they always did, fading back into laughter just as swiftly.

"Wet roads multiply the streetlights, giving the city street eyes."

"It's like Christmas, all these lights." He drew on.

I nodded in affirmation. "The sky really is falling, Chicken Little."

"Only for you. Always for you." He squeezed my hand, the world growing smaller, cozier.

Our train of thought spun into multiple storylines and memories of childhood. It wasn't that late, but we were delirious. Everything we said was suddenly the funniest thing *ever* said.

I saw his smile reflected in the window, and I loved him so much in those little moments. Maybe I was sixteen, and he wasn't 'the one,' and I was too young to know better. Maybe there was someone else meant for me but *fuck* them.

Their knuckles wouldn't look like his curled around the steering wheel. Their leg wouldn't bounce in the same rhythm when they got nervous. Their Adam's apple wouldn't stand as prominently in their throats or bob up and down like a sexy bouncy ball when they talked. They wouldn't hold their bodies with the same loose springiness or pop their wrists every so often to work out a sprain that went untreated from when they were a kid.

Perhaps that's what love is. Understanding all the ways a person differed from everyone else on the planet. Knowing these tiny gestures, tiny actions can be duplicated by thousands of others all over. Yet no one can replicate them in *his* exact likeness.

I'd forever be searching for him.

now, july

DOWNTOWN LONDON IS BUSTLING EVEN in the rain. Libby was right; I should get a job. It would help me pass the time until school starts and could help me feel less aimless. I cross the Tower Bridge and pause to take in the view. Joggers pass me in a hurry, and I hope I never become one of those people who go for a run on their lunch break. I scoot closer to the railing so I don't get knocked out of the way.

Out past Parliament, on the side of the Thames River, sits London's tallest building, Empyrean Tower. Empyrean was my father's company. The company he started with straight out of medical school here in London before returning to work for them again years later. Empyrean was the name of the hospital chain I grew up in.

The building is the first of its kind architecturally. Two twin helixes, the symbol for DNA, are firmly rooted in the ground, spanning floor after floor of offices. Glass hallways connect the two halves. According to my dad, it was a modern marvel when it came to fruition in the eighties. Seeing the symbol in person, solidified and not on the wall of my room or the paper of a pamphlet, is surreal. The twin helixes were the backdrop to my entire youth. I don't want a job here where every time I look out the window, there they are, a backdrop to my adulthood as well.

I don't know why I expected to find a job 30 minutes away from Libby's. Shuffling to the tube every morning for the commute would drive me crazy. The itch I used to have to travel has waned to nothing. The meaning of adventure feels lost when I have no one to tell the stories to. These days, I prefer to stay closer to home. Easier to escape to for my breakdowns.

Subconsciously, I know I am here because I never intended to get a job at all. I throw the resumes Libby printed off for me into the nearest trash can. I buy admission into the Tower of London instead.

I want to be absorbed by tragedy that is not my own. It is not long before my wish is granted. Burying my nose in my scarf, I blend in with the patrons of a guided tour I did not pay for. The guide lowers her voice like a camp counselor about to launch into a scary story with a flashlight on her face. She tells the tale of two princes murdered by their uncle, who feared they threatened his claim to the throne. Sometime later, they were found buried beneath a staircase. One of the princes was only nine. I pull my coat tighter around me to get warm, the chill in the air suddenly more ferocious. Thinking of a dead nine-year-old brings forth images of Gigi's gap-toothed smile and stringy brown hair.

She was the fifth Kingsley. Five when I met her, nine when she died. Numbers I've struggled to come to terms with. After the fire, I was diagnosed with dyscalculia. It's like dyslexia, but instead of words being jumbled, it's numbers. It was the excuse I told my mom for passing on

Berkeley. I couldn't read the music scores anymore. Left and right were reversed. I was playing songs out of order—the "Dead at 9" headline from the local paper stuck in my brain. No amount of therapy or songwriting could purge it. Everything became too unfocused when I tried. My mother had recycled my old essay to Berkley when she applied on my behalf to Jubal School of the Arts. I tried not to think of how I would manage to pass classes.

I leave the tower. I don't want to hear any more about dead kids. I board a hop-on/ hop-off bus and go from site to site until I'm exhausted. I don't get off the bus, preferring to listen to the driver's weathered voice telling me the city's stories. When the driver talks about the Great Fire of London, which burned for four days and demolished St. Paul's Cathedral, I decide I'm done touring for the day.

When I get back to the flat, it's dark. Libby is out; there is no note to tell me where she has gone. We don't feel the need to communicate every detail to each other, which is another thing I like about living here. My mom would have gone crazy if I had left without an explanation.

I thought coming home to an empty house would have put me at ease. I was free to grieve without sympathy or questions, free to go to sleep early should I choose, free to scream or binge eat the scones I had picked up on my way home. However, sitting at the table alone, the emptiness echoed through me.

Without knowing what I am doing, my feet carry me back to the bar from last night. Being Saturday, tonight is even more packed than the last. I feel underdressed in my father's old university crew and my jean shorts that barely poke out from beneath it. I quickly find my spot at the bar and relief washes over me that it's still empty.

Same nod, same raise of eyebrows. Different bartender. An odd feeling of disappointment comes over me.

"Whiskey sour."

He makes no move to make my drink.

"No?" I ask.

"No." He smiles, cheeks flushed. I feel his eyes rake over my face. His smile grows warmer, making me uncomfortable. "Jack and Coke?" He asks.

"That you have?" I laugh. "Tennessee whiskey but no sour mix?"

He shrugs. "I'll get some for next time." Then, realizing what he said, his face turns a darker shade of maroon.

Bartender #2 has black hair, which is thick and standing up at all angles. His tan skin is flawless, and I wonder if he has Korean or Chinese heritage. His smile is sweet as he hands me my drink with, of course, no ice.

"Anything else?" His eyes are bright. Hopeful.

"No, thank you." I offer a small smile. He matches it for a few seconds longer than I like before a man down the bar demands his attention.

I was once a pretty girl, so maybe some of my good features have clung to me like residue. Perhaps not enough time has passed for them to rot away like the rest of me.

I still remembered it clearly, the trying. How my perfectly curled hair was always falling elegantly down my back, seemingly without effort. How my blue eyes once stood out against the dark set of my winged eyeliner that took forever to apply. I had worked hard at it then. After being "the sick girl" for so long, I valued being a pretty girl instead. So, I dressed in my pastel skirts and flowery blouses. I acted like a daydream, like a Disney princess harvested from overturned pages. Back when fairy tales were my only dating experience.

It wasn't until I got older that I realized men weren't picturing a wife when they looked at me. They weren't picturing a life beside me at all. They were picturing themselves inside of me—a much less idyllic image. Luckily, I had met Grey before ever having to subject myself to dating, or hooking up, or whatever the apps are that exist out there now to facilitate meeting people.

I don't feel like a pretty girl anymore. My hair falls in messy blonde waves, more frizz than curl. My eyes are always red, with deep purple circles set beneath. None of my clothes are made to fit my body. My curves have gone flat from poor nutrition over the past year. The attention I get now feels misplaced like it doesn't belong to me somehow. I'd fall more in line with the likes of a drug addict than a Disney princess in my current state. My doe-eyed innocence was gone. I don't *want* to look like a fairytale. I want to look like a warning, someone to stay away from. Conversation takes too much out of me. I'm no longer made of sentences to spare.

The piano begins to play, stirring me out of my thoughts. I didn't realize that the place had live music. The instrument looked so old that I had assumed it was just for decoration, there to add character. I closed my eyes and let the tune soak in. A beautiful Celtic melody filled the room, rippling with sadness. I grabbed a napkin and scribbled down some words.

"Grayson!" My head snaps in the direction of the name. The bartender shoots up in attention. The liquor he was pouring has overflowed from the glass onto the counter. His eyes glance back to me, and he flushes again.

"Sorry." He apologizes to a man, the bartender from yesterday. *Shit.*

Following the attention of Grayson— go figure—

Bartender #1 meets my eyes. I glance around, trying to find anywhere else to look, but the room seems to center around him, so I settle into his gaze.

I realize suddenly the piano is empty. The music has stopped. How long had I been lost in my own world?

"Back again?" His strong jawline dips under the lighting, and he leans over the bar to clear the drinks of neighboring patrons. I notice other details about him for the first time like the stubble framing his sculpted chin, his thin but perfect lips. I nod once to avoid conversation. Habits are hard to break, and watching him has become a bad habit.

Bartender #1 tenses as he lays a drink in front of me. His jaw is fixed in annoyance as if he hopes I'll ask him to take it away. I haven't placed an order. Confused, I tilt my head when he waves his hand toward the guys who sent the drink. I nod my thank you without smiling or zeroing in on anyone's face. I'd rather be considered rude than inviting. The bartender unsuccessfully tries to conceal the dimples forming in his cheeks in response to my reaction and resumes pouring.

I have covered over ten napkins with lyrics when Bartender #1 places another drink before me. This one is water.

"You're cutting me off?" I ask.

A toothpick hangs from his mouth like some British James Dean. Damn it, now I'm thinking like the other girls.

"Last call was an hour ago." He says.

I look around, unsettled, to find that the bar has mostly cleared out, give or take a drunk and a few stragglers.

"Oh," I say, taken aback.

The smirk grows. His T-shirt is white today, looser than yesterday's, though it still clings to the shape of his shoulders.

"You can hang out a little longer. I have to clean up before we shut down. You seem pretty absorbed in your... napkin novel?" He lifts one of my napkins and lets it float down before I can yell or snatch it back.

"Are you getting a good look then?" I quip, using his line from the night before. He rolls his eyes.

Bartender #2 begins to head out the door after mumbling something to Bartender #1, who shrugs and continues sweeping the floor. I mentally battle whether to grab my work and go before he can say something or if that leaves the opportunity for him to walk me home. I don't want to encourage either notion. I stay seated and keep scribbling.

"I'm heading out. I can walk you home if you'd like?" Bartender #2 asks, hopefully. I refuse to refer to him as Grayson. He should get a new name. Until he does, he is Bartender #2.

"No, thank you." I smile politely. My brain scrambles to formulate an excuse.

"Oh, okay." He shifts uncomfortably, and his shoulders fall, defeated. It pains me to see him upset. There's already more heartache in the world than I can stomach, and I don't want to be on awkward terms if I decide to return tomorrow.

"Can I tell you a secret?" I whisper. He perks up and nods. I lower my voice and lean in. "You're so sweet, and if I didn't already have a crush on the other bartender, I'd love you to walk me home." I wink at him. He still looks disappointed but slightly less defeated. There is a spark behind his eye that wasn't there before.

"Oh, Derek?" He asks. "Derek doesn't date." He kicks the ground like a little kid.

"We'll see." I smile, hop off my stool, and walk to the

piano. I sit down before he gets it in his head to pursue things further. He steps in my direction, so I let out a breath and lay my hands on the keys. I never thought I'd start playing again to deter a boy, but the moment I do, it feels good. Really good.

All the lyrics I'd been writing for the past hours become entwined with a composition. I don't sing while I play, letting the keys become my communication. It feels haunting, like the player before, but more grieving, the loss evident in the melody. The door clicks shut sometime later. More comfortable in the isolation, I hum the words before singing them outright. The verse I had written earlier and then the chorus.

"I swear the quiet's worse than the screaming,
All that's left are my bad dreams and
They all have your name, they all have your face,
Pleading to be saved, but I can't do a thing.
It's been a long and lonely year.
I haven't left the graveyard; I fear you'll disappear.
Then there will be nothing left to haunt me here.

Who am I? Who am I without my ghosts?
Where will I, where will I feel at home?
Panic when I wake up, panic when they're near.
Panic when they touch me, panic when I hear
Anything that reminds me, you'll never be right here.
I can't breathe; I can't see anything clearly.
Who am I? Who am I without my ghosts?
Where will I, where will I feel at home?"

I play and rearrange the lyrics on the napkins in front of me. My phone buzzes with a text from Libby asking where I am. Reading the time, I come to a halt. It's 1:41 am. The bar closed almost two hours ago. I'm never out past one. Bartender #2 left nearly an hour ago. I've forgotten how music eliminates the element of time. It disappears when I write and when I play. These past few nights have reminded me how much I've missed that.

I suddenly realize that all the lights, except for the ones on stage, are off. A surge of panic rises within me as I fear being locked in. There's no way they could have forgotten about me. I haven't exactly been quiet. I quickly gather my things and head for the door, but it doesn't budge.

"The latch is up top." Bartender #1 answers. He's sitting in my spot at the bar. My face grows hot in embarrassment. I play nonchalant and brush my cheek with the back of my hand trying to gauge what shade of rouge I've turned, tulip or tomato. My soul has been undressed before him. He *heard* me.

I searched for some clue into his thoughts. Did I hold him up? Was he watching because he felt sorry for me? Did he hear what I said to the other guy and think I was, in fact, into him? Why did he *stay*?

Slipping off the stool, he walks with cool confidence, shoulders back, in my direction. His jaw tenses like earlier, making his bone more pronounced under the stubble. I can see how his emotion changes as he nears, how it rearranges his features into something more dangerous. Endearing.

Stepping into my space, so close I can feel the heat lifting from his clothing, he comes to stop inches away. As he reaches up, I have the crazy idea that he might run his fingers through my hair. I close my eyes. My foot hits the door as I stumble against it, but I don't look. I can't.

All my nerve endings have been ignited, compelling me to remain completely still or to move towards the heat. I can't decide which urge is strongest; I'm too incoherent. My heartbeat is pacing the moment in a series of thump, thump, thumps. It sounds like a drum gaining tempo. Surely, he can hear it, too. I gasp softly as his temperature affects the rising goosebumps across my arms and neck, his touch less than a second away. I hear the lock click above my head as he undoes the latch.

The warmth leaves as he backs away. I open my eyes to find him smirking, of course. It's a different kind than his usual. Less sardonic, more intentional. As if he knew what I was thinking or *had* been thinking moments ago. If I wasn't flushed before, I certainly am now.

"Free to go." He comments from a safe distance, his accent heavily lacing the words. I watch as he returns to the piano where I had been sitting and plays my song.

"What are you doing?" I ask, winded, my curiosity gaining the better of me.

"The lyrics are good. Really good. Your composition was getting caught up, though. What about this?" He asks before singing my lyrics in a sped-up version of the music I had played.

His voice is incredible. Sinatra meets Jack the Ripper is the comparison that pops into my head. It makes no sense, but to me, it does. Rough and gravelly, like it had been fucked up in an alley, but then it transcends to fluid, melodic, like a harp from heaven. It makes my head tingly. When he stops, I want to ask him to play it again. I've moved to lean against the instrument where I can watch his fingers skim across the keys, dipping so often to press one down almost suggestively.

It dawns he was the man at the piano earlier. It was his playing that inspired my song. This isn't his first rodeo. It's clear by how effortlessly he's reworked the progression. He may have a whole catalog of music lying around, music I'm suddenly desperate to get my hands on.

What would it sound like? He didn't seem like the type to be harboring love songs, so what then? I begin to process something new: I've never collaborated with someone before. It's exhilarating. Almost as exhilarating as when I thought he was going to touch me. He stops playing then, tilting his head as if to ask what I think.

"Why did you speed it up?" I question.

"Sing." He beckons as he plays it again. I do, shyly at first. My modesty fades quickly. The change reveals passion, and the panic becomes more apparent. It is a captivating switch, and I hate to admit, I love it.

"I see your point." I concede, attempting to retain whatever stubbornness is left in me. I'm in a power struggle, unsure of myself. I keep losing control around him, and it's freaking me out. Accepting my remark, he nods quickly, standing. While he retrieves his jacket, I retreat for the door. The moment of civility between us is over. I don't wait for him to follow me out. I'm about to cross the street when I hear the hinges creak.

"Are you going to wait?" He yells before I can flee.

I look around to see who he's talking to. It's only me. "Yes, you." Amusement reigns over his tone. He shoves his hands into his pockets, almost nervous. Then, it turns to annoyance again. "Well?" He prompts.

"*Excuse me*? Wait for what?" I am baffled.

"I'm walking you home." He says, a matter of fact, his fingers fumbling with the lock. I stand stunned.

"Let's go." He gestures onward, appearing in front of me. Under the streetlights, his eyes have taken on a lighter tone, more like honeycombs. I'm reaching out like *I* might touch *him*. I catch my hand and bring it back to my side.

My composure rushes back, the lapse in judgment forgotten.

"Look, about what I told your friend, I'm not interested in you. I just wanted to let him down easy." I explain, sounding like a liar. I hadn't thought I was. Crossing the street, I follow his lead even though we're heading to *my* house.

"You told him you fancy me?" He boasts, laughing as he hops onto the raised stone wall separating planters from the sidewalk. I'm caught off guard by his playfulness, a third side to his personality; another that seems out of place from my original interpretation of his character.

"To get him to leave me alone. That's it." I declare, keeping my voice formal, almost scolding. This makes him laugh louder. I groan. "Please just go away. I can walk myself. In fact, as fun as your company is, I'd rather be alone."

He clutches his heart as if I've wounded him. It takes less than a second for the anticipated eye roll to follow.

"I don't give a shit. It's two am, and we're in the city. I'm not letting you walk home alone, unresolved desire for me or not. You want to have this attitude the whole time?" He waves his hand up and down to showcase me. "That's fine. As soon as I drop you off, it's no longer my problem."

"Whoa, whoa, whoa. Unresolved desire?" I scoff.

He shrugged, running his hands through his hair to push the strands out of his face. I knew he was frustrating from our small talk in the bar. He was sharp. Quick-witted. Quickly agitated. Despite his weird magnetism, he wasn't someone I cared to have walking me home. It enraged me that he thought I had "unresolved desire."

I stew while he jumps down from the stone wall that is beginning to rise, adding more privacy to the garden yards.

He keeps pace, his long legs moving in half strides to stay in time with my own.

"Why don't we spend the rest of the walk in silence since you insist on being here?" I request. He says nothing as if to prove he was already saying nothing and my statement was unnecessary—a*rrogant bastard.* A minute later, we arrive at Libby's.

"This is me." I proclaim, stopping in front of her gate.

"Aren't you going to invite me in?" Eyebrows. Smirk. *Asshole.* It's my turn to roll my eyes. He's not funny.

"Goodnight—" I hesitate, failing to remember his name.

"Derek." He says. *Oh, yeah.*

"Derek." I taste the word on my tongue. It feels conspiratorial, a secret. I know more about him now than any of the other girls from the bar. "Goodnight, Derek." I turn to the flat without looking back.

now, july

"YOU'RE HOME LATE." Libby accuses but fails to hide her smile behind her coffee cup, giving away that she had, without a doubt, been peeking out the window.

"Mhmm." I torture, harboring details she so clearly craves. I pull open the fridge and search for my real milk. *Glass of milk* flutters in my head, and I block it before it can resonate.

"He was ridiculously hot, or at least his shoulders were. That was all I could make out. A guy from the bar?" She pries, feigning disinterest.

"Yes. I know what you're thinking, and it's not going to happen." I retort. The cap unscrews easily, and the white waterfall fills my glass. Placing it back in its cubby, I take a sip and allow our eyes to meet.

"Why *not*, Allyson?"

I cringe at the use of my full name.

"Why should I, *Elizabeth*?" I take another sip, leaning against the cabinets.

"Don't call me that." She shoots me a death glare. She despises Elizabeth almost as much as L.

"You picked this battle, Libs."

"You don't have to keep closing yourself off to the world, you know?" She says lightly, her eye contact holding steady. Something in her always pulls things from me—things I don't usually say.

"I played the piano tonight. I sang." I pick at the peeling paint of the sage-colored cabinets.

"Al, that's great! How did it feel?" Her smile brightens the room. I hadn't assessed how I felt yet. I shrug and kiss her on the cheek as I head to bed.

It felt like I lost time, I finally thought as I closed my eyes.

now, july

THERE IS a hollow ache that accompanies each day's arrival. This one is worse than most. The memories from my dreams are encapsulated in my every thought. I can hear his tone, his laughter. Again, I reach for him, and he is not there. I grip the pillow that has taken his place, and a whimper rips through me. I remind myself that I will never have the luxury of touching him again. The ache grows.

I compel time or whatever controls the universe to spin back. The urge, the demand, is so strong beneath my skin. For a moment, I believe it is possible. If I work hard enough, I can make it real. I can change it. I have never wanted anything as much as I want this.

Bring him back, I beg. I squeeze my eyes shut.

When I open them, there is just a deflated pillow and a deflated room from which I have stolen the air. The loss of hope is immediate.

There is nothing to look forward to.

Today is a bad day. Today means I will not get out of bed.

Libby peeks in once to check on me. When she sees my face, she crawls under the covers beside me and reads a few chapters from *his* book before leaving me be. She leaves a sandwich on my pillow for dinner, but she doesn't wake me. She doesn't require more of me. Not today.

now, july

TOMORROW.

Tomorrow is the word that echoes when I wake. It is finally tomorrow. I reform it. Tomorrow is today. Today, my bed doesn't feel like a coffin. It doesn't feel like I will choke on smoke when I breathe. This is a good sign.

I grab a fresh set of clothes and head to the bathroom. If I can make it to the shower, I can make it outside. I say it like a mantra.

Repeat actions. This is what my therapist had advised. The therapist had come after the first incident, after I first confided in my mother about seeing Grey again. He had been Not Grey 03, buying pancake mix from a grocery store. My mother didn't view it as poetically as I did; she only saw the delusion. Once she'd told Michael, it was game over. On to therapy, I went.

My therapist, Michelle, had been working with me to drive thought patterns through behavior, create consistency, and make little promises to myself—the bare minimum of what I could commit to. That way, even incrementally, I had accomplished something, and tiny achievements were still progress.

I turn the knob on the shower and wait before remembering I have to press the stupid button to make the water flow. Stepping in, I silently curse the mechanics of European plumbing. To move away from my thoughts of therapy, of replaying my sessions, I list the differences between the two continents. It holds my focus the entire shower.

I think of Grey when my foot touches the cold, checkered floor, and I wrap a towel around myself. Then, again, as I plan my outfit and dry my hair. I prepare for rain, lining my lashes in waterproof mascara. I think of him as I get dressed. I make more small commitments as I walk through the door.

Day two on the job hunt is another failure. Day two did not involve sight-seeing due to the rain. Day two pretty much sucks, just like yesterday. I shiver. No, day two is better than the bottomless pit of yesterday. I got out of bed today. It was a small accomplishment. I give myself additional praise for calling it out.

I deserve a drink.

I end up back at the bar, which is less congested than I had expected it to be. There is no traffic coming in and out, and there are no crowds with pints standing around the outdoor ledges built along the wall of windows. The sign on the door shows they open at 6, but it's only 4.

"You can't stand out here for two hours, Ally." I think out loud. Pinching the bridge of my nose, I begin to pace. "Now what?" I hadn't thought of what to do next. Thoughts of the apartment, *flat* rather, are attached to yesterday's stint of sadness and give me anxiety.

"You wanna talk to yourself for a few more minutes, or you wanna come in?"

Derek's accent is almost American today, and it cuts through the spiral I had started to go down. I briefly wonder if he has spent time in the States before wondering how long he had been standing there. I hadn't heard the door creak open. *Focus, Ally. You need to respond.*

"Uhm." *Do better at not being weird*, I criticize.

"Or you could stand out here and enjoy the rain?" He asks, squinting and tilting his head towards the sky.

"The sign says you're closed." I point to the square hanging from the glass as if explaining my reason for not following him inside. I sound like an idiot.

"I just invited you in."

Right. Obviously. *Out loud, Als.* "Uhm. Right." I say under my breath. *This is going well.* He steps back from where he is peeking out the doorway, allowing me access.

"Just you?" I ask.

"Just me. Grayson will be here shortly." He says. I wince.

"Bartender Number Two." I correct on impulse. He cocks his head to the side and raises his eyebrows.

"Is that what you reduce us to?" He asks seriously, but his eyes are light with humor.

"No. You're Derek, but I don't like his name."

"What's wrong with Grayson?"

I close my eyes as he repeats it. My dreams flash behind my eyes. There is no pillow to cling to.

"I'm going to go." I move backward. I can't hear it again.

"Bartender Number Two isn't here for an hour." He modifies. "I have work to do. Have at it." He gestures towards the stage. He throws the towel he had been using to wipe the table over his shoulder and leaves.

I stare at the piano. Is that why I came here? I don't have

to answer my question to feel it in my bones. I brush my fingers along the keys after stepping up the platform. Something in me falls into place as I sit on the bench and tie my hair back.

"I heard their voices in the wind beggin'.
'Little Red, Little Red, please don't go in.
You won't change a thing; you'll only burn again.'
I ignored their warnings said: 'I've never met a monster that wasn't my friend.'
So I lied there hurting, content to deal with the fallout in the morning.
Little Red, don't be nervous; we're all both beast and burden."

I don't know if Derek placed the pen beside me or if it was here already with the napkins. Each verse fills a new square, and everything falls out of me in the correct order for once. I furiously scribble, disregarding my worry about whether it will make sense to other people. This isn't *for* other people.

My dreams of Grey are fresh, and I'm trying to write my way out of the nightmare. The piano keys pull the blood from my wound, draining its life as it takes a new form. A weight is lifted as the overwhelming sadness is reduced, cut away to live outside my body instead of in it.

Bartender #2 is leaning against the counter, watching me. I check the time. God, I've been at this for over an hour again. I didn't hear him come in. He mumbles something to Der—Bartender #1, and they nod in unison. I close the cover. The song is done. It's precisely what it was supposed to be.

Feeling like it's unavoidable, I walk over and order a drink before I head home. Exhaustion hangs off of every particle of my being. Sleeping all day yesterday, I barely got in two hours last night.

"Whiskey sour?" I ask, approaching the counter. Bartender #2 widens his eyes, clearly violating his promise to have it next time. *Liar.*

"Coming up," Derek says as he pours.

"Wait— you have it?" I ask in surprise.

"Always have."

"You're a dick," I say to the other guy. He smiles sheepishly and walks away quickly. This solidifies it. I will never call him by his real name.

A smirk finds its way onto Derek's face as if he's had the same thought. He quickly places the glass in front of me before staggering backward slightly. Suddenly, seemingly changing his mind, he leans forward again, gripping the edge of the countertop.

"How old is this place?" I ask, sipping the tangy liquid.

"The building? Over a hundred and fifty. This bar? Probably the same."

"How do you know?" I probe.

"It's my grandfathers. The history's been passed down."

"So, you own it now? Or you work for him?"

"I work for him." Derek's smirk becomes a genuine smile. I wonder if it's my nosiness and decide to push my luck.

"You hiring?" I ask. I glance down at my fingernails, a foreign distraction but the only one I can think of to hide my desperation. Libby would be thrilled, and this pub has been the most comfortable place for me outside of home. I must fail at faking distractions as his laughter breaks into the quiet air.

"We have enough bartenders." He says, leveling with me. "There is even a Three and a Four."

I feel the desire to push his shoulder jokingly, a reflex my body has forgotten how to act on. I stare at my arm, limp against my side, like it should have moved.

"Okay." I sigh after a beat. Partly to him and partly to my immobile arm.

"We could use an entertainer, though." He replies.

"I don't do that kind of work."

"I meant the piano."

"I know what you meant." I snap. It holds less venom than I'd intended.

"Why not?" He asks, coming out from behind the bar to lean against the column beside my stool.

"I don't play in front of people." I will him to stop pressing.

"You played in front of me. Twice now. Total stranger." He says, the dimples forming in his cheeks.

"You're Derek." I remind him.

He lets out a frustrated huff and I think of Libby as I smile into my drink. Laying the empty glass on the counter, he steps forward, reaching for it. His fingers cross over mine in the pass. The buzz is back tenfold. *So, this is what it's like to touch him.* The thought comes from nowhere, and I reprimand myself for thinking it.

"I don't know your name," he says. It comes out hard in more of a statement rather than a lure. I can tell it's not a pickup line, but the way his eyes are set on mine and the feeling of his fingers still resting over my own create a jump in my heart. It's hard to believe that wasn't his intention.

Jeez, those eyes. They really are more of a melting brown. Impulsively, my free hand stretches for his chin. I jump when my fingers graze the stubble there. I had only *thought* of touching him; I hadn't intended to do it. I want to tilt his head back so his eyes catch the light, but he moves of his own accord, ever the mind reader. I watch the color change as they flood Juniper and then amber with more exposure.

"They're not shit brown," I whisper.

I fully planned to remove my hand, but his wrapped around my elbow, pulling me to stand. My fingers fall in synchrony with one another, dragging lightly across his jaw. He inhales sharp, staggered breaths. I had only wanted to see the color of his eyes, but now that I'm touching him, there's something more. I'm compelled to *keep* touching him. I shift forward so our bodies are nearly pressed together. His heat wraps around my frame like my favorite sweater. I hadn't realized I was cold. I shiver then, unable to look away and start to raise my other hand.

"Grayson!" A guy snaps from the background. A cramp forms in my stomach, and I flinch. His eyes leave mine as he seems to notice as well. It breaks the spell. I jerk away.

"How much?" I ask.

"What?" He fumbles the glass in his hands.

"The drink?"

"Oh. It's on the house." He mutters and returns behind the bar to carry out his tasks. I drop some bills on the counter anyway and slip out the door.

then, july – october

MY FIRST CRUSH on a boy was this kid from the hospital. He was one of my dad's other patients. I used to beg my dad to let me tag along when he'd treat him so we could spend time together. He'd let me hang out in the boy's room while he did his rounds. I was probably six or so, and the boy was about eight. Nurses and doctors would bustle in the hallways while we played cards and talked over whatever movie played in the background. I liked how he didn't seem to care about growing up. He never tried to act older than he was. Never said "That's kid stuff." When it was us, we were just children building forts and playing pretend.

I've only had the one crush. I was never close to any of the other boys to find them cute enough to like. I suppose the ones I partnered with for school projects were nice, but they didn't measure up to that first boy. None did, until *him*.

My second crush had been the most annoying. The bad crush. The crush you wish you didn't have. The crush that could end all crushes.

Grey Kingsley wasn't just funny around other people. He was funny all the time.

At dinner with Gigi, he placed carrots under his gum line and told her he was the vegetable walrus. He made up stories about the green things on her plate that enticed her to eat them. Milk came out of my nose the day she asked about broccoli, and he said broccoli was cool because they had the same haircut. He proceeded to eat the top of the tiny tree so "the hair" was shaped like his own.

"See?" He had asked her, and she ate around her own, trying to get the details just right. He told her it was wrong, so she tried another. Eventually, the broccoli vanished from her plate, and Marilyn was thrilled.

After dinner, Grey was always the first to gather the plates. Charlie naturally followed his example, and I watched years of teamwork as siblings unfold before me. Gigi hopped up, eager to help and to be useful. They'd found a way to make clean-up part of the event. Marilyn turned up the radio under the cabinet to her favorite station. Everyone danced while they cleaned, each trying to upstage the others with their moves.

Grey cleared the plates, disposing of uneaten food, which was never a lot, and put it into the trash while Charlie rinsed. Gigi staffed her position, ready to load the dishwasher. She had developed a meticulous system for how she liked things loaded. James put them away in the morning after his run.

Charlie and Grey were adopted when they were twelve. They'd gained two parents at the same age I was when I lost one. While Grey and Charlie are fraternal twins and had always been together, they'd only been the Kingsleys for three years. I wondered if earning their place drove their sense of responsibility or if they appreciated it more in knowing what it was like to be orphans. Regardless, I was thankful. They had challenged my perspective on what was important.

True to his word, the night we first met, Grey *did* push to get to know me. It started simple. Whenever I'd enter a room, his face would light up, and he'd pause what he was doing. He'd lay down the controller if he was in the beanbag in front of the couch fighting a death match on the PlayStation.

"Ally!" He'd exclaim. "So, settle a debate for me. I think chocolate ice cream is better, but Gigi claims strawberry is. What's your take?"

He went about it strategically, much to Marilyn's enjoyment. She'd smile knowingly every time he'd rub his cheek before making up a story for why he needed to know this or that. His interest in me pleased her greatly while it annoyed Charlie to no end.

After a few weeks, he stopped making up stories and started asking outright about my favorite book, a favorite song, and what my parents were like. He'd ask again the following week. When I asked why, he said it was because favorites change every day, and he wanted to know who I was now, not who I was a week ago. I always really liked that answer.

* * *

As the summer passed, the three of us started high school together. They were the new kids in a small town where new didn't happen often. I watched as people reacted to the Kingsleys. Patiently, I waited for them to leave me.

I anticipated Charlie and I falling off when she picked up Drama Club. Her time was then consumed with dreaming up costumes for the fall musical. I was sure that with so many new friends, it would only be a matter of time before I ended up in the background. But she never let me.

On Mondays and Wednesdays after school, Charlie put on a show, begging me to wait in the auditorium while she fit the actors on stage. She forged bonds between the cast and me, asking how a costume fit or what I thought of their performance until the conversation didn't have to be prompted; it was natural. While she worked, I'd set up a picnic blanket in the aisle and prepared PB&J's for the crew, courtesy of Marilyn. I think being the snack bitch is what cemented my spot *in* the club without a title of any official capacity.

Like Charlie, I was also confident that the impact of school on our lives would deter Grey's interest and that it would lessen it as he learned how many options he had. After he joined the football team, I watched cheerleaders giggling at each other as they scribbled their numbers on tiny, perfectly folded sheets of paper before slipping them into his locker. Yet, to my utter disbelief, the hair flips, and short skirts did not waver his advances towards me.

I hated to admit he was wearing me down.

When Grey spoke, he did so with energy and charisma. His entire body was invested in what he was saying. If he was telling a story, his hands would wave wildly, reenacting details. His head was always tipped back, ready to burst into laughter. He was complimentary, finding every opportunity to return the conversation to the other person and never failing to say something nice about them. People left his presence feeling happier. I'm not sure if they ever knew why, but I did.

Even without using words, he communicated everything you needed to feel like you knew him. His body language was open and laid-back. He'd tap someone gently with the back of his hand when he wanted to interject or pat them on the back when saying hello. It was fascinating to see how people responded to him, their faces changing and lighting up, unable to resist smiling.

How he listened, though, nearly ripped apart my resolve to stay away from him. He listened with his heart. Holding your eyes, he'd lean in like what you had to say was the most critical piece of information he would ever hear. He tried not to interrupt; instead, he made small sounds of acknowledgment. If it was a group discussion, you could be the quietest person at the table, but he'd still hear everything you didn't say. He would comment on your actions as if they were part of the conversation.

He was unusual for a teenage boy; he retained everything. He'd remember the names of teachers' kids despite them only mentioning them once, and he'd take the time to ask about them before class. He remembered Gertrude, the grandmother of a girl who sat at our lunch table, was in the hospital and often checked in on how she was doing. For all this, I would have adored him even if he had shown no interest in me at all.

* * *

On Tuesdays and Thursdays, Charlie and I would set up camp on the Jeep's tailgate while Grey attended practice. This was my favorite time: talking through the day, absorbing the sunshine while distant voices from the field floated over in the warm autumn breeze. Virginia Octobers were full of color as the leaves began to change, but the summer heat tended to hold tightly to the daily temperature, often waiting until November to truly drop.

It was one of these days when Grey Kingsley changed everything again.

The humidity had started to seep through the fabric of my clothing as the sun changed direction and began to sink into the horizon. The rays came to rest exactly where we sat. Strolling leisurely from the locker room, Grey chatted animatedly with a teammate. I shrugged out of my pastel cardigan while we waited for them to reach us. When they were close enough, a boy named Chris Tandy held out a hand to introduce himself. I chose not to remind him that we had been lab partners less than a year ago and had shared classes since the sixth grade.

"So, Homecoming King, who are you taking to the dance? None of the girls will say yes to me until they know who you're taking." Chris pressed, trying to draw out the details of Grey's non-existent love life.

Chris was slightly shorter than Grey, his chin starting where Grey's shoulders did. He had frosted tips in plain brown hair and a round, pinkish face. Most girls considered him a heartthrob, but I never saw it.

Not missing how Grey's eyes flickered to me before he answered, I shook my head subtly. Dances were so not my thing. Whether it was drilled into me from my sheltered life at the hospital to be careful or my total lack of coordination, dances were a social event in which I struggled to participate. The one dance I had attended in 8th grade added titles to my name, the weird-awkward-sick girl, as I stood in a corner bouncing while everyone else busted a move on the dance floor.

"Yeah, I think I'm gonna go stag." Grey squinted in the sunlight. His mouth remained slightly open. Another

Greyism. When he felt like a debate was coming, he kept his lips parted, ready to jump in with colorful, light-hearted objection. It was starting to stir me how much I kept note of everything that set him apart from everyone else.

"Come on, man." Chris pleaded. "I need you to get a girlfriend so the market can open back up for the rest of us."

Charlie laughed. "He's not wrong. I'm tired of girls trying to be my friend to get close to you." I looked at her alarmingly. She didn't think *I* was doing that, did she?

"Alright, alright." Grey threw his hands up. "Convince the girl I want to be my girlfriend, and we all win." He shrugged.

Wait— *what?* One of the girls had done it. They finally worked their way into his field of interest. Grey *wanted* someone to be his girlfriend. My hands began to shake, though I had no right to be upset. I knew this would happen eventually. Taking a deep breath, I forced myself to relax. It never could have been me anyway, I rationalized. I *never* would have done that to Charlie. There was relief in that thought. An excuse I was going to live by.

"Dude. *Easy.* Just give me a name." Chris said confidently.

"Allyson Parrish."

"*Ally?*" Charlie exclaimed before busting out in laughter. "No, Grey, you have to pick someone without taste." She joked.

His eyes remained fixed on me, examining my every reaction. I felt my flush light up my face like a Christmas tree. I focused on the others, evaluating their notice, and found no relief. To Chris, his features frozen in shock as if to say: *All the hot pieces of ass you could have, and you want her? Really?* Then to Charlie, whose face was still creased in laughter, thinking it hilarious that Grey assumed I'd ever even consider him.

Seeing her head tilted back in amusement reminded me how much she'd changed my life. All of my previous prospects, girls who I think could have been my friends if they weren't so affected by the gossip, already had a *best* friend. A girl they went through kindergarten and every princess-themed birthday party with, a person to confide all their secrets. I've never had a best friend before. Charlie is my first.

I've never had a boyfriend, either. But I have read about them. I've seen the movies. Enough to know romantic relationships don't last the way friendships do. If it didn't work out, this could ruin Charlie and me. A risk I wasn't willing to take for a boy. Even one as rare as Grey Kingsley.

Charlie was rare, too. She was kind and loyal and shared Grey's charisma. Her sense of humor was darker like mine, something people didn't always understand, but she did. She understood me perfectly. I wasn't going to put myself in a position to lose her, even if it would cause me some jealousy or discomfort down the road when Grey did finally give up on me.

"Well?" Chris asked, fully recovered. "Ally, will you be a dear, and please, please go out with this man so daddy can get some again?" He asked like a true gentleman. I cringed at his use of the words "daddy" and "get some" in the same sentence.

Luckily, I didn't have to answer. A book flew at his face from Charlie's hands, saving me just in time.

"Gross. You, stop trying to set my friend up with my brother." She waved her finger at Chris. "And you, stop hitting on my friend." She turned to Grey. "You guys are freaking me out. Come on, Al. Let's go home." She said, moving around the vehicle to take Grey's place in the driver's seat.

I shrugged at them like that settled it. "You heard the lady."

* * *

Later that night, Grey met me in the kitchen. When we couldn't sleep, which was becoming common for both of us, we'd go for a glass of milk. A new tradition we carried on, like a small echo from the night we met. The night he accosted me in the kitchen. It seemed so long ago now that I truly knew him.

Most times, our trips would overlap. He or I would be sitting at the counter already, an empty glass set out on the granite just in case the other showed up. Our conversations became more intimate in the refrigerator light. It was easier for me to lose my guard rails while everyone else was sleeping, and it was easier for me to ask *him* the questions.

This night was different. He appeared not smiling cheek to cheek the way I had grown fond of. Instead, he offered me only a slight tilt of his lips. His oversized black shirt hung loosely off his torso. All his shirts were oversized, and he seemed to prefer that fit. *I* enjoyed that it gave the cheerleaders less to ogle.

I was unused to a less exuberant Grey. The kitchen felt emptier somehow without his energy to fill it. He poured himself a glass of milk, screwing the cap back on before pushing the glass forward, unsipped. He leaned against his elbows, letting his hair fall into his face, obscuring his eyes.

"So." He let the word hang in the air as he reached for the milk again, sliding it from palm to palm as he tried to formulate his thoughts. "You don't want to go to the dance with me."

My heart began to race in my chest. He flirted with me in front of the others, but when we were alone, our tone differed. We'd fall deep into conversation about philosophy or moments that had shaped who we are. This was a change. It felt more meaningful without eavesdropping ears. I was going to have to tread carefully.

"No, I don't want to go *to the dance*. I don't like dances." I went with the short version of the truth.

He nodded, lips pursed and pushed out to his cheek in consideration.

"My girlfriend doesn't need to like dances." He'd said then, his ear-to-ear smile finding its way back. I rolled my eyes and scanned the counter for something to throw at him. I settled on the pen I used to write lyrics in my journal.

"She doesn't need to be polite either." He quipped once the pen bounced off his shirt and back onto the counter. I reached for it, and simultaneously, he reached for my journal. We both pulled back with our desired artifact in hand. He tried to hide it behind his back.

"Grey! Come on, give it back!" I circled the counter, reaching for my pages. My chest leaned into his arm as I attempted to get the book from behind him. He kept moving it so it was mere inches out of my grasp. After a second, I stopped fighting. The front of our bodies were pressed to one another, and I could feel his heart beating beneath his clothes, racing, a continuation of my own. We stilled, both breathing heavily.

This would only work once. That's what I told myself as I shifted forward, causing him to back into the cabinetry. His arms fell loosely to his sides. I turned fifteen in August. Still, I had never kissed a boy before or tried to. I had no idea how to be sexy. So, I stopped thinking about it. I thought instead about what I wanted to do, what I would do if I allowed myself to like him. I raised my hands to his beautiful head, twisting his curls between my fingers before sliding them down to grip the back of his neck. It was my mistake. I looked up. His open expression showcased his vulnerability. My heart turned erratic.

I was leaning in, allowing his frame to support my weight. One hand fell to his waist, and the feeling of leather brushed against my fingers. The target had been acquired. I pressed my lips to his cheek, changing direction at the last second and stealing the book from his grasp. I returned to my seat victorious.

It took him a moment to turn around. His expression wasn't the playful challenge I had expected. He looked heartbroken, and I hated the rush of guilt that accompanied it. I didn't intend to be mean, and I certainly never thought I could hurt him.

"That." He laughed shakily. "That was really cruel, actually." His voice sounded hoarse.

Grey ran his finger across the rim of the glass to keep from looking at me. He tapped it once and pulled back before dumping the milk and placing the glass in the sink. I quietly left my stool to put the gallon in the fridge, an excuse to be closer to him. Typically, at this time, we would have been sitting beside empty glasses facing each other, one of my knees between his two. I pondered the change from our usual, unhappy with the distance and even more surprised by *how much* I disliked it.

My stubbornness peaked as I leaned against the stainless steel of the refrigerator door and waited for Grey to say something else. It was a game *he* had started when he took my journal in an attempt to read my personal thoughts, many of which were about him. Reading them would have revealed everything about my true feelings. At that time, my lyrics detailed his curly brown hair, sun-kissed skin, and kindness. Kindness I wasn't repaying in this moment as I offered no explanation for my actions.

I *hated* this.

"I'm gonna head to bed." He smiled but it was off. It was a smile, not *his* smile. "Goodnight, Al."

He passed me, and I blocked his path. I wrapped my arms around his neck and tucked my nose against his collarbone. He didn't hesitate to hold me. It was one of Grey's best attributes: he didn't let hurt or anger block him from his true intention. One of his arms wrapped around my waist while the other gently held me against him by the back of my neck. The last time I had felt so safe was when my dad was alive. Grey and I had never done this before. Just the casual side hug at "hello."

"I never meant to be cruel," I told him.

He exhaled, inhaled, slowly. "*I know*, Ally. You're not a cruel person. It's why I like you so much."

I let go of him before I could decide never to let go of him. It was too pleasant to inhale him, to feel his body cocooning me in security. I knew in my core Grey Kingsley wouldn't break my heart. I wished for the millionth time that loving him wouldn't break Charlie's.

The scar on his chin that I had spent so many dinners admiring was too close, and the temptation to touch him again while I could was too great. I pressed my lips against the pale drag gently before pulling away. His air staggered as if I had kissed him on the lips. It was somehow just as intimate. I removed myself, giving my brain the oxygen it needed to think straight.

I questioned if I could have kissed him, *really* kissed

him. Would it have been so different? *Charlie. Charlie. Charlie.* I repeated her name in my head the way people repeated Bloody Mary standing in front of bathroom mirrors. Hoping she would appear to scare me back into my place. But more so, hoping she wouldn't, so I could go on pretending.

"Goodnight, Grey." I turned to depart. He caught me by the waist. *His* smile was back in full force, back to his playful, exuberant self.

"Can we both stop saying goodnight and just talk? No funny business. Just us on those two stools," He dictated, pointing his slender fingers toward our spot. "like any other night."

"Okay." I sighed in relief. I wasn't ready to go either. I liked our kitchen conversations.

Staying up for hours, we talked about my sociology class and what drove human behavior. We talked about my dad, and I told him everything I could remember about who he was and briefly about how he had died. His eyes fell closed as he comprehended my loss. He shared how he never knew his parents, how he was orphaned as a baby, but the system was so bad it created the infinite wonder of "what if." What if they had parents out there somehow who showed up one day to take them back to a life of love?

We launched into a discussion of our dreams and how our subconscious shaped them to highlight our desires and crushing truths. Like how I still had dreams that my dad would show up at the door to my house but could never cross the threshold without turning to dust, just like the ashes we kept in an urn with his name etched into the side.

I tried not to fall for Grey then, in our midnight magic. The moonlight poured through the window, and like light reflecting off the water, it bent the same way to compliment every angle of his face. The purple glow from the buttons on Marilyn's stereo tinted the space lilac, and I felt that if love had a color, it would be the same shade. I don't know what prompted me to tell him this, but he seemed in awe of it, perhaps part of him realizing I had just confessed my true feelings; I quickly changed the subject. As the sky was beginning to brighten, I had to return to bed before Charlie noticed I was gone.

now, july

EVERY MORNING, the loss hits me differently, but there's always the same anxiety, the same black hole within me pulling the person I was into oblivion. I believe I'm still in withdrawal. I always have the same connection to Grey that can never be met. Muscle memory is destroying me. I have to stop my arm mid-extension from where it is reaching for the phone to call Charlie. To confide in her my secrets, better kept than in a diary. I'm battling with my brain to break chemistry.

It's written that every seven years, all the cells in our bodies are replaced with new ones. I wonder if I have to wait another six years for this to end or if it will only amplify my loss. Then, no part of me will ever have touched a part of them.

I pull myself out of bed before another day is swallowed by another night. Before I lay here again, making no progress for the second time this week. I try to make myself functional. I pretend that useful and functional are the same thing.

I move through the day in order of chores. I make the

bed. I shop the grocery list hanging on the fridge while I ignore the funds Libby has left in a jar labeled "Grocery" on the counter. I call it my contribution, though it still feels too little for all she's done for me.

When I return, I put away the groceries, dust, and vacuum the floors. I find being busy doesn't mean being present, that it doesn't prevent me from feeling only half human. When the clock strikes four, I breathe a sigh of relief and lock up quickly before heading to the bar.

My days seem to revolve around my nights. I tell myself music is the only reason, and it has nothing to do with the staff, but as I pull open the door to the pub, I understand more thoroughly. These nights by the piano are the only place I feel safe enough to confront myself—the only place where all of the feelings do not eat away at me. Here, I give them a voice to scream.

It's a small shift in my mindset, but being fascinated by my pain has become much more enjoyable than being devastated by it. Even in a new country, I fear the culture and history are all wasted on me. I'm too self-absorbed to appreciate them.

Sonnie, previously known as Bartender #2, acknowledges me with a smile. I've been coming here for over a week now, and Derek let my nickname slip. "Grayson" did not like "Bartender #2", so Sonnie was a compromise we had worked out. I'd adapted quickly, loving how it slipped over my tongue as if stolen from a different era. The more I used it, the more he gleamed, enjoying the word like a secret we passed back and forth. I was glad for it, afraid that I would never be able to call anyone else by *his* name, or even an extension of his name, without flinching.

"Hey, Rebecca." Sonnie greets me by *my* new name as I approach the bar. Behind the counter, he struggles to hide how pleased he is with himself for his quick thinking. He makes a feeble attempt to cover it up by drying off a glass that wasn't wet to begin with. I roll my eyes but chuckle anyway.

Because I've been evasive of all personal questions, Sonnie and Derek have turned who I am into a game. Their favorite play is guessing my name. So far, I've gotten Brittany, Beatrice, Penelope, Zena, and the list goes on. Ultimately, at the night's start, they decide on their favorite and call me that for the evening. I've started to like the game. I get to be so many people other than myself.

They give me a name, and I give that name a history. Penelope was from a farm in Idaho. She grew up raising cows. Her dad never died; he trained racehorses. Zena grew up in New York. She attended boarding schools, which her wealthy parents sent her to, but they spent every holiday together as a family. For Christmas, she received puppies that arrived under the tree in boxes with blue bows. I prefer their histories over my own.

Tonight, I've become Rebecca.

Who would Rebecca be? I start building her profile until I bore of it and instinctively, my eyes search the room for my piano. My usually empty seat is occupied. The keys play in a complicated succession that sparks a raging conflict inside me. War plays out within my mind as I work out the feeling it has evoked and what words would be attached to such a sound. The piano man's shoulders hunch, and his passion reigns in my ears. I wonder what his original intent was and if it was meant to be anything more than a composition piece. I wonder if he'd be offended if I made it more.

"He's pretty good, huh?" Sonnie asks, interrupting my thoughts.

"Derek's always good," I confess, sipping the whiskey

sour he had laid out. I've heard him play enough now to recognize his signature.

As if he could hear me speak his name over the music, he stopped and turned to us. His charged gaze landed directly on mine. Holes burned through my head. I contemplated getting my sunglasses from my bag to relieve some of the intensity.

"Piano is all yours, Bex," Derek says, strutting off through the kitchen door, which continues to swing back and forth. They must have decided my name before I arrived tonight—a new twist to the game. I would smile at his cleverness, at his given nickname to my given false name, but I'm too shook. How was he able to speak so casually, as if he didn't just play a masterpiece? The keys replay, a phantom of the melody in my head. I sit on the bench, still warm, and try to repeat the tune.

"That's my song." I jump as his voice materializes beside me, a whisper in my ear.

"Errr. Yeah." I say through pathetic lips.

"What is your name?" Derek asks again. I let my fingers drift across the black and white, resisting the urge to push down. I give in too soon, allowing the note to fill the room. He lays the hood down gently, forcing my fingers to move from where they were dancing moments before. "If you're going to play my song, I deserve to know your name."

"Why do we have to do this every night?" I sigh.

I don't want to be Ally again. Rebecca, "Bex," as he so charmingly dubbed me, would have been raised in California by beach bums. She would have grown up surfing in salt water that drowned every worry she ever encountered. I bet all of her friends were still alive. I like being Rebecca. I stay resolute in my stance.

"Why avoid telling me such a basic fact?" Derek's eyes

center on mine, and I try to avoid the annoying moment when I get lost in them.

"What is your obsession with labels?"

"It isn't a label, it's a name." He rebuts.

"A name is another word for a label." I throw back.

"There are better things to protest." He argues. "Why the secrecy?" He leans forward like his domineering shadow will somehow make me answer. Wrong. He doesn't know that I like existing in the shadows.

"I'm happy not being noticed," I say, hoping to resolve the matter.

"But you are noticed. More so for being strangely over-protective of what you're called. You know it takes more than a first name to steal your identity?"

"Yes, Derek." I roll my eyes.

"Further proof that you know *my* name, which is hardly fair."

"Ally." I blurt out. Permission is apparently unnecessary. All my other names float out the door, and I miss them immediately. *Come back*, I silently beg.

"What?"

"My name. It's Ally. God. I tell you, and you still ask questions."

"Ally." He tries it out. "I liked Rebecca better." He says as he walks away. I see the smirk form on his lips and know he is lying.

now, august

WE'VE DEVELOPED A ROUTINE. I show up at four and work through my music. Derek stops by my station regularly, advising me to try this note or that. He sweeps the floor, returns to take my pen, and scribbles his own lyrics on my napkin without asking. He knows he doesn't need to; his additions are always good. They eliminate whatever my block was, and I can never find objection to them, especially when they make the music so much better. Halfway through the second week, Derek, Sonnie, and Big Mike (Bartender #3) have convinced me to stay and play through the night for tips.

When I tell Libby I have a job, she is thrilled, and I know I have to do it. Her happiness alone would have been reason enough for me to push past my stage fright, but I don't do it for her. I do it because I can't seem to want to do anything else.

The first night I play for a crowd, I'm beyond anxious. Derek lays my whiskey sour in front of me while I take in the size of the crowd, attempting to predetermine what will win their favor. Will they tolerate me or boo me off the stage? Butterflies attack my stomach in angry mobs. No, not butterflies. Wasps.

"Nervous?" He leans across the counter that separates us and studies me, trying to get a read on my energy.

His attention, paired with his dimpled chin, tug at me. He always looks like a hurricane held at bay only by the skin on his body. I don't know what draws me to this conclusion besides his consistent propulsion. That and the eyes I can't seem to get enough of, constantly plaguing my thoughts over what shade they'll be. How they lighten and darken, both calm and storm. There is so much going on inside of him. Enough to cause worry, to sound an alarm. Maybe it would if I was a regular girl, but if he's a hurricane, I'm a tornado. We're both natural disasters; perhaps this is why I've felt most comfortable here, in his presence. Where I'm most free to be myself with all the shingles hanging off my house. I'm at ease in the contradiction, in somehow being the storm and the result of it.

His face is within reach, less than two feet away. Taking a risk, I place my thumb into the divot of his chin that divides it. I'm curious if it is smooth or rough, if he's shaved or not. It's both. The usual stubble is too shallow to be seen but is still felt, nonetheless. The rest of my fingers fall gently on his jawline.

He has such a devastating face, the kind that inspires quotes like "the face that launched a thousand ships." I hardly know him, but I feel like I'd fight in that war. His breathing is shallow, and our eyes lock. What color are they tonight? Before I can move him, he tilts his head, already knowing what I want. His eyes shift in the light. Pine trees.

"Pine trees?" He laughs.

"I didn't realize I had spoken," I confess, feeling timid. I flush momentarily before I'm caught up again. My fingers find a new path and trace the creases that have formed in his cheeks. He's made a frame for his smile.

"Your eyes," I whisper. "They're the color of pine trees. Juniper. Like fall, when the needles sprout from the branches before they fade to brown. Yours are always changing seasons." I puzzle.

He stares at me for a while as if I've said something exquisite or troubling. I can't define which way his confusion is leaning.

"Ally." He whispers softly. It leaves my skin tingling as if he were the one touching me. It's breathy and full of implications that I'm starting not to mind. I watch some internal dilemma play out in his head before he comes to a decision. Sonnie clears his throat behind us. We both pull away quickly as if we've been caught doing something we shouldn't.

"Ally, you're up." Sonnie's expression is discouraged as he waves his hand towards my stage. *My* stage. I like the way it sounds. I find the piano and feel relief before I take in all the bodies, the faces that will be watching, judging— panic twists in my stomach, sucking the air from the room. I feel like I'm going to throw up.

"She needs five minutes," Derek growls before coming around the bar and taking my hand. He guides me through a door to the kitchen, then another to the back alley.

"Derek, what are we—" I begin to ask. His back falls against the building's aged brick, distracting me as he pulls a pack of cigarettes from his pocket and lights one.

"You smoke?" I ask instead, stunned.

"Helps the nerves."

I extend my hand for a cigarette. I'm ready to try anything if it means I don't have to feel like that again. To my surprise, instead of lighting a new one, he offered me the slender stick that had just been pressed between his lips. Slipping it between my own, I fight not to run my tongue across the filter to see if I could taste him on it still. I fail and taste nothing but the bitter tobacco. Serves me right.

Pulling from the filter, I choke as the smoke fills my lungs. Cigarettes are turning out to be very different from the joints I used to sneak outside and smoke on the back porch while my mother was sleeping. A habit I only started after the fire. It allowed me to remember the Kingsleys without the pain. In a sick way, it also helped me to feel closer to them. Breathing in smoke the same way they had.

Thinking of them stings, so I focus on inhaling. I try to pull again with more success. Flicking the ash like I've seen in movies, I let my arm rest by my side. The head rush hits a few moments later, making me feel like I'm floating. The ground becomes less steady, and the cigarette falls from my fingers.

A pair of arms jolt out to stabilize me, changing my trajectory. Instead of falling backward, I fall forward against him. Derek chuckles, light and childlike. It helps to soothe the fear and unease building inside me. I debate straightening myself out to stand, but his grasp on my waist feels like a security blanket. Gently, he lifts my fingers back to his face.

"Don't stop." He pleads.

My breath picks up; it hitches. My gaze comes to rest on his shoulders, too wide, too tall to be Grey. A soundless sob rises in my throat. I feel unstable again. This is wrong. He's wrong. Why is everything upside down again? I'm rattled. All of our old memories are shaking free from this angle. Grey's slender fingers twisting the knob on the radio to turn it louder, his voice off-key in the Jeep. Grey smiling brilliantly at Charlie as she jumps on the couch, spilling popcorn for the millionth time. Grey flipping pancakes in the kitchen. I shouldn't be here. Flames overtake the area. Smoke from the cigarette on the ground spirals up in tendrils, clouding my vision. I wince and turn away.

"Ally." Derek's accent comes out thick. He holds up his hands where I can see them. His knuckles are bruised. He pins them between his back and the wall. "I won't hurt you."

Confused by his actions, I search for his eyes to find an explanation. When I meet them, that sense of security returns. The air tastes fresh again. I hate the inconsistency living inside of me. I go from fine to fractured too quickly. He doesn't seem to notice my instability. Or he doesn't care. His face is calm and sure.

I begin to relax. I trust him, I realize. Derek always seems in control, but he's relinquished it to me. He's trusting me as well. My fingers press into his cheeks, touching him, and the tingle has turned to a buzz. I think of ghosts draining batteries to be able to draw enough energy, like a life force needed to be seen. Derek is that life force, filling me with static.

He maintains my stare as I trace his face. I run my fingers across his chin, his cheekbones, his eyebrows.

"I'm going to place my hands on your waist. I promise not to move them." He says breathily. He gauges me for an objection, but if I had any, I've forgotten them.

I gasp when he touches me. The sound causes him to furrow his eyebrows as if concentrating on maintaining his delicacy. It's becoming natural to lose control of myself around him, and something like a moan passes through my lips.

"Fuck, Ally." Gripping my waist, he pulls my body

tighter against his own. I feel like someone has jolted me with a thousand watts of electricity. My forehead falls against his, and we both pant for air, savoring each other's oxygen. "Every time you touch me..." He whispers, droning off. My hands have found his neck, exploring, tangling in his hair. Our mouths begin to part.

The door to the kitchen flies open.

"Yo Derek, have you seen Al? Crowd's getting impat—" It's another bartender, Big Mike this time, not Sonnie. He stops mid-sentence when he sees us and blows out a whistle. "Nice night, innit?" He asks, his laugh bellowing through the alleyway.

Appalled at myself, I shift out of Derek's space, and he drops his hands from my hips and stares at them. I push past Mike into the bar.

"Mate." Mike scolds loosely as I pass, addressing Derek. "Bugger off." I hear him snap in reply, now far away.

I'm not singing tonight. I feel icky like I've violated Grey's trust somehow. I don't have it in me to put on a show. I pass through the second door. I'm back in the crowd when I see the piano again. At once, I know it is the only way to free myself.

"It's not about the people; it's about the music. It's about soul." Derek reassures, softer with me than he had been with Mike. Now less than a meter away, he must have trailed in behind me. Ignoring the guilt, I focus on his words. Closing my eyes, new words take their place: *Isn't that the essence of who we are? What we love?* I open and nod, sure this time. "Go." Derek offers, smiling gently.

The moment I begin to play and sing, the crowd falls away. It's all about the song. I'm the half-woman now. Only this time, I'm living in a memory everyone can see. I finish the first number, and the room breaks into applause. I search for something, someone.

"Soul." Derek mouths from across the room. It's disconcerting how the shame disappears behind the sparks still lingering from where he touched me.

Before I know it, we're closing up. Big Mike lifts me like I'm no heavier than a sheet of paper and swings me around. "Al, that was incredible! The whole room went silent when you started to sing. I've never heard the pub that quiet before." He ruminates.

Big Mike became a fast friend after our introduction. He liked how I roasted the guys and found my American accent hilarious. Apparently, I say a lot of words wrong. He likes to pick out the differences in our phrasing. The easy banter has become a highlight in my days. When he sets me down, I thank him and say goodnight so I can make my departure.

Libby has been waiting for this night. I know she will be up when I get home, starving for all the details, and I am eager to divulge them. She was still upset that I wouldn't let her support me, but I had been too worried it would amplify my nerves worse than they already were.

A few lingering girls stop Derek and ask him to take a photo with them. *Huh. So, girls really do ask him that.* It's different than I expected. Not that I'd expected anyone to be like, "You're so hot; can we please take a photo with you?" which is why I had been so appalled the first night he'd accused me of wanting to. No, these girls clearly thought he was something to look at, but it was something else. They were *fans.*

I took the opportunity to sneak out, feeling uneasy as discomfort played across his face at the attention. I had just reached the handle when a pair of hands covered both of my own. Derek's pine trees catch the light, taking on their familiar yellow hue; I watch as they transform into honeycomb. The cool London air pours in from the outside, even this time of summer, but I don't feel it. All I feel are his fingers wrapped around my palms and the buzz of him touching me. I wonder if this is what addiction feels like.

"It's frustrating when you don't wait like I ask." He speaks in a low volume that causes heat to stir between my thighs. *Fuck.*

He steps away from me, and the air loses its thickness. I want it back. I liked the anticipation. I hear tires on wet pavement as the street falls back into my peripheral. I planned on replying, but my instinct is to be sassy. If I tell him I can walk myself home, he might let me. I keep my lips sealed. It isn't worth the risk.

We pad down the street softly. Both of us lag, slower than our usual rushed pace.

"Mike was right. You were phenomenal up there." He chuckles, and it comes out shaky. He brings his arm up to scratch the back of his head—a gesture he mostly reserves to use in my presence. I can't be sure why, but it pleases me. Derek shoves his hands into his pockets and says nothing as we continue the short hike to Libby's. We're about a minute's walk away, and I'm scared the quiet will turn awkward, so I try another route of conversation.

"So, you're like *somebody* then?" I inquire, hoping to get him talking.

"We're all *somebody*." He replies quickly, like he'd rather discuss anything else.

But I can picture it too clearly. Derek on a stadium stage playing pieces like the ones I've stolen and turned into something else. I picture the bright spotlights casting his shadow bigger, creating its own entity. Peter Pan and his lost shadow, all grown up. The crowd would hold up their cell phone flashlights like fairy dust as he made thousands believe again.

"Derek." I scold.

"Ally, must you insist on digging into my life every night?" He shoots me a pointed look over his shoulder.

"Fine. I'll just Google you. What's your last name?" I asked, ignoring his question and also the fact that he regularly digs into mine, my name being a prime example.

"God, don't Google me." He warns, but his humor is back, the evidence in his dimples.

"So, you're a full-blown big-deal musician." I laugh.

"I don't like labels." He smirks. I push him. My hand betrays me by lingering on his arm. Beneath the layers, the warmth of his body radiates through the fabric. The contact feels like someone has hit the defrost button. We've stalled out. No longer frozen but motionless. I remove my hand with effort. I don't want to mess this up. The alleyway was a close call. We could have ruined everything. I like his scribbles on my napkins and his pep talks. I don't want them to go away. Without mention, we resume our stride.

"Yeah, I *was* somebody." He says after a beat, shoulders falling.

"Not anymore?"

"Not anymore."

"Yeah, me either." I acknowledge, glum. That part I understand more than he will ever know. A gust of wind blows my hair, the strands dancing around my face. Derek hesitates, and then a decision is made, and he tucks them back into place.

"Maybe you're not who you used to be, but you're definitely *somebody,* Ally." He says quietly, leaning forward. The butterflies have returned. I'm almost enjoying them before they begin to boil in my stomach. One by one, they die and turn into something toxic. Anxiety, what I feel is anxiety. Derek is going to try to kiss me, and I don't want him to. He is the wrong guy. He is not Grey.

I take a step back and cough. My first friend since moving here, and I'm blowing it hard. Is that what we are? Friends? I've spent practically every night with him writing songs over the past two weeks. Yes. Friends seems like a good place to start.

"Hmm." He muses aloud and looks away. At first, I believe he is upset, but then I see his smirk and find that he is amused, as always.

"Do you never get angry?" I ask.

"You'd think I'd be used to this randomness by now, but it still scrambles me." He snickers. "Yes, I get angry. Usually I function on angry."

"Like the night I met you?" I quiz.

We lean against the concrete enclosure of the garden gate in front of Libby's. His leather jacket crinkles, and he squints towards the sky as if expecting rain.

"Did I seem cross then?" He asks.

"You were clearly annoyed. I think you thought I was prissy." I admit.

"I thought you were beautiful." It's a compliment, but he says it like he is recounting a grocery list: *I thought we needed milk.* "And obnoxiously American, yes." There it is. This time, there is some emotion behind it—humor, I think.

"Hmmm," I say to fill the silence because suddenly I've forgotten what we were talking about and can only focus on how he was attracted to me. The buzz is back. Butterflies revived.

"I should go." He says, pushing off.

This has become our routine. Derek walks me home; we exchange a few words, and he goes away. Every night, though, we find ourselves speaking more at length. My intrusive questions met with intrusive questions. Sometimes we answer, sometimes we don't. Either way— it's always okay. Our music has become more intertwined. His arrangement to my notes or lyrics as he adds, changes, makes recommendations. He's been the instructing hand behind my needle and thread, sewing together the best music I've ever made.

I wait for him to head down the block and disappear around the corner. Instead, he turns.

"I want to show you something. Tomorrow morning. Are you available?"

"Yes," I say without thinking. I answer quickly, too quickly. My feet guide me backward, my body in shock of my mouth. I'm familiar with "no." It has become a core word in my vocabulary. More popular than all the others. "Yes" feels foreign on my tongue.

"Derek." I move back into his space, wanting to touch his smile again now that it has reappeared.

"Ally." He moves back into mine, inviting me.

Libby cuts the outside lights on, peeking out the window. He begins to step away, always dancing around this thing between us. I'm overcome, not ready for him to disappear. Taking his arm in my grasp, I pull him into the gate behind the banister out of her sight so his body is pinning mine to the bars. His eyes widen in shock at my change of character.

"I don't know," I say breathily, answering the unspoken question. "I don't know what I'm doing. I guess I don't want you to go yet. Or something." *I am so not playing it cool right now.*

"Or something? You want me to sneak through your window, Ally?" He teases, running his fingers through my hair before securing them to my neck. *Why the fuck does that feel so good?*

"What? *No.*" I retort flabbergasted. He snickers. I pout, my hand leaving his arm to pull at his hair in childhood retaliation.

"Don't do that." He says seriously, moving my hands back to his face like in the alleyway. "*That* makes me want to fuck you. *This.* This is safe."

Breaking out into chills, I shudder. My body had freaked out over the idea of kissing the guy, but now he talks about fucking me, and it's in overdrive. *What the hell is going on with me?* I should go inside. The last thing I want is to rile him up, but my actions argue back. Like before, I run my fingers along his chin, thumbing the single black hoop hanging from his left ear like some washed-up 90's front man. On him, though, it works.

"You *want* me to touch you?" I ask.

"Yes. Pretty much all of the time." He exhales.

"So you like being touched?" I follow up, not entirely understanding my question.

"Not normally, no. I like it when *you* touch me. I'd kiss you right now if you didn't seem so damn opposed to the idea." He admits.

Vulnerable is a rare look on him, and it makes my stomach flip wildly. Somehow, my hands have come to rest on his waist, him now the one gently tracing my features. Under his shirt, I find his skin and draw him near. He groans, his nose brushing against my own. His breath is hot on my lips, smelling of cigarettes and soap.

"Meet me tomorrow morning." He rasps in reminder like he's scared this interaction has changed my mind. It may have.

"Why?" I ask warily.

"Christ. You don't trust easily, do you? I'm not trying to sleep with you. I told you I want to show you something."

"Friends don't sleep with friends?" I pry suspiciously, running my palms across his stomach in contrast to my words.

"No. And friends don't go for a grope in the garden either." He accuses, stepping away, the phone from my back pocket in his hands. "Tell me you'll come."

I nod, giving him my passcode to enter his number. I remain frozen against the gate long after he's left. My phone buzzes in my hand, breaking my stupor. A message from an unknown number appears on my screen.

GO INSIDE, ALLY.

I roll my eyes at the screen but follow his instructions, opening the gate to head in. Moments later, a follow-up text appears with the address and the time.

then, november

CHARLIE DECIDED we should have a sleepover. I had never been to a boy-girl sleepover before, with the exception of Grey, of course. My parents would never let me have a party like this. They were too afraid of teen pregnancy and coke-addicted youth. Luckily, this was just another night at the Kingsleys, and as far as Mom and Michael knew, nothing out of the ordinary.

I loved how James and Marilyn saw things differently than my own guardians. Grey had a friend over, and Charlie had a couple of friends over. They embraced that their children wanted to spend time together rather than apart, and it wasn't like they wouldn't be in the house to chaperone.

The five of us sat around the massive coffee table. The sectional was a wide U-shape, plenty big to accommodate all of us with room left over. We played a version of Two Truths and a Lie. Only versus sharing facts about ourselves, we were asked questions and then voted on which answer was false.

Grey turned to me, my face going red in fear of what he'd ask.

"Is it true that you grew up here?" He posed for his first question.

"Here, as in Matthews? The state? The states?" I laughed.

"Yes."

"No," I responded quickly, causing him to rub his chin in doubt.

"Interesting." He said in his best accent which matched no origin I could identify.

"What was that even supposed to be?" I asked, cracking a smile.

"Hey!" He yelled playfully. "I'm answering the questions here!"

"Answering?" I mocked, giggling.

"Hey!" He tried again. "I'm asking the questions here."

I was even more obsessed with him than I had been. Our moods had become shared. When Grey was in a good mood, which was always, I was in a good mood. Our close encounter in the kitchen a month ago became a memory I regularly tapped into. It's what I daydreamed about in class. I acted my age, scribbling his name in hearts on the bylines of the notebook I prayed no one ever saw. Charlie giggled beside me and scooted closer to Ollie, a boy she had a crush on from our grade.

"Is it true that when you're alone you..." He paused. I gazed at him skeptically. "try to shove as many marshmallows into your mouth as possible?"

"Yes," I said seriously.

"Very good. Final question." He took the tone of a detective.

"Is it true that you want to sleep with me?" He asked.

Charlie threw a pillow at him, causing the popcorn

basket to spill in a heap on his lap. I was thankful for the distraction, afraid my flush would give me away. Only in speech have I learned to deny.

"Let—hey! Hey, let her answer!" He waved off Charlie's continued attack. His eyes locked on mine. "Well?"

"Oh, yes. It's really all I think about." I mock with an eye roll.

"That's definitely the lie," Elizabeth said. Elizabeth was Charlie's friend and sat at the desk next to mine in English. She bats her eyelashes at Grey.

"I second that." Charlie agreed.

"You guys are trying to ruin my night, " he said, but his smile remained plastered across his face.

"No, I think it was the first one." Ollie mused. He stood, stretching as he prepared to launch into his reasoning.

Charlie took my hand, whispering how cute he was for the thousandth time into my ear. With his skater-boy style and curly blonde hair that hung down to his shoulders, Ollie was one of those guys who always had a girlfriend. Charlie was hoping to be the next.

"Yo, listen up. This is gonna be good." Grey picked the popcorn off his blanket, popping it into his mouth. He shushed us for the speech like it was a grand finale.

"Shut up." Charlie threw an M&M at him. He caught it effortlessly in his mouth.

"The man is trying to make a speech, sister." He stated dramatically, gesturing to Ollie. I liked the way he drew on certain words and subtly repeated others he had stuttered on. I watched his mouth as he spoke, and he smiled when he caught my stare.

"So," Ollie started. "She says she wants to sleep with him and then rolls her eyes, but," He emphasized the 'but.'

"that's a proven tactic to make us second guess it. She wants it to be obvious that it is the lie."

Grey began to clap slowly while the three of us girls scowled.

"You can't argue with that logic, ladies," Grey said, waving his hands way more than necessary to get his point across.

"However, it is highly unbelievable," Ollie added, and we all clapped as Grey shrugged it off.

"Doesn't make it less true." Grey pouted.

"Bro, would you stop interrupting me?" Ollie pulled at a curl as it gained his attention momentarily, then turned back to us. "As I was saying, the first one is clearly the lie. She has no accent! She is the palest out of all of us. Plus, we have only had classes together since 6th grade."

"Actually, I'm Canadian," I said, remembering what a douchebag he was in the 6th grade. He would steal answers from my homework and cut me in the lunch line.

"See? She wants me." Grey fist-bumped the air.

"I don't know why my parents insisted on adopting both of us," Charlie whispered loudly. I snorted.

As the night wound down, we all faded off as a movie played on the screen above the fireplace. Once again, I admired the Kingsley's sectional and its ability to sleep five comfortably.

Charlie had curled up in a ball with one leg stuck out, and Ollie held it like a teddy bear. His mouth hung open, and every few seconds, his head cocked back unattractively in a snore. Elizabeth was stretched out as close as she could get to Grey. Her head sat practically in his lap, annoying me to no end.

Grey was sitting upright with one hand resting lazily by

my leg, his head tilted back against the couch. I stood and stretched, reaching for the remote to turn the volume down as explosions roared to life on the television. A crunch stole my focus as I took in the popcorn mess on the floor. I kneeled, trying to pick up each kernel, but it was useless.

"You know they invented a suction device for that. It's called a vacuum." Grey said drowsily, keeping his voice low.

I jumped, startled. I hadn't realized he'd woken up.

"I don't like messes," I explained.

"Fair enough. I thought I'd have a wittier response, but I'm too tired." He rubbed his chin, his voice full of sleep.

"So go back to bed." I snarked, throwing one of the kernels at him.

"Not without my sleeping buddy." He grinned, patting the couch beside him. My eyes involuntarily shot to Elizabeth.

"I have to pee," I said awkwardly as he took notice of my gaze. I didn't. I was unsure what to say to my best friend's brother, who kept flirting with me. "Don't you hate that no one has found a better way to announce that?"

He leaned forward, oddly intrigued. "Well." He paused, moving his hands in the air as if he could pull the ideas from there. "There's 'I have to use the restroom,' 'I need to freshen up,' which I never understood. Oh! There's 'I need to potty,' which is a classic, but that kind of sounds like you're pooping." He joked. I briefly wondered if I would recognize him without the smile that seemed to be permanently fixed on his face.

"I have to pee," I repeated. He sent me on my way with a two-finger salute before settling back into the couch. He subtly inched away Lizzy, sending a shockwave of satisfaction through me.

As soon as I reached the hallway, I felt a sinking in my stomach. The anticipation had diminished, and this escape from his prying eyes felt less rewarding than I had imagined. There was no relief.

I opened Charlie's door, examining her turquoise walls, her shag rug, and the flowers that decorated her pillowcases. A pang of guilt hit me as if I had betrayed her. I backed into the hallway and heard movement from the living room. Grey coughed, and my thoughts filled back up with him.

Suddenly, I was standing in front of *his* bedroom, pushing open the door. I'd passed by it plenty of times but had never been inside. Walls of light barn wood bookcases met the low-paned windows. His room had been painted charcoal gray, and his headboard was adorned in rich cognac leather that offset its tone. Each shelf had a light inside, showcasing his collection like a library of rare books.

Most cases were covered in published works, but the top two shelves were filled with pages bound together by clips and folders. A typewriter and computer sat on his desk, with well-worn keys. Seeing all the books without spines, I realized these were the works Marilyn had mentioned over the summer.

Curiosity got the best of me, and I reached for one, sitting on the floor by the window. I mentally mapped the room, looking for hiding places should someone walk by. I began to flip through the pages and became immersed in the story in seconds.

```
One look, and I knew he deserved it. It was
a frightful sight, this man before me. If
you could even call him a man. His sticky
```

skin glistened like a July night. How had I been made of him, and did this mean I, too, was ruined?

I devoured the words, settling into my spot on the carpet.

then, november

"PEOPLE TYPICALLY ASK before going through someone's things," Grey said from above me. I gasped at the intrusion. Mine or his, I was unsure of. His lips parted, waiting for me to speak, but I was too embarrassed to remember how.

"If you're going to read my writing, you at least have to tell me what you think." He sighed, stretching out across the bed. His shirt lifted slightly and my mouth dampened at the exposure of his muscled abdomen.

Clutching the baseball from his nightstand, he tossed it into the air repetitively. I waited for it to fall in his face. It didn't.

"What is it about?" I asked, the pages in my hands feeling like trade secrets.

"A man with no virtue and how that impacts the world," Grey answered.

I nodded, processing the new information.

"Do you like it?" He stared up at the designs etched into the plaster ceiling. The moonlight bounced off his scar.

"It's incredible."

He turned to face me, the tick of his lips revealing pleasure at my answer. Extending a hand, he motioned for the manuscript.

"Where did you stop?" He asked once I handed it over. I pointed to the spot on the page, scooting closer to the bed. As he started reading, I rested my back against the nightstand.

"*Micah had always believed that men weren't born bad; they were made. It was Jeremy who changed his mind about that. Jeremy who delivered the blow so swiftly that Micah couldn't even register the crack of bone splitting. These were children, for God's sake. They were not soldiers. They were not disposable. Yet, Jeremy looked at them as if they were.*

Micah spit out the blood that had formed in his mouth. He stood and looked across at the boy he had grown up with. He watched as his friend transformed into something else—something simpler, an opponent.

Jeremy smiled wickedly. He did not care who was the victor. It was the fight he had wanted, and so, for him, he had already won." He reads aloud.

He continued for five minutes before saying, "You can sit on the bed, you know. I won't even try to hit on you." He added for good measure, his infectious smile back in full force.

Scooting over to make room, I climbed into the spot he'd made. My muscles started to relax in the warmth he'd left behind. A few more pages and I began to fade. As if Two Truths and a Lie was a prophecy, I fell asleep in his bed.

now, august

I STAND in front of the mirror and twist my hair this way and that, trying to get it to do what I want. My will doesn't seem to be strong enough to command it, and the blonde strands stick out in every direction. After a few moments of this, I decide to leave it down.

I brush my teeth for the second time this morning and then change clothes for the third. I'm unsure what to expect, so I dress cutely in a plaid pencil skirt and chucks. I pack some jeans and a shirt I don't care about, just in case the day takes a turn and we end up in the mud shooting plastic ducks. I don't know what English people do for fun. I just came back to society. I'm so not ready for this date.

Not a date, Ally. I remind myself. Libby must be getting to me.

When I came inside last night, my suspicions were correct. She was waiting up with a cup of tea in her hands. When she motioned to the cup beside her, she smiled widely, like it was the best joke ever.

I groaned.

"Libby, you know 'Spill the tea' literally came from women gossiping over tea in England. It's not clever; it's just on the nose."

"Which is what makes it clever, nonetheless. Now, sit. Spill." She pulled out the chair from next to her.

I gave in and sat, pouring myself a cup of Earl Grey. I added cream and sugar while she put on a show of patiently waiting for me to finish. When I could delay no longer, she wore a smug expression. *Gotcha,* it said.

"Have you sent your new collection to Italy yet? That Pompeii exhibit is going to be insane. That one statue gets me every night." I made a meager attempt to change the subject.

"Yes, I did. So, you like this boy?" She asked, taking another sip though her eyes never left me.

"Okay, wow. Going straight for the meat and potatoes, huh? No 'Ally, how was your night?' 'Ally, how was singing?' Straight to the boy. I expected more from you, Libs." I mocked, attempting another route of evasion.

She waited. Oh, she was good. Silence was often the best tactic when trying to get one to reveal their secrets.

"Yes, Libby. I like the boy, and I feel guilty for liking the boy because the boy is not Grey, which makes it feel wrong, but when he looks at me, I forget why it feels wrong." I said in the longest run-on sentence ever.

"Are you going to see him again?" She asked thoughtfully. She didn't engage in any other part of my confidences.

I focused on one of the four mismatched chairs across the table. The table was round and made of natural oak. The wood rings were visible through the stain, indicating it had been cut from the trunk of a very large tree. It seemed less likely it had been bought and more likely that it had fallen through a portal from a storybook realm only to land right in Libby's kitchen. I felt comfortable in the small space, her tiny breakfast nook cradling us and my confessions.

"Tomorrow," I said like it was the biggest secret yet. "I'm seeing him again tomorrow."

"Will you go even though you feel like you're betraying Grey?" Her casual use of his name felt foreign. She said it the way you say someone's name who is still alive, not in the way you tip-toe around someone who has died.

It was an interesting question she posed. Interesting, because I hadn't considered not going. After Derek left, the guilt of what had almost happened smacked me in the face. But even then, I had never considered changing my mind.

"I didn't realize I had a choice." I had admitted to her then.

She smiled knowingly. "You must really like him, Ally. Opening your heart to someone new doesn't dishonor Grey. The very best way *to* honor him is to share the love you had for him and then love some more."

I was thinking over what she said and trying to find fault. I couldn't. I still don't think it's as simple as she makes it sound, but I liked the idea.

"Go on your date." She added.

Wait—*what?*

"Date?" I laughed. "It's not a date."

She stood, placing her cup in the sink. "Goodnight, Al." She squeezed my shoulder and sauntered down the hall.

"Not a date, Lib!" I called after her.

Now, here I am, brushing my teeth, changing outfits, and packing extra clothes, thinking of it as a date. I step away from the mirror. I need to stop overthinking this.

I grab my keys from the hook and climb into my gently used car, which I bought when I moved here. In the city, I can travel by the tube, but where my university is, having a car will be much more effective. I drive down the wrong side of the street, the left side here, and follow my phone's GPS. It's a two-hour drive—about as far away as my stretch to school will be.

I'm happy Libby talked me into securing a dorm. I would not want to make this drive every day.

England uses more roundabouts than traffic lights, and I don't have an opportunity to text Derek and ask him where the hell he is having me meet him. When I pass the millionth rolling hill, I'm convinced he entered the address wrong, and I've driven all this way for nothing. A tree line in the distance marks the beginning of a wood. The small dot on the GPS signals that's where it's taking me.

"You have arrived." My phone announces.

I slow the car.

"Arrived where?" I ask it. It doesn't answer.

Then, I see. Shortly ahead is a driveway. I pulled in and was blocked from going further by a large gate. An aged brick wall spans out on either side, seeming to stretch for miles. A black box on a post has a call button and a keypad. He didn't give me a code.

PLEASE TELL ME YOU DIDN'T BRING ME OUT HERE TO KILL ME.

I type and send the text, hoping my phone has enough service to go through. If I'm mistaken and have the address wrong, I don't want to press the call button.

ALLY. BE REASONABLE. TAKE A LEFT AT THE END OF THE PATH.

I roll my eyes. Good to see his tone hasn't changed through text. I studied his number last night after I got in bed. Obsessed over if I should text him and ask him what to wear, what we'd be doing and if he had thought of kissing me again after he left. Settling, I added his name to my phone and went to bed. Seeing the letters on my screen now makes my fingertips fizzy. They twitch every few seconds in anticipation. Fizz, pop. The gate opens before me in time with the ding of his message. I guess it's the right address.

I drive slowly. The road seems to go on forever before the wood line finally tapers off and opens to a path. The sunlight was cut off under the trees. Making the left I was instructed to, it now blares through the windshield, blinding me. The dirt road has turned to stone, and the landscaping is well worth marveling at. Each side of the stone is enclosed with boxwood bushes framing the larger-than-average driveway. It finally ends at what appears to be a massive museum—the orb of a conservatory peeks over the stone blocks of the mansion.

What the hell is this place?

Derek steps through the massive doors. I can't stop ogling them. The door has a wrought iron frame, encasing stained glass inside. When they shut, the doors meet in the middle to form a tree trunk that branches out from the middle. It's stunning.

He steps around to the driver's side, again, the wrong side, and opens my door for me. I've been so transfixed by the doors I hadn't bothered to get out yet.

"Kill you? Where's your originality, Ally?" He asks, poking fun at my earlier message.

"Derek, where are we?" I'm still gawking at the building before me.

"Well, uh, in a manner of speaking, I guess you could call this home." He appears bashful before he nods in the direction of the house. "Come."

He leads me up to the doors which are even more breathtaking up close. He smiles as I stop to appreciate them. The glass casts rainbows along the stone floors inside.

"That's one of Duke's, my grandfather's, prized creations." He says from a few feet away. He's squinting up at the doors as he speaks. "It was inspired by the Sainte-Chapelle in Paris. He said being in that chapel was the closest he had ever felt to talking to God. He wanted people to have the same experience upon entering his home. It sounds ostentatious, I know, but that was never his intention. He liked the idea of creating a place where people could come to discover themselves. He used to open the place to the public before—" He pauses before picking up his story in a different place. "It's the same glass from the Chapelle. Extra they kept under the church in case they ever came to need repair. Duke can be quite tenacious when he wants something."

I have been in awe of the property since I pulled up. The doors are exquisite, but Derek gives them a voice. I've been so captivated by their beauty that I hadn't taken notice of *him* yet.

A silver chain hangs around his neck, holding a ring at the end. Today is the first time I've been able to see what's on the end of it, as it is usually tucked into his shirt. I'm curious about the ring, who it belonged to, and what makes it so special that he wants to carry it.

I slip my pointer finger through it and spin it around, the rest of my fingers resting lightly against his chest.

"It was my mother's, " he whispers before taking my

hand and ushering me forward. This spawns many more questions, but I put them on hold for later.

The "date" jitters have faded and been replaced with... excitement? Yes, that's the right word. I'm excited to be here. Eager even. Eager to explore more of this place with him.

He guides me down a massive hallway. Ferns appear to be growing from the floor up to the glass ceiling. I stop and reach out to take a leaf between my fingers. I gasp.

"It's alive," I whisper. To maintain this seems impossible. I've seen moss walls on Pinterest and Instagram. I've taken photos in front of the ones at the yogurt shop back home. But those were always fake replications. They pale in comparison to this.

"How do they get them to grow like that?" My jaw is on the floor, and I'm sure I've never been anywhere so enchanting.

"Water and light. It's all about balance. It took years of patience for Duke to finally work out the proper irrigation to keep them alive—the proper glass to deliver the perfect amount of light from above. The ferns are grown off-site horizontally and imported in when they reach maturity. Their roots tangle to give them stability. Look." He pushes the leaves away so their roots are on display.

Derek gauges my reaction to everything. His face is aglow and carries a peace I haven't seen in him before. "Duke is quite proud of this. It's his favorite place to bring people to brag." He chuckles warmly.

"A place like this shouldn't exist." I look at him wide-eyed.

"My grandfather is a believer in creating such places." Admiration laces his tone. I'm seeing Derek in a whole new light. The way he knows every story behind this place, a keeper of its history, adds another layer of beauty to him.

"Do you want to see more?" He looks at me from under his lashes, and I see my eagerness reflected.

I nod drunkenly. I *am* drunk. I'm drunk off the beauty packed into every detail surrounding us. I'm drunk off his energy, the openness he's adopted for the day. He takes my hand and doesn't let go when we start walking again. I reach a point of intoxication I don't know I can recover from.

We pause in front of a large stone archway. "The Music Room." He declares in another whisper to my ear. I don't feel like an adult with him now. I don't feel like we're on a date. I feel like I'm with my best friend, sneaking around a castle and going places I'm not allowed. I feel like an explorer of places unknown to the rest of the world.

A giant organ is the focal point of the room. It sits against the back wall.

"Do you play?" I hum back quietly.

"It's not too different from piano. I'm sure you could learn it quickly."

I want to. I want him to teach me how to play. I want to stay up all night in this room, twirling around the ornate wood floor.

"If you lit a bunch of candles in here, it wouldn't even feel like the same time period. This is amazing. Thank you for bringing me here." I swell with gratitude.

"I've been wanting to, Ally. I knew you'd appreciate it." He squeezes my hand, and some emotion is masked under his expression. His gratitude, perhaps, that I appreciate it in the same way he does.

We continue moving forward. "The Ballroom." He

announces at the next archway. The ballroom was plucked right from Beauty and the Beast. Fallen from the same portal as Libby's table. Almost too perfect. Almost animated.

I want to know what inspired this, too. I want to know the story behind the room and the man, what it's been used for, and the occasions such a room has played backdrop to. I picture partygoers in ballgowns and how *they* would have reacted to everything that has been brought to life here. I am about to ask, but there will be time for that. The end of the hall has captured my attention as it appears to open to an endless indoor garden.

"I'll tell you every story in this building, but there's something I want you to see first." He leans low and speaks softly, responding to statements I haven't made. I have my usual reaction to him, and I learn the butterflies are actually bees. It's the only way to describe the buzzing I feel when he is this close to me.

We pass out of the hall, and I am stunned when we step out into the gardens. A stream runs through the center of the gigantic room. Its low gurgle mingles with the sing-song of the birds trapped by the glass ceiling above. The roof is vented, its steel frames embraced by pulleys, allowing someone on the ground to operate its opening and closing. I like that this process has not been mechanized.

Beside the stream, trees grow indoors; they seem not to know or care that what is natural is different from what they've been given. Small blue bricks are outlined by red ones, forming paths that lace their way toward other rooms and spectacular places. These paths are framed by flowers I have never seen before. Tiny gold-plated posts tell you what they are and their origin—countries like Peru, Greece, and Australia. This room showcases a collection of the most beautiful parts of the world.

Derek appeases me by ambling so I can look at everything. While I look at it, he looks at me. I feel afraid that I might fall if I look back. Everything about him plays into my greatest imagination.

I'm lightly holding his arm with one hand, while the other is entwined with his own. It's as if we have been doing this for years, not minutes. We stroll naturally, without effort, and with a grace that is foreign to me.

"Close your eyes." He says as we get closer to our destination.

"Mmmph." I huff with a smile so he knows I'm teasing.

"Please," he asks with perfect politeness. When he says 'please' like that, I want to give him anything he wants. I close my eyes, and we travel synchronously as we had been.

"Don't open them yet." He lets go of me, and I hear the fabric of his clothing swish before a heavy creaking. Metal rubbing against metal.

"Okay. You can look."

When I open my eyes, he is standing next to one of those pulley ropes. The sound I heard must have been one of the vents. I find it on the ceiling, pleased that I guessed correctly. I look back at his face and catch my breath.

The beams refracting off the pool dance on his face, and his brown eyes are golden in the light. All the yellow specks came together at once and illuminated. They look like halos surrounding his pupils. The dimple in his chin and his unholy, rosy lips are astonishing. He glances up from beneath his lashes again, and all of his physical traits dissipate, so there is nothing left but his soul laid bare before me. Every time I've seen him before this exact moment, it suddenly feels like a mask. Now that he's shed it, I don't know if I'll ever be able to look away.

"What do you think?" he asks, a hint of fear in his voice, as if he's afraid I won't like it.

"There is a heaven," I say to the angel, and he rewards me with a radiant smile. It breaks his face into creases, and I desire to touch each one.

He approaches me and moves his arm around my shoulder so he can point to things. I missed his skin on mine and how powerful I feel when he touches me. It makes me believe in magic. It makes me believe I'm *made of magic*.

He seems to forget himself before regaining track of what he was pointing to. I follow his finger and finally take in the room around us. I was wrong before. *This* is the most beautiful place I've ever been.

Without Derek distracting me, I can fully appreciate the space in all its glory. A pond of water is encased by columns overgrown with ivy, and in the center of it, a piano sits on a small raised round platform. The instrument's legs are underwater. The light from the vent falls upon it perfectly, and I'm certain I'm in a dream because the water sparkles like glitter around it.

"Whoa." I muse.

He points beyond the piano to what looks like the wall of a house inside the conservatory. "The balcony there, that's my room when I stay here. I wanted to show you my favorite place in the world, Al." It's the first time he's called me Al, and I love the way it sounds.

"Is that why you brought me here, Derek?" The black spot in my mind grows, coating everything else and tainting the experience. I can't find a reason for why my head grows clouded. A thousand stories have taken place in this room, and I'm suddenly overwhelmed by them.

It's Grey, I realize. He's the black spot. This is the kind of place I would have wanted to show *him*. To watch him invent its history, writing out each one of those thousand stories. Maybe one about this place being ripped from Wonderland. That being the secret behind its beauty. None of it is crafted; the whole structure is pieced together with relics of other worlds more dreamlike than our own.

I'm close to crying. Derek looks from his bedroom back to me and I can see the false connection he just made. His eyes go wide.

"No! Not that. I told you last night." He runs his fingers through his hair in frustration with himself. "I didn't bring you here to shag. I thought maybe you'd like to write a song together in a place like this, and as soon as I got the thought in my head, I couldn't shake it."

His assumption behind my panic was wrong but maybe not misplaced. Is that what stirred my grief? The idea of moving on from Grey in such a complete way that I'm ready to give my body to someone else? Yes, I suppose that was a part of it. Everything I learn about Derek deepens his appeal to me. I have been so elated since I walked through those doors; it's like I don't recognize myself without the pain. I'm moving on in other ways—more permanent ones.

"Ally." Derek's voice cuts through my thoughts. He sounds as mournful as I feel. "I never meant to give you the wrong impression." Regret coats his features. "Duke built the room based on the Roman baths. He wanted a place like that, designed to heal you. The piano was my idea. When I proposed it, he had said there was no better way to heal than through music."

He changes the course of my thoughts so quickly. I lose

sight of the stories Grey would have made up and focus on the real one. I like that it wasn't made to please me. It already was, and that pleases me more. Both magic and reality converged; a real man with real blood and bones labored to make this exist. It's already the better story.

"Last night, at your door, I thought about that. I thought about you and I writing at *that* piano. *That's* why I brought you here." Derek continues.

I press my palm to his cheek. His face is cold and smooth as if he had shaved this morning. His eyes meet mine, like his soul is meeting mine, grounding me back to now. "I'd *love* to write a song with you here."

It's funny to see Derek in his leather jacket, rolling up his pant legs to his knees. I lay my boots to the side and straighten my skirt before we wade through. On the bench, we sit side by side with our feet above the shallow water. The pedal to change the key is elevated to the same height as our feet. When Derek lifts the hood, his notebook sits atop the keys from where he had tucked it away when he was last here. I itch to read the lyrics he's hidden within its pages, but not as much as I wish it to take away the conflicting thoughts forever terrorizing me.

Derek presses a pen into my palm and again places his trust in me. It was a risk to allow me to take control last night, to bring me to his most personal space, and to give me access to write in his journal where he buries his inner-most thoughts. Yet, he did it all without hesitation.

I glance at his face; it is relaxed and happy. I forget why I'm supposed to be nervous. Turning to an empty page, I scribble the first lines that pop into my head.

If I had a world of my own, it would look like this room.
It would look just like you.

He stares at the page for a long moment before his fingers find the keys, and he plays the perfect melody for it. Then, he takes the pen from me and adds his own words.

It's heaven, heaven if you let it be.

It's the perfect end to the verse and sits like clarity on the page.

then, november

I STARED OUT THE WINDOW, taking in the pitter-patter of the rain falling between the pine trees that framed the side of the yard. I breathed in deeply, trying to memorize the smell that was home.

My mom had cleaned earlier in the day, and I had poured oil on the wood floors the way my father used to. A candle flickered from the hall tree behind me, painting the walls a dusty yellow and infusing the air with calla lilies, my mother's favorite scent. I waited patiently for Charlie to pull up, trying to remember what I filled my time with before the Kingsleys.

When Grey, not Charlie, pulled into the gravel drive, I fought to keep the involuntary smile from filling my face. Grabbing my duffle, I yelled a quick "bye" to my mother in the kitchen and sprinted across the wet lawn to the Jeep. Grey held open the passenger door, his hair black under the dark clouds, rain straightening the curly strands against his forehead. He grinned, unfazed by his dampening clothes, and offered me a hand. I hoisted myself into the seat by placing my shoe on the foot rail.

While he ran around to the driver's side, I admired how well he kept his belongings. Grey was meticulous, tending to his things as if they belonged to someone else, and he was only borrowing them. Everything he had appeared new.

A chill ran up my spine as the cool leather seeped through my leggings, making contact with my thigh. The newscaster had claimed it would be in the low forties the past few days, but it had been warm all week. Naturally, the day I picked to wear thin clothes, the weather decided to disagree with my wardrobe decisions. Shifting out of my raincoat, I reached into my bag and pulled a hoodie over my head; I was glad I had chosen to pack it.

Grey climbed in and shook out his hair, water droplets flying in every direction.

"Grey!" I shrieked, annoyed that the dry clothes I had just slipped on were now wet, too. He turned to greet me, my favorite version of him. Lips curled up at the corners, teeth pulling on the edge of his smile. My breath caught in my throat. He was so heartbreakingly beautiful.

No, Ally. Best friends' brother. Best friends' brother.

Ignoring my annoyance, he opened his mouth, and his words poured into the silence.

"Mine. All weekend." He shook his head, beaming as he cranked the heat.

"I'm here for Charlie." I reminded him, rolling my eyes despite his words' effect on me.

"Keep telling yourself that, Al. Are you ready?" He asked. I fought another eye roll and settled for a curt nod in response. He started the engine and pulled onto the road. I hooked my phone up to the auxiliary cord, plugging it into the radio, acquiring full DJ privileges.

This was our ritual. He drove in his laid-back style, with

only one hand on the wheel, while I scanned through my playlists, matching the music to my mood. I picked a song, and he turned the dial, raising the volume. He effortlessly sang along, knowing every word, although he failed to stay in tune. I laughed carelessly as he stunned other drivers at stoplights, making them turn their heads to find where the horrid sound was coming from. He always found ways to entertain me.

As the songs we knew shifted out, I stared out the window. The skies were darkening and starting to cloud, a storm in the making.

Later that night, the rumble of thunder grew closer, and lightning flashed outside Charlie's window. My fingers fell like feathers across her blush duvet. As much as I had felt at home next to Charlie when I fell asleep, I woke to the storm with my stomach dropping. My hands began to shake as the feeling grew inside of me. It was similar to fear, though I wasn't afraid of the storm. I tried to place it.

Sitting up, the feeling subsided when I saw Charlie's form asleep inches away from me. Our feet were tucked under the same cocoon, and I could feel her warmth radiating. It calmed me momentarily until another boom shook the room. I jumped, and pinpricks started in my stomach again.

I stood, the light from outside guiding me. A flash from the window laid streaks across the room, making the details prominent before leaving me in darkness. I guided myself along the wall, down the hall to the second door on the right. The room rattled again. I knew I shouldn't. My heart hammered in my chest. My fingers rounded the door-knob as I pushed it open.

I blocked off the protests of my conscience as I stepped

in and shut the door behind me. The fluffy beige of Grey's comforter was gathered around his face. My feet thought for themselves and carried me across the room.

As a branch smacked its leaves across the window, my racing pulse stopped and restarted. Lifting the comforter, I climbed in between the sheets. The crisp cool of the linen kissed my skin, and air filled my lungs. I took a breath I hadn't realized I'd been holding. Goosebumps raised the hair on my arms. I shifted towards him and buried my face in his chest. The warmth hit me instantly.

His arms wrapped around my torso, pulling me closer until my chest came to rest against his own.

"You're in my bed, Ally." Grey's words webbed in my hair as he pressed his lips to my forehead. His stomach vibrated with the sound. "Your heart is pounding."

I opened my mouth to speak, but nothing came out.

"Can you admit you like me yet?" He whispered, low and rumbly.

I shook my head, hiding my smile. This was my *best friend's brother*. I shouldn't be tracking him across every room he enters. I definitely should not be in his bed. Again.

"You will." He said with finality. It continued to echo in my head, even minutes later.

His hand reached down and effortlessly looped around my leg, bringing it to rest over his so we were intertwined. The pinpricks in my stomach turned to sparklers. I lay half on top of him, half on the mattress.

"Hmmm." He sighed. I shivered.

Pressed to his chest, the tension I had felt dissipated. The anxiety was released. The pull to him was inevitable. I couldn't admit I liked him because the terrible truth was that I was already in love with him. It had been happening so gradually I couldn't see it until I was right there in the thick of it. Wrapped up in him, I was completely consumed.

"Grey?" I said, but he was already asleep. I snuggled in and held my secret tight for another night.

now, august

THE SKY GROWS into a dusty purple outside the conservatory windows. When the rain begins to fall, it cascades through the open vent, landing in the water around us. Derek lights a few candles on top of the piano as the shape of the plants dim and fade around us. My memories diminish as I lean into the warmth of the space.

"Are you hungry?" He asks a while after we stop playing. We had been quiet in the still room, neither of us speaking as we turned to face out over the dark pool. Our toes pointed down, tracing patterns across the water while we listened to the rain. My stomach growls in response. It reminds me I haven't eaten all day. I had arrived here around noon, too nervous for even a small breakfast. It had to be at least eight or nine now.

"I'll go hunt for some food." He laughs, hopping down with a splash before disappearing down a corridor.

I should have told him it was late and past time I got going, but I didn't. The storm outside booms, a welcome excuse to my logic. As much as I'd like to lie to myself, I know I wouldn't want to leave even without the storm.

Each flash of lightning cascades a spotlight onto the gardens before me. The water on the leaves catches the light and makes the plants sparkle. Even in the dark, this place provides no trace of sinister. I'm dying to explore more rooms, but it's too vast a space to trust my sense of direction. I'm not sure I'd be able to find my way back.

The real reason I don't want to explore follows quickly behind the first one. It's Derek. He's what casts a spell over everything. The way his eyes drink in everything I do is always so full of emotion, saying things his mouth can't. Not yet. I don't want to see another room without his stories of why it was created.

A glow from beyond the balcony he had pointed out catches my focus, and I notice the one room I don't need more information on—his room. I grab a candle from the piano to light my way and find a staircase off the open sitting room overlooking the shallow water we were sitting in. I take the stairs slowly, trying out how each step will creak with my weight adding pressure to the boards.

When I reach the top, there is a door, and I pull it open. Whoa. The wall beside the door I entered from had a large, paned glass window overlooking the side yard. From here, you have a bird' s-eye view of the hedge maze below and the fountains that circle and weave around it.

Straight ahead, a massive fireplace is nestled between two doors. I assume that one leads to his bedroom and the other to his bathroom. The wainscoting is a dark greenish-gray, contrasting the lighter tones of the paint above its border. It adds to the British narrative of the home.

Greenhouse glass panels encase the door to the balcony on the far wall, which I had seen from below. The room is a comfortable extension of the conservatory, seamlessly incorporating all its details.

Dark mahogany shelves extend up to the ceiling in the corner next to a single table housing a record player, the only furniture in an otherwise barren room. Boxes are scattered about, and the only things that appear unpacked are the books lining the top shelves and the countless records that fill the bottom. I like that this is what he chose to unpack first. It tells me what is important to him.

I look to see what he was listening to and place the needle, satisfied with his choice. *Are You Lonesome Tonight* fills the air in Elvis' voice. I open the balcony doors and crack the windows to hear the rain mixing with Elvis. I scan through his other records: Sinatra, Def Leppard, and Prince are just a few that I flag to listen to later. I pull them out slightly further than the others so I can find them easily. Among his books are titles like *Music Theory, The History of Music,* and *Music Composition.* Lord, he's a music geek.

His footsteps startle me out of my careless manners, and I remember I'm supposed to be downstairs at the piano where he left me. Derek leans casually against the door frame, showing no sign of irritation.

"Because it was in there? Or because you like it?" He asks, intrigued, waving towards the record playing.

"Yes." I smile. He extends his hand to me. Whatever prompts me to take it, I let it lead. He spins me across the room and dips me before pulling me close into his arms. Everything is warmer here.

"You really love music," I say.

"What gave it away?" His face is entirely at ease. His voice a hum.

"You're moving in?" I ask. These are his most prized possessions. I can't imagine him being separated from them for long.

"Once Duke decides he's done in the city." His face

pales, and the tension that usually masks him is pulling at his features. It's *his* dark spot, spreading. The wreckage we both carry inside of us. It is the look I had recognized the first night in the bar.

I practice Libby's patience. I wait. It works, and after a moment, he speaks.

"He's sick." His voice breaks. "Really sick. He had people in the city he wanted to say goodbye to. Affairs he wanted to tie up to prepare for what happens next."

I expect the words to create a sinkhole and swallow us in sadness. Somehow, it only feels lighter. I watch the burden lift from his shoulders as if he can feel it too, how the confession eases some of the tension.

"It's not curable," I say as both a question and a statement.

"No." It sits hollow in the quiet now that the record has ended. The heaviness still hasn't returned. The vinyl skips, and the needle scratches, prompting him to step away to rectify it.

A creeping sorrow fills me alongside the solace. It's an odd feeling, the two things mingling. Awful and bearable at the same time. Duke, who bled this place from his fingertips, would soon be gone. What would become of it? Who would carry on the legacy of creating such things? I became afraid to meet him should Derek ever decide to introduce us. Afraid to love yet another person I would lose.

"I brought food," Derek says.

"I'm not very hungry anymore," I admit. I let my legs carry me to the balcony doors and pull them open.

I admire the piano in the pool, the ivy columns, and little details of the planting I didn't see before. Downstairs, I hadn't noticed ornate benches tucked into the room's edges. Derek follows behind me and takes a seat to my left. Without thinking, I reach out and take his hand in mine. The warmth immediately spreads through me. I like how I don't hesitate before I touch him now—a small smile forms on my lips.

"I like how you do that." He says quietly.

"What?"

"Embrace the darkness. Make it lighter, " he murmurs. His consciousness appears to be on the same wavelength as mine as he once again vocalizes my exact thoughts. The now familiar electricity has turned comfortable—more like a vibration under my skin instead of a zap.

"Is it weird that I love him too? Just for the things he's created." I ask. I hope it doesn't offend him to speak of Duke like this. I have no claim to this stranger.

Derek shakes his head. "No. The only weird thing is how you seem to understand better than anyone else."

We sit listening to the storm for a while. His thumb traces patterns on the back of my hand. I wonder if things will change between us once we leave. Will he still hold my hand like this back at the bar, or can this 'us' only exist here?

When we settle out of the silence, we return to his room and eat the pizza, unconcerned that it has gone cold. We sit on the floor atop a pile of blankets he's pulled from the closet. The TV mounted above the fireplace is showing a rerun of *Doctor Who* when he turns it on. I ask him not to change it.

I used to watch this with my dad as a kid, and being here with Derek, I feel connected to every version of myself —past, future, and present. We talk about which Doctor was our favorite, and I worry he'll kick me out when I say

Matt Smith, considering most people prefer Tenant, but he sticks with the habit of surprising me and says, "Me too."

Libby left for Italy this morning and won't notice my absence, so I don't bother to text her that I'll be home late. Before I can register what's happened, I am asleep.

then, december

IN THE KITCHEN, Charlie stirred the pancake mix. The room was lit only by the light from the Christmas tree set up in the living room. It was 1 a.m., and we were trying not to wake her parents.

Charlie and I had finished two bottles of Marilyn's Moscato and had just popped our third. I wasn't used to drinking wine, especially not in such large quantities, and it was starting to affect me. My fuzzy brain made me laugh out loud at the orb that had appeared, floating around the cabinets like a spirit. It was probably a consequence of staring at the pendant lights too long.

Whisking had caused Charlie's body to move in funny ways. Her fuzzy socks were slick on the tile as she paraded about in a dance. The pancake batter seemed to have a life of its own, bouncing energetically in and out of the bowl like Flubber. Drunk and uncoordinated, she slipped as if in slow motion, landing with a thud on the floor. The bowl she had managed to save victoriously flipped forward at the last second, coating her face in the batter.

"No! Flubber!" I whisper-yelled, sliding across the floor to the crime scene.

"I don't think he made it, Al." She said, laying in its remains as she convulsed in uncontrollable giggles.

"What is going on in here?" Grey walked out of the hall in a white tee and boxers. His socks were halfway up his calves.

He stopped short when he rounded the counter and saw Charlie. She sobered up, and a quiet fell over the room. He hadn't yet noticed her face. She sat up suddenly, causing him to jump. I straightened, curious at how this would unfold.

"Jeez, Char. Is this one of those weird ass face masks you girls like to make?"

"What's with your socks?" She asked, setting us off into another fit.

"Whoa, whoa, whoa!" He held up his hands in defense. "They keep my feet toasty." He said in the most adorable way, knocking his heels together like Judy Garland in The Wizard of Oz.

She reached into the bowl and lifted a glob of mix. Without a second thought, she flopped it on his socks.

"I don't like them." She scrunched her nose.

I couldn't contain the laugh that bubbled out of my lips. His mouth fell open.

"It's on," he said as she scrambled to get off the floor and run. I was relieved that most of the mix had landed on Charlie's face, leaving little for ammunition. I had ducked behind the counter for safety when the kitchen became unnaturally quiet. I peeked around the corner.

"You didn't think you would get away that easy?" Grey asked my shocked expression. He palmed a hefty glob down the side of my cheek. I gasped.

Charlie chuckled conspiratorially somewhere out of sight before the bowl, and the remainder of its contents appeared above Grey's head. Seconds later, his curls became thickened by the batter, heaps dripping down into his face. I covered my mouth to hide my snorts.

He was mid-spin to tackle her when Marilyn stepped in.

"What on earth..." she trailed off. Her dark hair fell angelically across her silk robe. She held up a hand. "I don't want to know." She stepped carefully around the goop scattered across the floor and grabbed a glass of water from the fridge.

"Ally, dear, please make sure my hoodlums clean this up."

"You got it." I smiled sheepishly.

A slight grin played on her lips as she left the room. Sighs of relief reverberated off the tile as her door clicked closed down the hall.

"I'll clean. You shower. This is not what pancake night was supposed to be." I grumbled to Grey, grabbing a towel from the drawer.

"Too dirty for you?" He winked.

"Grey, she's never going to go out with you." Charlie sighed.

"You're wrong. She likes me." His smile grew bigger.

I could feel her annoyance from here. It was a relief to have her focus on him. One look at my wide eyes and flushed cheeks, and she would have known he was right. Anger surged through me. Who did he think he was to assume my feelings in front of her? What an arrogant prick.

"Grey, I know you think you're God's gift or something, but not every girl likes you. Besides, Ally's too cool for you. Why don't you let her decide for herself instead of clouding her head with your nonsense?" She snorted, raising her eyebrows sternly.

"I'm going to shower. Als, you don't have to clean all this. I'll take care of it if you want to hang out in my room. Grey, don't harass her!" She scolded as she flipped her hair and walked off. She was such a little hothead.

I wet the towel in the sink.

"You do like me though." He leaned easily against the island counter a few feet away, screwing off the cap of his water bottle. I gripped the ledge. The alcohol was making my head spin. These accusations were not helping.

With all the courage I could muster, I turned to face him, smirking with confidence I didn't have.

"You've been at this for months, Grey. And again, I tell you: no, I don't."

Feeling the high of a false win, I got on my knees with the damp rag and resisted the urge to glance up at him. *Just wipe the floor, Ally. One tile at a time.* The evidence of our food fight was almost gone. One sweep of the Swiffer should finish it off. *That's good. Focus on the mess. Try not to make a bigger one.*

I stood and rinsed the batter caked onto the towel. Grey lingered in place. Charlie's head popped around the corner, making me jump for the second time in one night.

"Grey, be a gentleman and let her use your shower. Preferably without making any crude jokes." Her eyes narrowed, softening as they turned to me.

"I put some of that conditioner you like in there!" She chirped, disappearing once more.

I stared at where she had just stood until the water cut on upstairs. I let out the breath I had been holding. Grey cleared his throat.

"Let me show you where the towels are."

Following him down the hall, we entered his room—the room I had snuck into three times already to sleep, curled up around him. I shut the door behind us out of habit. His smirk did not escape my notice. *God, Ally. This really is a problem.*

I gazed at the bookcases lining the walls, yearning to open them all and reveal his innermost thoughts. I had observed him highlighting his favorite lines enough to know these books held his secrets.

He dipped into the attached bathroom and flicked on the light.

"Towels are here." He opened the cabinet by the door to reveal a stack of perfectly folded white towels. Turning the shower on, his curls fell in his face, springing loose from the dried mix.

"You can use my body wash so it's less conspicuous when you smell like me tomorrow." A coy grin lit up his face.

"Grey, you can't keep saying things like that." I sighed. The counter dug into my thighs as I sat on it by the sink.

"Why not?" Warm brown hands approached the counter on either side of my thighs. He pushed my knees apart and stood between my legs. My breath hitched. I stared up at him, my chest heaving as steam filled the small space. With a finger beneath my chin, he lifted my gaze to him.

"I don't want to hurt Charlie," I confessed. We locked onto one another, and warmth pooled in my palms, making me dizzy.

"Charlie doesn't want *me* to hurt you. But I'm not going to hurt you. We should tell her about us because you do like me, Ally. I'm going to be the one." He said, full of faith.

"There isn't an us." In my mind, it sounded assertive. From my lips, it sounded uncertain.

"There will be. Honestly, it's about damn time you admit it to yourself." His smile was full of assurance as he exited the bathroom, leaving me in a fog of feelings. *I'm going to be the one* repeated over and over in my head as I undressed. I didn't doubt that, like everything else, he was right.

then, december

THE HOT WATER fell in waves down my back. The heat cascaded across my sore muscles from cleaning the pancake mix off the floor, from the stress of secrets, the strain of repression. Repression?

I groaned out loud. I even sounded like Grey. Standing in the shower, I washed quickly with his soap and the conditioner Charlie left me. I tried to get in and out as soon as possible. The effect of the alcohol on my stomach, combined with the steam in my lungs, made me feel like I was suffocating.

When I stepped out, I invited the coolness as a welcome reprieve until the air grew dense and the mirror began to fog. Afraid I was going to be sick, I wrapped a towel around myself and flung open the door. Trying to level my breathing, I leaned against the wooden frame and closed my eyes.

When I opened them, Grey was looking up at me from over his book. I hadn't realized he would still be in the room. Feeling self-conscious, I readjusted my towel, pulling it higher to shield more of my chest.

"Drinking's fun, huh?" He mocked. I groaned, wishing I

had something within reach to chuck at him. The wine had absorbed my energy, so I reached for another towel to dry my hair instead. I desired nothing more at that moment than to be in bed.

"Come here." He smiled warmly, laying his book on the nightstand by a glass of ice water. Water I was suddenly craving. Noticing my stare, he extended the glass to me.

"I have to get dressed." I protested.

"You can grab a shirt from my dresser if you need something to wear." He said, toying with me. I was determined not to take the bait.

"I've got a bag in Charlie's room. I'm sure she's waiting on me."

"She's asleep." He replied. "So, I guess you'll have to sleep here again." He patted the bed.

Ignoring him, I padded over to the chest of drawers and searched until I found a red VANS tee that seemed long enough to cover me. I slipped it on over my towel, letting it fall.

Grey whistled from behind me.

"Jesus, Al. Can I veto Ally clothes from now on? Because I *love* you in Grey clothes." He said, jubilant. Turning to face him, I crossed my arms and rolled my eyes, which only deepened his shit-eating grin. "By the way, Charlie left you some clothes on the desk," Grey said, humor leaking into his voice.

Annoyance filled me, and I threw the closest thing on his dresser at his face, which happened to be a football. He caught it easily and fell backward, laughing. His brightness diminished my anger at once.

"You're an ass— " hole was what I had started to say before my insides turned and lurched, forcing me to make a run for the bathroom.

"Not the effect I was going for." I heard Grey say as he jumped out of bed and followed me.

While I emptied the contents of my stomach, he stood behind me, pulling back my hair into the elastic I had left by the sink. When he finished, he sat on the floor leaning against the tub while he rubbed my back between vomiting sessions. I begged him to go, but he shook his head no.

"I'm never drinking again," I murmured, hanging my head over the toilet when I felt it might finally be over.

He laughed heartily. "I think everyone says that their first time."

I slid into the floor, enjoying the coolness of the tile as it seeped through the fabric. He gently slid me towards him so I could use his thigh as a pillow to rest my head. I felt grateful that he had brought me a pair of panties earlier, so I wasn't entirely indecent. Not that I would have cared. I was so far past having dignity at this point. I wrapped my arm around his leg.

His fingers worked through my hair, brushing it away from my neck. He pressed a cool washcloth to my skin, the fresh dampness absorbing the sweat. Beside him lay my "sick kit," as he had called it.

The first time I took a break from throwing up, he had left to retrieve the essentials: saltines from the kitchen, ice water, Pepto, the iPad for entertainment (we learned I liked 80s movies when I was sick), and finally, a toothbrush, which was my favorite by far. Grey was a good caretaker.

While *Back to the Future* played in the background, Grey continued playing with my hair.

"Can you admit that you like me yet?" He asked quietly.

I smiled into his leg, nodding. His sweatpants smelled faintly of Downey and mint from my breath. I must have gurgled mouthwash a half dozen times after retching last.

"After this, I think I love you." I joked, my voice hoarse.

"*Finally.*" He sighed. "I was getting really tired of acting like I don't love you, Ally." He responded, his voice heavy with exhaustion.

I swear my heart stopped beating. I laid perfectly still for what felt like forever, frozen in place.

"Crap. I guess you're not supposed to tell a girl that before you've even kissed her." Grey said, suddenly more alert, embarrassed even. Before then, I had never heard Grey embarrassed over anything. He was always sure of himself.

I rolled onto my back to stare up at him and the scar on his chin that I adored deeply. It had become the signature of his face, the thing I always noticed, the thing no one else shared. His scar made him distinct, and I loved it like I loved every other part of him. I was stupid to think we could ever be just friends. What we were becoming was inevitable. I was naive to think otherwise.

"Grey Kingsley, are you actually nervous?" I teased.

He nodded, his cheeks turning red.

"Why? *You're the one.*" I reminded him, reaching out to trace his scar.

"Uh—duh." He confirmed, his character fully returning. With that, he readjusted and wiggled happily onto the floor beside me, pulling my leg over his like usual. He pressed his lips to my forehead as I snuggled against him.

That's how Charlie found us in the morning, still cuddling on the bathroom floor.

now, august

THE ONE. *The solitary words echo in my head as I run towards the house.*

My feet hit the floor, and I am sure this is where I am meant to be. If I can make it upstairs, I'll be able to see him again. I long to hear him say the words "I love you." He has the ability to ease this panic I'm feeling. He has a way of making everything better, just like he always does. All I need to do is reach him.

I rush to his door and find it open. Grey isn't there; he's in the bathroom, leaning against the tub just like he was that night, the night he told me he loved me. I call out but he doesn't see me. The moment I cross the threshold, I am back in the downstairs living room, and everything is on fire. I try to run up the stairs again, but something falls and stops me. I try to scream to warn them. Nothing comes out.

Hands are shaking me awake. My eyes pop open, and I take in my surroundings. Everything is unfamiliar.

"Ally. Ally, look at me." Derek says. Derek?

"Hey, focus on me." I don't understand why he is in my bedroom. My shoulder burns. I scratch at the fabric of my shirt. Mangled cries escape me, and I panic as I try to get the material off.

Derek's fingers find mine at the hem of my shirt, and he pulls it over my head. The moment I am freed, I reach for my shoulder, hissing as my fingers brush over my scar. Derek's eyes turn to full moons, wide in shock.

"Bloody hell." He says under his breath. Tears are pouring down my face, and I can't get comfortable. Every angle stretches the skin, irritating the old wound, and it is agony.

He stands and runs his fingers through his hair. He paces once and then disappears. I am reduced to a mess of memories of Grey. Charlie. The Kingsley's. The fire. I can feel Grey's arms still wrapped around me before they're ripped away, replaced by flames. Then, the searing of my skin under the beam. I whimper; the burn becomes the strongest feeling. Gone. They're gone. That ache is worse than the burn.

I shake, searching the floor for my phone. If I can call them and hear their voices one more time, I'll be okay. *They won't answer, they can't.* I remind myself. My heart accelerates. My thoughts race faster, turning into a spiral. One memory immediately replaces the last, each twisting me into a tighter knot. It's wringing out my heart, like hands wringing out a bird's neck. I can't breathe.

Derek reappears with ice and presses it to my shoulder. I cry out, gasping as oxygen reinflates my lungs. The cold sinks in, and the burn loses some of its potency.

"Ally." His expression is alarmed.

"Mmm?" My whole body is shaking. Small convulsions as the nerves overtake me. I feel the tears threatening to overflow again.

"Do you know why Matt Smith is my favorite?" He asks

abruptly, sitting beside me once I take over holding the ice. He sits casually with his arms tossed over his knees, trying not to touch me.

I shake my head, no, but I am barely listening. The memory of the beam cracking reappears, and for the first time, I can vividly recall the sound of it splintering. I wince, squeezing my eyes shut.

"He's my favorite because they put so much detail into his storylines. The way they looped into each other was brilliant. I think he is the only Doctor ever to say his real name."

I don't engage, so he keeps talking.

"My favorite episode is probably the one with the little boy's bedroom and the nightmares he brought to life or the angels; it's tough to pick a favorite, innit?"

I think the Christmas specials were my favorite episodes, and I want to tell him so, but *my* nightmares are still being pulled to life.

"Oh, and the companions, Ally! Best of all the seasons hands down! I used to watch it with my grandfather when I was just a boy. It's become a bit of a comfort show now, yeah." He smiles, and his hair falls into his face. I imagine pushing it back. For a moment, I start to, but I don't want him to stop talking.

"I hope one day I am as talented as that. That I can bring stories to life in such an intricate way. Only I want to do it in a three-minute song. Ambitious, eh?"

Pulling the ice from my shoulder, I lay it on the rug. The cold was becoming a distraction to my listening. This time, I do move his hair out of his face so I can see his eyes. Faltering for only a second, he rants on. I'm glad. I don't want to miss a detail. Maybe it's the juniper, or maybe it's his words that have started to calm me like a lullaby.

Last night swims to the front of my mind, how perfect everything *was*, and I hope I haven't ruined my first date with the only man I find remotely interesting. Fascinating, in fact.

I wish I could speak, but I can't find my voice. Someone has stolen it. My embarrassment, perhaps. So, I stay mute while he rambles, comparing the Tenth and Eleventh Doctors.

"Duke and I used to sit on the floor just like this. We'd lean against the couch in the living room and stay up into the morning watching episodes. We'd pop some corn and binge. I had to swear I wouldn't tell my mum how late we stayed up." He beamed.

I tell him my dad and I did the same thing. If he's surprised that I'm speaking, he doesn't show it. *I'm* certainly surprised.

We continue discussing shows we watched as kids and how they influenced our personalities. I told him about *Charmed* and how, as a seven-year-old, I experimented with mixing various chemicals and shampoos in the bathroom, pretending to create potions. I used to take the tiny bottles and toss them at squirrels in the yard, imagining that I could somehow turn them back into humans, as if they had been cursed to live as cute rodents forever. I viewed myself as their rescuer. The squirrels, however, had a different opinion.

His face breaks into familiar creases when he laughs, and I find myself thinking he's beautiful once more. We ramble on about this and that as the subject constantly changes, seemingly without cause. Soon, the ice has fully melted on the floor in front of me.

"I can take it." he grabs the bag of jiggly water and heads off through a door that I assume leads to the kitchen.

I cringe as he touches the plastic that was just on my shriveled, wrinkly flesh, but I bite back my objections.

He falls back to his seat beside me, turning on what he calls the "tele." I want to make fun of him, but I don't have it in me.

"Derek?"

He glances over. I can't tell what he's thinking; probably that I'm a nutcase.

"I'm sorry about all of—" I gesture around me.

"Don't." He warns as if he were scolding me for apologizing. It's as simple as that. He flips through the channels. I look down and realize that I'm shirtless.

Fuck, Ally. Thank God I chose a modest bralette. The lace covers me up more than a bathing suit would. I let out a sigh of relief and reach for my blouse. It is wet and ripped from my clawing at it. This is what I get for buying delicate things. I pull the blanket around my shoulders to cover myself.

"Now you're feeling shy?" He jokes.

I smile sheepishly. I'm out of witty comebacks.

"Hold on." He runs into his room and grabs me a shirt. It's a plain black shirt, exactly his style. Slipping it over my head, I can't help but catch his scent. Saltwater and linen. Like summer sheets that have been left outside to dry. There's a hint of cologne around the collar, but I can't place it. I wonder if he sprayed it with something. I hold it out and examine the material, looking for evidence that he did. I can't find any, so I look up at him and smile, hoping he didn't notice.

He stares at me a moment too long and becomes awkward, rubbing the back of his head again. His arm flexes as he moves it back, the definition of his muscles showing.

"I need water. Do you want water?" he asks, his voice raw and shaky. He doesn't wait for me to answer, leaving me confused.

I want him to know he doesn't have to be awkward around me. I catch my reflection in the glass of the balcony doors. Flushed, wild-eyed, and in his shirt, I look different. I look like *me*. I begin to wonder if his departure was due to another reason. I try not to linger on the thought. The bees are congregating in my intestines enough as it is.

He stays in the kitchen for a while. When a minute turns to ten, I stand to explore before I spiral again. His walls are empty. There are no pictures, no paintings that make it feel personalized. Throwing a glance toward the kitchen, I sneak back to the shelf containing his record collection.

I flick the switch to a wall sconce, and when it flickers to life, I bypass the records to where he keeps his books. I learned from Grey that books are where you keep your secrets. *Who are you, Derek?*

I feel like I already know, but the longer I dote on it, the less it feels like I do. I know how he communicates and that he seems to feel strongly about the right things. Until now, that has been enough, but I find myself thirsting for more common knowledge, like where he grew up, whether he has siblings, and which one is his favorite. Most importantly, I want to know what thoughts he keeps hidden. Noticing the binding of what appears to be a children's book, I lift it from the shelf and crack the spine.

D E r E k R I v E r A

His name is scribbled on the back of the cover in child's handwriting. I smile at the sloppy print. My fingers graze the capitalized and lowercase letters that have been placed all wrong.

Rivera. It sounds Spanish but his accent is more American with a heavy British influence. It's mostly like mine, with certain words catching, and there are some phrasing differences here and there, like how he's used the terms "bloke" and "cheeky" to describe people.

I flip through the pages. They are browned at the corners from overturning, and there are random scribbles and stickers on the pages. They are careful to avoid the words and pictures, showing that even as a child, he respected what this book had to offer. I skim the words enough to understand the story is about a talking tree. I make a note to ask him why it was his favorite. A rush fills me as I imagine what his explanation will sound like.

I slip it back on the shelf and reach for another. His copy of *The Great Gatsby* is worn, and like the last, the pages have browned at the corners. I flip through, noticing that everything is kept clean. There are no highlights or underlines. There is no writing on the pages, pondering what the author felt when he wrote a particular line, or working out the true meaning of it all. It's not stamped with character like Grey's copy was.

I try to decide if this is good. Then, I criticize myself for comparing them and promise not to do so again. Yet, I feel an overwhelming sense of déjà vu as I scan his shelves and flip through his books exactly as I did with Grey's years ago. I wish it stopped me or made me feel guilty enough not to be so invasive, but it doesn't. I haven't felt *curious* about anyone in so long; I don't know *how* to stop. I've learned nothing about boundaries. I reach for another and another.

Finally, my hands touch a slim book. It is on a shelf towards the top that I can barely reach. It sits in a row of 10 or more, just like it. I pull it down, careful not to make too much noise, and flip through the pages.

Every single page is covered in Derek's handwriting, holding his lyrics. Some are brimming with concepts for new tracks, while others outline themes for future albums or potential global tours. Detailed notes, dating back a year, are meticulously listed alongside various cities across England. I didn't realize that Derek had toured. Given his talent, it makes complete sense.

I can't stop flipping through the journal, craving the information it holds. It feels like I'm intruding on something deeply personal. As I go to close the book, I notice a page with red writing - the only one not in black ink.

They're lyrics. Really fucking good lyrics. These are the words I've been searching for. I slip the book into the waistband of my skirt and start to creep downstairs. Derek still hasn't returned from the kitchen, and I wonder if there's another way out. Perhaps he left, needing an escape from me after all. Then, I hear the kettle whistle and know he has not. I return to my mission.

The piano taunts me from across the moonlit water. Now that the storm has passed, it appears like a reflection pool under the bright sky. I could use some healthy reflection.

I stand in front of the keys in a trance, barely remembering how I got here, my legs still wet from wading over. I press down on the black-and-white. The notes echo throughout the hollow room, and the sound waves reverberate, inviting me to play more.

I sit at the bench and work through the song stuck in my head, finishing the work Derek started years ago. It's the song I've been trying to write this whole time.

"I live on the island of misfit toys.
I never wanted to stay; it's not a choice I made,

Though I must admit, I feel at home among broken things.
Please don't be afraid; my furs matted and aged,
But I was once loved before these terrible days.

Please, don't look away; it's so nice to be seen
by eyes as gold and pure as yours.
Do you think we could play for a little while?
Before the night steals the sun from the sky and it rises,
somewhere in India.
I'm forever young when you touch me like that,
Forever new.
When ya coming back? How about tomorrow afternoon?
I'll be seeing you."

I stop singing to add my lines beneath his on the page. It snaps together like a puzzle piece. The music always sees what I'm not quite ready to.

now, august

A SLOW CLAP startles me out of my bubble after I play the final chord.

It must be after 2 a.m., so I am shocked when what appears to be a gardener stands from one of the benches at the edge of the wall. He is wearing soft gray coveralls with dirt stains on the knees. I would feel threatened if his face were not weathered with age. His small body is withered and deteriorated, barely seeming to support itself without the cane in his hand. His features are wrecked with kindness, and I assume that's the real motivation behind my ease. *Kind is different than nice.*

"That was lovely." The man says. His voice is rich, penetrated with layers of warmth.

"I'm sorry, I didn't realize anyone else was here," I admit.

Usually, I'd feel out of place. Like I had been caught somewhere I shouldn't be. I was the kid in the castle again, too comfortable in a place that was never mine to feel comfortable in. This man doesn't make me feel caught, though. As he tilts his head and gazes at me with admiration, he makes me feel like I'm the most significant part of the room. Something he wishes could stay so he could enjoy it whenever he liked. I understand at once that he's a collector of such things. Such moments.

"You're Duke." I realize.

"And you must be Ally. You're everything Derek said you were. I'm already a fan." He smiles affectionately.

I laugh in disbelief. "I'm a fan of yours." I gesture to the room around me.

"Hmm." He chuckles as he considers this. "Would you grant a dying man a wish and stroll with me around the room?"

Another laugh escapes me. "I see the relation now. That's quite some leverage you have there."

I poke fun but cross the pond anyway. I take his arm when he offers it to me.

"Do you always take walks so late?" I ask him. It's the first on my list of questions for this man.

"When the pain prevents me from sleeping." He answers in his gruff voice. I picture him as an Indian chief in a past life. Imagining the frail man beside me adorned in feathers and a smock, I smile. Then, his statement registers, and my smile feels misplaced.

"Are you always this honest?" I pose a new question, feeling more comfortable with my expression.

He pauses beside me, and his face breaks into a large grin. I'm reminded of Libby, then, how he turns from eighty to eight with that one action. I look around at his home, and it makes more sense that an eight-year-old created it; adults too often lose the function of their imagination. They settle into what is and not what could be. Not Duke. He knew how to erect a dream. I want to ask him if he feels trapped inside this body, this wrinkled flesh, and if it's ruining him. Suddenly, I wish I had another squirrel potion, one that could free him.

"I try to be." He answers my question.

He had said "the pain," hinting at his illness. He had said it as if I had known for a while and not learned of it only earlier today. He had such trust in Derek. Such faith that he had already told me. His suffering was not kept secret. Instead, he seems to have embraced it as part of himself. He shared it freely, knowing full well that it was not his burden alone to bear. The pain a connector, not a gag. It feels like an epiphany, and like the song, I'm not quite ready yet to understand it.

"You knew my name, " I say. It isn't a question, but I hope it will require more explanation. I want to know what Derek has said about me.

We walk slowly, and I don't mind the pace. I enjoy the quiet shuffle of his footsteps and the shallow *huhh huhh* of his breathing.

"You're the first girl my grandson has brought here in quite some time. You think because I'm old, I'm not curious? I've asked more about you than he's cared to share. I use my—what did you call it? Leverage."

Duke has a quiet way of revealing himself to me. I knew before meeting him it would be this way. We would get on. We're both dreamers speaking in subtle truths. I think about what Derek would have given away and how he may have described *me*. I can't come up with anything good enough to have granted me this conversation. I'm not used to such effortless communication.

Our silence is comfortable. It pairs well with the stillness of the gardens. When he finally breaks it, it's as if we had never stopped speaking. I nickname him "The Tailor," something about how he stitches together nature and conversation: the two somehow converging to be the same thing.

"Your pain. It kept you up as well?" He inquires. Once more, he appears more like a child than an adult. More invasive, more to the point than what is usual for grown-ups.

I stare back at him, shaken. Unlike Duke, I am not in the habit of revealing myself to strangers. Like with *Not Grey 406*, an unadorned "He's dead." is enough to end my conversations. My pain does not connect with people the way his does. Or, possibly, it's me, and I do not connect with people as easily. I feel at a loss for how to provide him with an answer. I'm unable to present my tragedies in the same universal way.

"Your songs expose more than you think, child." He says, absorbing the shock that must still be clinging to my face.

"A year ago, I was in a fire that killed the people closest to me. I haven't told Derek yet. I don't know how to tell someone it still burns every time I wake up." I confess.

Duke ponders this for what feels like hours. When he decides to alleviate my tension and respond, I know his words will stick with me forever.

"All phoenixes rise from ash."

now, august

AFTER DUKE and I parted ways, I returned upstairs, still haunted by what he had said. Derek is out on the balcony, and it's clear he's witnessed my interaction with his grandfather. He doesn't look displeased. The opposite, actually. He looks...relaxed.

"What wisdom did Duke have to embark upon you?" He stares knowingly.

"You could hear?"

"Only when you were playing. You finished my song." There is no trace of irritation that I read his innermost thoughts without permission.

"You're okay with that?"

"You made it the right song, Al." He sighs, and his head tips back with his eyes closed. He appears finally at peace with himself, something I don't think he's felt for a very long time.

The right laugh, I had thought the first night we met. *The right song,* he says now. Everything feels right with us. It *feels* like a very forward notion, and I try not to let it fester.

I start to sit beside him when he reaches for my hand

and gently pulls me into his lap instead. I immediately like this better. I like the cool bars of the balcony pressing against my scar. I like his arms, the arms I've ogled so many times, draped lazily across my waist. I lean into his chest, enjoying the warmth. I only have a couple of weeks left before I leave for university, but it's hard to imagine that reality, not now that I'm so submerged in this one.

"Thank you." He says, startling me.

I can't figure out what he's thanking me for. *I* should be thanking *him*. He's given me so much today. I believe in things again. I have hope. It's a wonderful feeling.

"For what?" My quizzical nature wins out.

"Coming here today. Letting me see things through your eyes. I like being able to see this place the way I used to." He hasn't opened his eyes, even when speaking to me. The weight of the world is a heavy load to carry. Now that it has fallen off his shoulders, he seems so tired.

"I think it's time for bed, sleepy boy," I whisper while running my fingers across his jaw, then his cheek, before tracing his face once more. He doesn't speak until I stop a few moments later.

I imagine leaning forward and pressing my lips to his. It seems so natural. The impulse is so strong that I almost act on it until he speaks, shattering the urge.

"Okay." His fight is gone, and he gives in. Pulling myself up, I extend my hand and hoist him to stand.

We pass our spot on the floor in the living room, and I follow him through a doorway. He falls against the made-up mattress, the only piece of furniture in his otherwise empty bedroom. He doesn't ask me to stay, and I don't wait for him to.

I climb under the covers on the opposite side of the bed. I place a pillow between us, wrapping my arms around it, and he doesn't try to move it away. Even after our closeness outside, it seems we both like the space. I certainly do. I'm still flustered from my almost slip-up.

Derek tucks a stray hair behind my ear, inviting back my rogue thoughts with his touch. He leaves his hand on my cheek, his scent comforting—the pulse in his wrist thrums against my neck, hypnotizing me to exhaustion.

The last thing I remember before falling into a dreamless slumber is the cover of pine trees, my safety blanket, protecting me from all the things I don't want to think about any longer.

now, august

SUMMER IS ALMOST OVER. University starts in less than a week. I've announced to the rest of the team at the bar that I'll be leaving. It feels like the last week of summer camp before returning home. Only home doesn't feel like the right word anymore now that I have a new place I feel so connected to, a new family. Everyone is their best and brightest selves.

Since that night in the conservatory, Derek and I have continued to grow closer. Gone are the days of him scribbling lyrics in passing. Now when I arrive early, he's already at the piano waiting for me. I brush my hand across his back, announcing my presence, before sliding onto the bench beside him, enjoying the feel of his shoulder against mine as we take turns explaining the ideas we came up with in each other's absence. It's him I'm dreading saying goodbye to the most.

Big Mike has turned my last week into a prank war. Somehow, he tracked down an old doll in some antique shop. He and Sonnie have been alternating who hides it, picking whatever spot they think will scare me the most.

They've hung it on the back of the bathroom door, where I spotted it mid-pee and screamed.

At closing each night, I stay and wash dishes, bus tables, whatever I can do to help out. Which is how they came to hide *her*— the doll, my nemesis, *Mrs. Potts*, in the supply closest amongst the cleaning supplies. Needless to say, I was rather startled. Tripping, I took down a cluster of mops and landed ass-first in a bucket, which had rolled all the way across the bar with me still in it.

The two of them slapped each other like little girls, sliding down the wall in tears, their laughter bellowing out. Derek watched from a distance, shaking his head at their antics, the faintest hint of a smile playing on his lips.

These people have become my friends, my salvation, and I am not looking forward to leaving them.

On my last night, I walk into an empty bar with a cake on the counter. I'm immediately suspicious. Then, I notice the Over-The-Hill candles on the cake as they jump out from behind the counter, yelling, "Surprise!" Seconds later, a dozen or more *It's a Boy!* balloons are released into the air from a net they'd been holding. I realized it was their final prank, and they couldn't resist the opportunity. Derek is leaning against the doorway to the kitchen, chuckling as he watches my reaction. I am going to miss them all immensely.

I play my final set. I hug the boys goodbye. Mike lifts and squeezes me in his typical fashion, warning me not to forget him. He promises Mrs. Potts will hunt me down at college if I do. Sonnie hugs me tightly for a beat too long, causing Derek to clear his throat, a request to break it up. I am so grateful for how they have shifted my summer, my existence, into something resembling a life again.

I finish my goodbye tour and head out. I try to escape

without saying goodbye to Derek. I don't know how I'd be able to. I don't like picturing my life without him in it. Almost comically, Derek catches the door behind me, halting me from going too far without him as my escort.

"Do you ever learn?" He laughs.

"I guess not." I match his spirits.

"You were going to leave without saying goodbye?" He tilts his head, waiting for me to answer as we keep pace, side by side. We fall into our comfortable rhythm.

"I couldn't stomach it," I confess.

"You don't lie, do you?" He's smiling now. I don't understand. He's in a relatively good mood, considering I was about to walk out without a word. It didn't matter to him; he knew he would walk me home regardless.

"Umm." I stutter, trying to make a sentence. I feel jittery, perhaps at what I know is coming.

"No. No more umm. We are removing that word from your dictionary. Okay? There are so many better words to tell me what you're thinking, and since you seem to have no problem reading my thoughts," I know he's referring to the multiple times I've gone through his journals, "the least you can do is be vocal about yours. Fair enough?" He asks.

"That was a long speech," I say, still looking down.

I'm finding it difficult to steer the conversation to where I want it to go. Normally, our interactions are purposeful, and we always know exactly what we want to say. But tonight, I'm struggling. I can't find the right way to tell him that I don't want to stop seeing him without it sounding like I'm asking him out. Do I want to ask him out? I'm not sure. I do know that I hate the idea of not spending my nights getting lost in his head and our music.

"There we go, much better than um." He laughs, and I want to push him again. I settle for a glare.

"Let's try again. You don't lie, do you?" He's pushing his luck. By his smirk, I can tell he knows it.

"I can't seem to lie *to you*," I say, deciding to answer him even though he is being Mr. Obnoxious tonight.

"Me either." He sighs after a moment, and I can tell he wants to say more but doesn't. He looks so serious with his hands in his pockets, eyes on the path ahead.

We're almost to Libby's when I shiver, and he unzips his jacket to give it to me. Before he can slip it off, I protest. "No, don't."

"Ally, you're cold." He says.

"It's summer." I laugh. "The breeze just caught me wrong, is all."

He shrugs but says nothing, still wanting to give me the article off his back. We've made it to the gate in front of Libby's flat. I move in front of him and unzip it the rest of the way. His eyebrows go up suggestively before I step inside and wrap my arms around his waist. Pressing my cheek to his chest, I breathe in his soap and linen scent for what I hope isn't the last time.

I can tell I caught him off guard by the way he stills before wrapping his arms around me and holding me close.

"I'll be home for the holidays," I speak into his shirt.

I'm instantly infuriated with myself. The closest holiday I'll have a break for is Christmas. I don't think they celebrate the pilgrim holiday of Thanksgiving over here. Though, I wouldn't want to wait that long, either. Christmas is months away. I could make an excuse for Labor Day, Halloween, or anything that's sooner.

"I know, Al. This isn't our goodbye. I'm going to see you again." He breaks away, his hand slipping against my neck as he whispers the words.

His forehead comes to rest against mine. His lips, like

feathers, brush against my own in a happy accident. It was too light, too brief to be considered a real kiss. We don't acknowledge it, and when he turns and disappears, the hollow ache returns as if my magic has been stolen away for good.

About twenty minutes later, my teeth were brushed, and I tucked myself in for the night when my phone vibrated in the sheets beside me. Derek's name lights up my screen.

WHAT HOLIDAYS, EXACTLY?

then, december

"SO, YOU TWO?" Charlie asked, towering over us. Even with the ibuprofen, my head was pounding from last night's drinking. I felt torn between wanting to explain and wanting to beg her to please, please stop talking.

Her eyes were wide, taking in the scene before her. I had rebuked every one of Grey's advances to date, yet there I was, found wrapped around him. I'm sure it must have been a shock.

"Grey, how could you?" She yelled, stomping her foot. I covered my ears and buried my face in the closest thing to me, which happened to be her brother. He stretched his arms out as far as they could go without hitting the wall as he always did when he first woke up.

"Charlie, she was sick from all the wine. We fell asleep on the floor." Grey said, yawning. "Nothing happened. Just cool it, okay? Ally's got a headache."

I glanced at him in confusion. How could he know that? Well, I guess my shielding my ears was a pretty good indicator. Taking in the hurt on Charlie's face, I tried to sit upright, putting some distance between Grey and me. My body felt like it had been in a train wreck.

"Charlie, we should talk." I croaked. I was starting to lose my voice from vomiting all night.

"Go ahead." She spewed in her fury. Her blonde waves were still frizzy from her pillowcase, and I felt worse knowing the first thing she did when she woke was to look for me. "Clearly, anything you can say to me, you can say in front of my brother."

"Okay." I nodded. I had only lied to Charlie as much as I had lied to myself. Now that I had stopped, I couldn't bring myself to be dishonest with her. I prayed this wouldn't destroy our friendship, but it was too late to change how I felt. "I love you, Charlie. You're my best friend, but I've been falling for Grey, and I'm sorry, I don't know how to fight it anymore. I love him too." I admitted.

Grey jerked his head in my direction. He had also readjusted to sit upright and was now staring at me. Gaping, really. I realized it the first time I had said I loved him. Last night, I had only said, "You're the one." While I'd implied how I felt, it was still very different from actually hearing the words out loud.

"I love you," I repeated, holding his apple eyes. Like limewire, they sparked contentment somewhere deep inside my chest. He smiled like he had won the lottery.

My contentment broke when Charlie addressed him, not me, with accusation.

"Grey, *you know*. You *know* you can't be with her, " she warned grimly. Charlie was cold and severe. It was a version of her I had never encountered. It felt like there was something I wasn't understanding, some secret sibling language passing between them.

Wait, what?

"Charles, you know this won't change anything with us," I assured her, hoping her nickname would break the tension.

"It already has, Al, but that really isn't the point here." She snarled. "Grey, we *promised*. No attachments, remember?"

It felt like a punch to the gut. My closest friend was labeling me as nothing more than an attachment and implying that as far as attachments went, she had none for me. It stung worse than I could have anticipated.

"Charlie, this is not the time." He said, taking on her tone. Calculated, cold, too cutting to sound like the Grey I knew. I wanted it to stop. Frankly, the whole confrontation was beginning to make the room spin.

"Char, I know you're hurt." Standing, I took her hand as I tried to reason with her. "Can we talk, just you and I? We can figure this out. I really believe we can."

She shook me off, prompting Grey to stand and step towards her. I couldn't understand why, but I moved between them. I felt the need to protect her, though I knew Grey would never even consider hurting his sister. His eyes hardened and locked with hers as they argued silently in some code I couldn't translate. Finally, she took a step back in defeat.

"No offense, Ally, but you have no idea what you're getting into here." Tears are streaked down her face. The tables turned as Charlie became the one pleading with me. Seeing the confusion written on my face, she gave up and redirected the conversation back to Grey. "She could get hurt."

He threw up his arms, exasperated.

"Charlie, you're the one who brought her here! You're the one who broke the rule when you decided to be friends with her. I can't help that I fell in love the exact same way you did, the way mom did, the way everyone does when they meet her. Okay?" He threw out.

"You love her?" Charlie asked, her lip trembling. Gone was the angry lioness; a harmless and scared kitten had replaced it.

"Yes. It's a full-on head-over-heels, knock-it-out-of-the-park kind of thing. I love her." He declared. "I can't stop. Please don't ask me to."

He relaxed, softening back into my Grey. I moved out of the way, feeling less defensive than before. The fight seemed to be over for now.

He pulled her in for a hug, whispering something in her ear. I couldn't be sure, but it sounded like, "I'll keep her safe." That didn't make sense. I was sure I had heard it wrong. Perhaps he had mumbled something more like "Thanks," and I had mixed up the syllables, my mind putting words in places where there were none.

"Well then. It's settled." She said, stepping away from him. As her smile returned to her face, I knew we had her blessing. "But you guys make me the best third wheel ever." She said, giggling as I tackled her with my own hug.

I followed them to the kitchen, where Marilyn was preparing a holiday breakfast. It was Christmas Eve morning, and she had gone all out with the French toast and seasonal table arrangements.

She reminded us we were supposed to be eating pancakes, but the mix had evaporated from the cabinet overnight. Marilyn zeroed in on Charlie and me. We laughed, taking our seats next to James and Gigi, who were already digging into the spread before them. While I ate, I tried to work out the weirdness of what had happened in the bathroom and why their words seemed so coated in double meaning.

I was on my last sip of orange juice when I figured out what had unsettled me so much. It was Grey. How he'd transformed from my boyish ball of kindness and wonder into the man who had accosted me months ago, that first night in the kitchen.

now, august

BRITISH UNIVERSITIES ARE different from American colleges. The rooms are called "halls of resi-dence" instead of dorms. There is a singular sink against the wall closest to the door and two twin beds along the opposing side. I have yet to meet my roommate, but based on her choice of decor, she seems to be quite a dark individual.

"Are you sure you don't want to look for a flat off campus?" Libby asks, not looking away from the altar set up in the corner as she finishes tucking in my new comforter around the thin twin mattress.

It isn't the altar that alarms her. It's the combination of the Ouija board sitting on the nightstand we share, the pentagram tapestry hanging above the bed, and the collec-tion of books on serial killers lining the shelves on the wall. I have to admit, it *is* a bit alarming how dedicated she seems to be. I'm all for the darkness, but ours seems pretty different.

"I'll keep you posted on that." I laugh, hugging my aunt close.

"I have to go so I don't miss my flight, but please call me, Al. I will worry." She can't hide how her eyes skate around the room one last time.

"Go Libs. I'll be fine."

"Love you!" She yells, escaping down the hallway.

"Love you more!" I call back. I picture her running to her car like her flight is in an hour and not several. She is a stickler for punctuality. My skills in procrastination unnerved her to no end this summer. The only thing I was ever on time for was showing up at the bar.

Turning back to my room, my side looks barren, plain. Libby and I had been shopping yesterday for sheets, comforters, and an air fryer because I apparently "need" one, even though I'd already purchased a full meal plan. She's filled my mini fridge with all my favorites and a few of her leafy things to remind me of home. I survey the room. I can't imagine this place ever feeling like home.

Classes don't start until tomorrow, so I pull my Mac out of my pack and start up a movie. I can't focus on the plot. It's a little after five now, and twilight is beginning to suck the sun from the room. The characters are setting up their backstories before the conflict, before the part where every-thing changes.

After all the planning, it feels wild to be here at uni. After all the campuses my dad and I had unofficially toured, window-shopping schools, we used to pick up our coffees and stroll the grounds, talking lively about what I wanted to study.

We'd started when I was maybe ten. We had driven up to a church in D.C. for Ash Wednesday and arrived early. Across from the chapel was a school, but I swear it might have been a castle. I begged him to let me look around while we waited. He humored me. I asked if there were schools prettier than that one, and that was when he told me about Princeton, Harvard, and Oxford. My dad was supposed to be the one to drop me off today. It was always the plan—before he died, before the part where everything changed.

Charlie and Grey were supposed to be here with me or FaceTiming me from their schools. Grey was supposed to be in my bed on the weekends and texting me GIFs that didn't make sense to anyone but him. He was supposed to be emailing me novels and telling me how he was picked up by a publisher.

I unlock my phone. It's empty of new messages and emails. I sigh and melt into my pillows. This is one of the moments I had imagined so many times, and now that I'm in it, it's empty. Anxiety eats away at my brain and my stomach. I'm facing a fear. I kept putting school off because I was afraid of *this* feeling. Of being alone in a time that should feel so full of hope and possibility.

I try to disorient my mind with other things like the drive here. It was eerily familiar to the drive I had taken to the conservatory a couple of weeks ago. I hadn't realized they were so close in proximity, but I traveled the same road almost the whole way.

I wonder if Derek is there now, officially moved in with Duke, or if he's still in the city at the bar. I click the address in our message feed, and the GPS shows it's a twenty-minute drive from my school. The idea of seeing him again before the holidays we've discussed makes me more excited than it should. I decided to text him tomorrow after classes and find out.

Thinking of Derek brings me a sort of peace. I leave some of the things I lost behind and think instead of the piano room. The morning will start another day of music. I have three classes tomorrow: Music Theory, Dance, and Performance. I review the syllabus for each class and remember why I'm at this particular school. It's not about the social experience; it's about the music.

I open my Music Theory textbook and read the first chapter we'll study tomorrow. Sleep finds me quickly.

now, august

MUSIC THEORY WAS as dull as I had expected it to be. I order lunch from a pub about a block from school, but the faces there don't matter. It isn't *my* pub.

I hope that all my classes will not be like the first. I have to like at least one. If *that* is what I have to look forward to, I'll end up dropping out in the first month in pursuit of an alternate plan: scuba diving in Australia, busking the streets of Paris, or anything outrageous enough to keep my mind occupied.

I have a few hours between classes. Since they don't assign homework here, I explore the buildings on campus instead. The library is vast and beautiful, with its theatrical arches and dark honey shelving. A plaque near the door reads that this was a set location for one of the *Harry Potter* movies, and I see why. I have found the school's first redeeming quality.

Time moves faster between the walls of books, and when I check my watch, I only have ten minutes to make it to Dance, which is all the way across the courtyard.

I burst through the door exactly as both hands on the clock come to rest at 12.

"Just on time." The instructor smiles at me. He's a handsome man. His dark skin stretched across his bone, defining his cheeks prominently among the rest of his features. He appeared almost too young to be a teacher. Causally dressed in his dance clothes (gym shorts and an athletic tank,) he would not be distinguishable if it weren't for his position in the front of the room. "Take a spot next to Riley back there."

A lanky boy in the back sucks in his lips, causing his face to balloon out like a pufferfish. His eyebrows raise in acknowledgment. He flicks out his wrist in what I can only describe as a sarcastic wave. I take my place beside him.

"Alright, guys. I'm your dance instructor, Mr. Chambers. Everyone take five and get changed. I expect you all to arrive ready to sweat for future classes. This means sneakers or dance shoes, clothing that lets you move, no loose jewelry that can fly off and hit your neighbor in the face." He gives Riley a pointed look.

"Come on, mate. It was one time." Riley says raising his finger. His tone feigns defense, but based on his leather studded wristband and the rings scattered across his fingers, I sense there's further validity to the accusations.

Once we change, Chambers puts us to work. I like Dance; it becomes my only focus. I have no room for anything else—only motion. He takes the routines slowly, and I've never been coordinated, but I seem to pick up the count quickly, falling into step. When it ends an hour later, I'm already looking forward to my next class on Wednesday —another sixty minutes where everything is blocked out.

I shower in the locker room where I'd changed at the

start of class, dressing quickly to make it to my last class a few minutes early.

now, august

I STUMBLE into the auditorium and look back at my schedule to verify the class. It's the right room, but it seems off. The others have their feet kicked up on the chairs in front of them. Some talk in groups with friends from previous years, while some sit alone texting or strumming guitar lazily. It feels more kickback than classroom, prompting me to check the plaque outside. Did I have the right building?

Sure enough, it mirrors my schedule sheet. Room 2002, Mr. Anderson's Music Composition and Performance. I step in and find my way to an empty seat in the middle of the clusterfuck of rows. It is close enough to the groups that I don't stand out but far enough that I still have plenty of space to myself.

I lay my bag in the chair beside me. Each chair is a royal red velvet, black in areas from stains or wear due to years of nearly adolescent abuse. I run my hand over a burn mark on one of the cushions. I reach for my shoulder and rub the burn mark of my own. *You and me both,* I think to the chair.

Once you have been burned deeply, the nerve endings

die. You can't feel touch anymore. I remind myself of this every time I run my fingers across it. It has become a nervous tick, a source of comfort. I touch it when I am anxious or sad, when I am scared, and when I don't know what to do with my hands.

My parents called it PTSD. Well, my stepdad did, and my mom pretty much went along with whatever he thought since he was paying for the shrinks. The nightmares I had after the fire? PTSD. The nervous scar petting? PTSD. Pretty much any behavior that was out of the norm could be contributed to that one time I ran into a burning building where people I loved died.

My real dad didn't say anything. He didn't have an opinion on it. Still, I liked to think that if he were alive, he wouldn't contribute all of my uniqueness to trauma. He'd have a much more creative outlook on things.

Oh, Ally? That isn't PTSD. That's all personality. It's really quite good that she is feeling things so heavily now. She'll be able to move on easier when she's ready. This is what I imagined he would say.

I take out my notebook and write the date at the top. I debate if this is a good idea. I should be introducing myself to people and connecting. You only get one chance to make a good first impression. Fitting in should be somewhat of a priority, right? Did people still care about fitting in once they got to college?

I look around. Based on the groups that have been formed and the loners that look intentionally lonely, I guess people did care. People always tried to fit in. I don't. I don't pull out my phone to look busy. I don't have anyone to text anyway.

My phone dings as if to prove me wrong. It's a recording. A song. From Derek.

I don't want to wait until Christmas.

The words are lit up in bold on my screen. *Wait for Christmas to what?* I searched my bag for my air pods but left them in my dorm. I'm mentally shooting myself in the foot. I can picture the exact spot where they're sitting on the nightstand. Another thought takes precedence: *He's thinking of me, too.*

My stomach flip-flops. Asking him if he's staying at the conservatory just got a whole lot easier. I might be able to see him tonight, even. The suspense is too much and I'm about to step out to listen to what he's sent when the lights dim. The song will have to wait. I tuck my phone back into my pocket without responding.

There is an energy in the room, an anticipation for what happens next. The oxygen smells faintly of smoke, the kind that comes from fog machines at Halloween. Music begins to play. Adrenaline pulses under my skin; I am trying to decide if I like it or not when a spotlight hits the stage.

A guitar plays while the player is only a silhouette, a shadow projected onto a large white screen. The light flashes off while the music continues. When the lights return, the player has switched to the piano, layering over the composition. Every time the lights blink, the same shadowed man flips between instruments on stage, using a loop to mix the tones. The musician begins to hum over the track he's created before finally adding words to the song. His voice is rich and velvety, his tone flawless while performing over the music.

The song becomes louder, intensifying in both volume and emotion. Abruptly, it stops and only the voice remains. The lights go out, enveloping the room in silence. It's undoubtedly the most incredible production I've ever witnessed. The audience seems to agree, as the room is filled with thunderous applause. I can't see past the standing ovation, but I assume the performer is our teacher based on the enthusiastic reaction.

This. This is what I came here for. If I can create a moment like that by the end of the year, then this class alone will have been well worth the tuition.

"He's quite fit!" The girl in front of me giggles. I try to peep through them to see for myself.

"This is only a flash of what you are capable of. As an individual, a creator, an artist."

There is finally a gap in the audience now that everyone has taken their seats. Now that the girls in front of me have stopped shifting and laughing. I wish they hadn't. It was better before when I was just a girl sitting in the crowd, thrilled for what this class had to offer. Before I saw that my professor, the person I had so much to learn from, was Derek.

"My name is Rivera, not Mr. Rivera, just Rivera. I'm not here to discuss anything you may have heard, so don't ask me. And I'm not your fucking professor, so get that out of your heads now. I'll be advising this semester while Mr. Anderson is on leave.

I will not be grading you. It is up to you to determine your success here. Your grade falls in the hands of your classmates, your audience. Outside of this room, it isn't the labels that define your worth— it's the crowd. Turn to your neighbor and examine them closely. That is who you are striving to impress, not me. Have you got it?

I'm just the guy that stands at the front of the room and tells you the prompt. It's up to you what you do with it. Up to them if it's good enough."

No. No fucking way.

I'd be impressed at how he maintains his harshness if I wasn't so stunned at seeing him here.

So, that's what his music is capable of being? Not all doom and gloom like Bar-Derek's was, but catchy, upbeat, layered. He really is a rockstar. But a *fucking professor?* Sorry, *'advisor.' My fucking advisor?*

He looks like a different person onstage under the spotlights and layers of deception. His voice even sounds different; too stiff, professional.

"I'm going to call roll and ask you a few questions about yourself. If you get shy speaking in front of others, shake it off. You'll be in the spotlight every week from here on out." He is staring down at the paper in front of him.

"Aberdeen, Pheobe?" He calls.

I sink lower in my seat, considering whether to sneak out in a crouch or to casually walk out with purpose while the lights are still dimmed. The longer I stay here, the longer I want to slap him. This changes *everything*, and I hate him for it.

"Dennison, Lauren?"

"Here!" A girl calls back. I tune out the rest of what is happening.

He's a bartender! Never had he mentioned teaching. Not once. I start thinking over the books in the upstairs apartment about music theory and stage performance. He had mentioned he was moving here to be with Duke, *not* for a job opening.

"Knight, Phillip?" He continues through the list, moving at a pace much too fast.

"Here." A handsome blonde guy shouts out.

"Why music?" Derek inquires, bored.

"My girlfriend says I need to be more expressive about my feelings, and chicks dig musicians."

"I don't even know how to respond to that," Derek says, moving on to the next name. How is he the exact same person and yet so different?

"Parasons, Riley?"

The guy from dance raises his hand in that "I'm too cool for this" kind of way. I didn't know you could achieve that with a hand.

"Why are you in my class?" Derek asks inquisitively. There are little more than twenty-five of us in here, a relatively small class for such an ample space. Most of my other courses have had fifty to a hundred students. *Lucky me.*

"I need music to breathe. I don't like performing in front of people, but my band booked a tour this summer, so it seems I'll have to change that."

I wonder briefly how he booked the tour without singing in front of anyone. I pray, actually pray, that Riley will elaborate or keep talking about literally anything. The anticipation of the next name on that list leaves a sinking feeling in my stomach. He doesn't keep talking, and my time is up. The moment I've been dreading comes too soon.

"Parrish, Allyson?"

There it is.

Fucking hell. Maybe I could have avoided this if I had stopped touching his stupid jaw and asked more questions.

"Do we have an Allyson Parrish?" *Fuck. Fuck. Fuck.* I don't have to answer. Yeah, I can ignore it and *then* sneak out. Master plan.

"Alright. No, Miss Parrish." He crosses my name off the list.

"Robleman, Tom?"

I stand and make my way to the back of the class, thankful for the cloak of darkness in the shadowed auditorium.

My phone lights up and vibrates in my pocket, followed by my ringtone for Libby. *Milkshake* by Kelis plays loudly through the speaker. Damn her for that being her favorite song! It was initially a joke. I don't think she knew how big of a joke it would end up being.

I don't have to turn around to know what's happening, to feel all twenty-five heads shift in my direction. I silence my phone and debate darting for the door, but what's the point? My hope of going unnoticed is gone.

"Going somewhere, Miss—?" Derek asks, waiting for a name.

"Parrish," I say without turning.

"Ah, the elusive Miss Parrish. Was my class interrupting your phone call?" He pries. "You can answer that, but not answer me when I call your name?"

Yup. Definitely the same person. God, he's a dick.

"Allyson, isn't it?" He taunts. I can hear the familiar smirk in his tone.

Fuck me. I turn.

"Ally, actually." I step into the light.

He jerks up from his pad, his eyes growing too wide for comfort. My only relief comes from his reaction being subtle enough not to draw too many conclusions, but still, it attracts enough attention to make me feel worse than I already do.

"*Ally.* Would you like to rejoin the class?" He says, his jaw tight. His lips land in a straight line.

"It'd be my pleasure, *professor.*" I spit back, taunting him. Taunting his stupid fucking speech.

He glares at me for a second before finishing the role.

I turn my phone off and pull out my notebook from my pack. I have no lyrics to write; my mind is too busy screaming. I pull a loose page quietly from the binding and fold a paper airplane to busy my hands, to keep my mind occupied enough that I don't try to walk out again the way my legs are itching to.

"As I said, you will get a new assignment, a prompt for a new song every week. You will be graded on the three factors mentioned. To recap, that is: written composition, lyrics, and performance. You'll have a sheet to turn in with your performance assessments." He pauses for dramatic effect, scanning all the crowd's faces. All but mine.

"This week, we're going to start with a feeling: anticipation. You can write about anything, but it has to be something that makes you feel amped up. You have the rest of the class to work on it. This will be a team project. Teams of two. Start now."

I imagine what it would be like to have the power of invisibility. I would disappear from this seat right now and not come back. Can I get through months of this? I mean, we never kissed. We never had sex. I can't say we never slept together but we never cuddled. No lines were *really* crossed. He could just be my teacher, right? The intimate moments we *did* share play behind my eyes. Touching him in the alleyway. Stripping to my bra when my scar began to burn. *That makes me want to fuck you.* Maybe he couldn't.

"You're in your own little world, aren't you?" A voice says from beside me.

I jumped. "Oh, er, hi." I say, lamely drawing out the "hiiiii" since I have no words to follow it.

"Riley." He reminds me as he takes the next seat over and kicks his feet up on the chair in front of him.

Dressed in his regular clothes, I have to admit, I like his style. He's wearing a green leather jacket and a V-neck tee with a few silver chains around his neck. His ears are gauged, and the metal squares on his belt come to a tip like little spikes. It's very 2000's punk.

"So, what's up with you and Rivera? You looked rather miffed, and he looked like he was going to shit himself when he called your name. Drama?" He asks mockingly. It matches his sarcastic wave from dance.

"For someone whose tone is so disinterested, you ask a lot of detailed questions," I remark.

"It's a small class. Most of these people I was brought up with. You're new. Shiny." He throws out jazz hands on "shiny" before turning to smirk at me.

"I'm not interested, Ron." I flip through the pages of my journal, skimming through my lyrics to find some that suit the assignment. My irritation peaks when I see Derek's scribbles on the corner of the parchment and slam it shut. Riley raises his eyebrows before continuing.

"I wasn't trying to pick you up. You're not my type." He says, looking me up and down. "And it's Riley. Not Ron. Ri-ley." He sounds it out like I may be stupid or slow.

"I know." My own smirk is inevitable. There's a whole lot of fucking smirking going on in here today, but our conversation is helping me to feel somewhat normal again. Riley assesses me for a beat longer, then pulls a Twizzler from his bag.

"We're going to get on, you and I." He gestures between us with the red licorice. A genuine smile finds its way on his lips as he takes a bite and rips the end off the candy. He seems part dog, part boy. I snag a piece from his bag and replicate the bite. He's unfazed, causal, like this happens all the time.

Feeling daggers boring into my head, I glance up. The girl in front of me, the "he's quite fit" girl, is glaring at me.

"Did you need something?" I ask her, annoyed.

She makes a delicate huff and turns around in her seat. I roll my eyes. I am not dealing with some petty, mean girl on my first day. I don't have the patience to entertain it. Her blonde hair is bouncy, all tied up in a bow. Entitlement radiates off of her. I resist rolling my eyes again.

Riley scoots over and whispers to me. "It's not her fault. It's all the hairspray."

I find myself laughing without meaning to. I cover my mouth, startled. It takes me a while to warm up to people, yet here I am, stealing this kid's Twizzlers and forming inside jokes.

"So, you do have a sense of humor. I'm learning so much today." He leans back in his seat and tilts his head towards the lights as if they are the sun, and he is soaking it in.

His skin was pasty like mine, almost translucent, and I imagined he had a better excuse than I did for why. The sun had barely shown itself since I had arrived in England, making my complexion appear even more sickly than it had back home. I pictured it with a greenish tint to it now under the current circumstances.

"Do you have a beach here?" I ask, hopeful.

He opens his eyes. "Um, yeah. The coastline is about two hours from here. Are you already picturing me in my knickers? It's good, innit?"

"Yes. I might die if I have to go without seeing your junk all wrapped up in a tight little package for me to ogle." I cue my third eye roll of the day.

"You're going to suffer a stroke or something if you keep doing that." He comments.

I make a note in my book to look up the beach. I hadn't thought about going, but it's been months since I've seen an ocean. I realize I have gone minutes without thinking about Derek despite being in the same room.

I glance up, locating him immediately. Jumping from group to group, he nods animatedly. He seems almost warm, waving his hands as he discusses the assignment with each pairing.

Derek *isn't* warm. Well, he is to me, but certainly not to other people. Sorry, not people, *students*.

His button-down is tight, clinging to him in all the right places. I don't know what brand it is, but it is tailor-made for him. It's foreign to the apparel I'm used to seeing him in. Nothing like the plain black and white tees I became accustomed to over the summer. So, he changed his wardrobe but not his personality. Not entirely, at least. Maybe the school employed some advisor dress code I wasn't aware of.

I've never seen him look so lively. This is where his passion is. My brain nags at me that I missed out. I should have gotten to know this whole other side of him. Then, maybe we could have avoided this situation altogether. Why am I thinking about this like I wanted to date him? I shake my head.

Riley chatters about the project, and I mutter the occasional "mhmm" and "yeah, that could work." I flip through the non-tainted pages, trying to find a starting place for the assignment. Anticipation, I remind myself.

"So, I typically go more rock, alternative. Can you hang with that?"

"Mhmm." I nod.

"How are things coming along?" Derek says from behind us, forcing me to jump.

I'm deciding if I want to turn around when Riley answers.

"Oh great. Ally has a lot of ideas. 'Um' and 'Mhmm' are

at the top of her list." I can hear the sarcasm dripping as he throws me under the bus.

"' Um.' Really?" Derek gave me a pointed look, and I knew exactly where his mind was. *There are so many better words to tell me what you're thinking.*

"We were thinking of beatboxing," Riley interjects, saving me from Derek's invading eyes. I examine Riley blankly before breaking out into laughter. His face is so serious and sure of itself.

Derek takes a seat beside us. His jaw is set. It's how he looked whenever Sonnie hugged me, or I'd get a drink sent over.

"Mr. Parasons, correct?" He asks.

God. Don't interrogate him.

"Yes. And Miss Parrish. Can't forget about Miss Parrish." Riley says, tilting his head to the side with a shit-eating grin. I almost snort. He can hold his own. Maybe we can be friends.

"Oh, no. Not many people try to sneak out of my class on the first day." He quirks an eyebrow at me. *Welcome back, Eyebrows.*

"Yes. Well, there seemed to be a mix-up in my schedule. I meant to take Piano Composition, not Performance," I notate.

"Of course you did." Derek nods as if it makes perfect sense.

"Then she met me, and now she'll be staying. I talked her into it." Riley winks at me.

Derek tenses, and something inside of me tightens in response. It's a small reaction but I notice, and I like it way more than I should. I still have the urge to touch him. To reach out and lay my fingers against his jaw like I have before. To smooth out the tension. This is a dangerous game we are playing, Rivera.

"Have you had an opportunity to discuss the project? What sounds are you wanting to incorporate?" Derek probes for information. This seems normal, though. I assume this is what he did with all the other groups. I like how hands-on he is. He should be more hands on me.

What the hell, Ally?

"We're thinking alternative. A nice drum core and some guitar to get it where it needs to be. We haven't discussed lyrics, but based on that book," Riley gestures toward my journal. "we have plenty to work with."

"You could start with piano and go darker. Amp it up with a guitar overlay and drums."

"Oh, I kind of like that." Riley cracks his jaw, thinking to himself. He scrawls some notes in the book in front of him.

"I'll leave you two to discuss. It was great to meet you both." He makes his escape and stops to talk to the girls in front of us—girls who are irritating me by flirting more than talking about the assignment.

"You're really here!" They squeal. "I can't believe you *know* Zach Goodhart! You wrote all his best songs! I was devastated when the band broke up!"

Derek's eyes narrow before flashing to me. I looked away quickly as if I could pretend I hadn't been eavesdropping on the conversation.

"My past is off-limits. Tell me about your assignment, or I will move on to a group that doesn't waste my time."

"I'm sorry. I'm sorry." They profess. "We're just so excited to be working with you. *Faint Lies* is like, my favorite song ever."

True to his word, he walks away, leaving them to

squirm over their mistake and leaving me to question what the hell just happened.

now, august

AFTER DEREK MEETS with each of the groups, he returns to the stage and lays out what the semester will look like together. I make plans with my partner to meet later tonight to begin on the song. When class ends, Riley steals my phone from my back pocket with a spin.

"What's your password?" He pops his lips and waits impatient, expectant.

I don't answer. This nut job cannot seriously think I will just *give* him my password.

"Ally, if we're going to be best friends, I need to know your password." He says. "Why are you being weird about this?" He leans back on his heels, trying his best to appear confused.

I punch him in the shoulder. I can't help it. He is a freak, and I *do* like him.

"Ow!" He yelps. "When did girls start hitting so hard?" He rubs his arm.

"You're weird. You know that, right?" I say, unlocking my phone for him. He adds his number under the contact #1 Weirdo.

"Yup." He lights up as he watches me read his chosen name. My lips stretch into a smile, and my eyes roll. "Stroke." He mouths to me as he moves towards the door. His brohawk grazes the top of the frame as he steps through.

"Miss Parrish, a word?" Derek calls from the front of the classroom.

Riley pauses and shoots me a look over his shoulder, telling me we will be discussing this over dinner tonight—dinner I am oddly excited about. He wiggles his eyebrows and then leaves. The kids got personality; I'll give him that.

I backtrack down the aisle reluctantly. Derek is on stage, shuffling through pages scattered across the hood of the piano. I stop at the front of the stage and wait impatiently.

"You can come up." He says without looking away from the papers.

"Oh, can I?" I snark. He offers me nothing, so I grind my teeth and mount the stage.

He speaks with complete animosity when I am a couple of feet away. Keeping his head down he says, "How is it you are in my class, Ally?"

"I go to school here, *Derek*." I spell it out for him. "To study music. You know, to practice the *thing* we did all summer? At the university I *told* you I was going to?"

"I thought you were going to uni in the States." He bites back. I have his attention now.

"Well, you didn't ask. How is it that I didn't know you were a teacher, Derek?" I quirk my head and steal his raised eyebrows move.

"I'm *not*. I'm an advisor, and *you* didn't ask. Will you be dropping the class?" He questions.

I instantly hate that he assumes I should drop it or leave to better suit him. I want to be defensive and kick and scream. I reign in the anger and try to think reasonably. It's his job. He doesn't exactly have the option to leave. I can stay and make it awkward, or I can switch to another course. It's early, I'm sure I could. I said earlier that I had taken this on accident—the perfect excuse. I really need to work on my misplaced anger.

"I don't know. I need the credit, but I can get it somewhere else. There are other classes." I shrug, proud of how it comes out.

Sighing, he comes around the piano and leans against it causally, his hands tucked into his tailored pant pockets. I want to spit on his stupid loafers with his sexy ankles peeking out of them. It's almost Victorian; how that small show of skin appeals to me. Given our change in circumstance, it's nearly cruel that he appeals to me at all.

"Ally, this was a last-minute thing. Jace— *Mr. Chambers*," He corrects. "he's been my best mate since we were young. Anderson fell ill, and Jace called in a favor to get me the gig. It pays, and it's close to Duke."

"And this Zach Goodhart, he doesn't pay for these incredible songs you wrote him?"

"So, you did catch that."

"I did. Does that have anything to do with why I shouldn't Google you?"

"Yes, and I still hope you won't. Would you be dropping the class solely because of me?" He asks, changing the subject, leaning forward to hear the answer.

We're on a slippery road. I'm on a crash course collision into him, my fingers twitching at my side. It would be so easy to touch him. He's so close, testing my will by peering up at me from under those dark brows. I resist taking a step back. It's habit to overcorrect when avoiding a crash. It feels like either way, this isn't going to end well.

"If I were to drop it, yes," I say, struggling to answer.

"Do you want to?" He goads. Pushing off the piano, he shifts further into my space.

"Drop the class?" I think this over, fighting to keep my wits intact. "I was excited about Performance, but I need to be realistic about the fact that I have almost kissed my *advisor* on more than one occasion," I admit breathily.

A half-smile appears on his lips, then disappears just as suddenly.

"Riley will be disappointed." He says curtly, pressing his lips into a thin, hard line.

"Derek, don't be petty." I instigate gently, placing my hand on his arm. My thumb is unable to resist tracing small circles into his bicep. We both stare at it for a beat, then wide-eyed at each other. "We're partners on a project *you* assigned. That's all." I try to reassure him.

Derek steps back at once. He removes my hand from his arm.

"Whatever you decide, we should keep our relationship strictly formal from here on out." The words escape his lips calmly and without attachment.

It stings. Derek had made me feel excited about something again. Now I'm cut off? I understand the circumstances and the consequences involved. I completely get why this can't go anywhere, but it also means we can't remain where we are. No more texting inside jokes back and forth. No more writing songs together on the piano in the pool. I am digesting the feeling when he begins to walk away.

"Derek." I stop him. His face is cold. Steel. It's warning me about crossing lines. Apparently, first names have graduated to red flags.

"Rivera." He corrects.

With that, I almost lose my nerve. Almost.

"Would it make a difference— if I did drop your class? With us, I mean?" I'm stumbling through what I'm trying to say. Suddenly, I feel as if I am talking to an actual professor, not the man I've been letting inside my head for the past six weeks.

Another sigh escapes his lips, and he raises his arm to rub the back of his head as he considers the question. I know that gesture. He still feels it, whatever *it* is. Before this, we *were* something. I want him to admit it before the new dynamic is solidified.

"No. You're still a student. It would go against everything I am. Ethically." The words are sure of themselves. His body remains rigid, only his stare is softer now. Does he know he's hurting me? "I'll see you Wednesday, Miss Parrish."

He exits the room and I say nothing to stop him from leaving. It is at this moment I understand that I have a crush on Derek Rivera. That I've *had* a crush on Derek Rivera.

I ponder it over. Now that a line has been drawn, is that why it's safe to admit? I have no risk of it, of us, actually happening, so is that why I can finally admit that I wanted it to? *Of course, it is.*

I was afraid of the low that would accompany the high. Only, I feel ripped off because I never got to experience the high—just the low, never on time, always too late or too early. I'm always too late to save anything. I'm always losing people too early.

It's like Derek is the worst *Not Grey* of all, the worst because I don't want him to be Grey. I don't want him to be anything but Derek. I certainly don't want him to be "Mr. Rivera."

Grey, Grey. His name screams out in my head. A pang that is much worse than the sting of today rises in my stomach. Guilt takes over like a migraine, consuming every function of my brain. Give me the distraction back, I beg. God. The universe. I don't know who I am begging, but I'd give anything for this to stop.

then, january

I HADN'T SEEN the Kingsleys since Christmas Eve morning when my mom picked me up with the car packed and ready for the long drive down to Florida. Since her marriage to Michael, we have spent every year in Tampa with his family. I had begged to stay home or with the Kingsleys, but I lost, like most battles fought against my mother.

It wasn't Florida I dreaded; it was where we'd be staying with *Michael's* mother. I despised that woman more than I despised him. She was a rather large lady who kept her house warm, even in the southern humidity, which had made her perpetually sticky. Her sundresses, which were so thin they could have been nightgowns, were all marked with permanent pit stains, forcing me to cringe every time she folded me into a damp embrace.

The woman wore red lipstick that was always smeared onto her teeth and refused to let me call her anything but "Granny Naeh." Neah, as in Nevaeh, which she repeatedly reminded me, was Heaven spelled backward. Only her name isn't Neveah. It's Petunia—Petunia Litoris.

I saw it on her driver's license when it fell from her purse the year before. When I confronted Michael-the-Stepdad about it, he shushed me, telling me there was no harm in letting the old woman go by what she wanted. I know this, but she's introduced herself as Neveah ever since I've known her. Not just to me, but to everybody. It killed me not to ask why she did this, but whenever I'd begin to broach the subject, Michael would give me the death stare, shutting it down. I halted myself from mentioning the flaws in his own name to him.

I was the only person to call him Michael. To the world, he was just Mike. Mike Litoris.

The swamp days, as I liked to call them, dragged on until, at last, I was back home where I belonged. It took half a dozen showers to get the smell of Granny off me. I was in the car recounting this series of events to Charlie and Grey, who were howling out the window.

"Gosh, Al, that's awful." Charlie barked.

"Dude, you should have just stayed here. With *me*." Grey smirked. Reaching over the center console, he took my hand freely. Being close to him physically was a new sensation, especially in front of someone else. But I liked it. I liked it a lot. He ran his thumb across each of my fingers, like he could somehow memorize my fingerprint too.

"With *us*." Charlie corrected from the back seat. She was still having difficulty adjusting to the new dynamic between Grey and me.

"Like my mother ever would have allowed that." I rolled my eyes. "What I want isn't important where Michael is concerned."

"Yeah, well, Michael kind of sucks. Hey, Grey, do you think Ollie will be there?" She asked, switching subjects. We were on our way to Grey's teammate Chris' New Year's

Eve party. Grey nodded his confirmation to her in the rearview, igniting a squeal of glee from over my shoulder.

When we arrived, the party was too loud. The air filled with the white noise of too many people trying to talk at once and be heard over the music. Sensing my nerves, Grey drew me closer to his side. It was our first time out as a couple, and I felt like everyone was staring at us, their eyes fixed on our hands intertwined.

"There's my favorite guy!" Chris yelled, pushing through the thrall of bodies to where we stood in the foyer. In his hand was a red solo cup that sloshed liquid onto the rug every time he bumped a shoulder or a piece of furniture, which was often. I stared at the wet spots forming on the carpet, questioning if they'd come out and how angry his parents would be about the mess. Grey had told me they were away, spending New Year's on a ski trip in Aspen.

"It's about Goddamn time!" He said when he was close enough, looking between the two of us.

"Charlie!" A girl I recognized from the drama club waved her over. Charlie looked at me expectantly to follow, and I usually would have, but Grey didn't let go of my hand. I hadn't prepared for this, for the split. I didn't know where I belonged when both places felt simultaneously right and wrong.

"It's okay," Grey whispered in my ear. "I'll find you before midnight."

I felt relieved that I didn't have to choose between them. I let go of his hand and followed Charlie to the usual faces. Grey stared after me, smiling until Chris dragged him away through an archway leading to the kitchen. The comfort I felt diminished as I watched him go, even more so as I watched a dozen pretty girls take notice that he was alone.

I turned my focus back to the group, where a girl named Morgan from my history class was talking about conspiracy theories with the others. Charlie leaped right into the conversation while I hung back. Someone offered me a drink, which I quickly refused. I meant it when I said I was never drinking again. The too-sweet cherry mixer tried to cover the scent of the liquor beneath it, failing. Just the scent of other people's cups turned my stomach. Nope.

It took a while for me to feel comfortable enough to begin to mingle, even though I knew everyone around us. About an hour in, I felt arms wrap around my shoulders, followed by the scent of Grey. It was crazy how I could identify him off his scent alone. He smelled like firewood and marshmallow embers, like a fall festival. I leaned back, the last of my discomfort evaporating.

"I missed you." He said quietly so only I could hear.

The group stopped talking. Half of these people shared a lunch table with us. Confusion appeared on their faces. Their thoughts couldn't have been more obvious than if they'd had a question mark floating above their heads: *What does he see in her?* I felt suddenly self-conscious as I asked myself the same question.

"Whoa, whoa. When *the fuck* did this happen?" Morgan asked, smiling gleefully. "Because I ship the hell out of this." She gestured to the space around us.

Soon after, Grey launched into story mode about how he'd plotted to make me fall in love with him since the first night we met. The people we knew and those we didn't gathered around to listen were eating out of his hand by the end of his tale. Usually, I'd hate the attention, but how he looked at me when he spoke, how he seemed to get choked up, melted everything away but him.

I was shocked that people started clapping when he

finished—shocked that Charlie was one of them. I had never told her about our kitchen rendezvous. I was afraid she'd be upset with me, but she appeared awed. My heart swelled with gratitude. I mouthed a silent "thank you" to her, not caring if she understood what I was thanking her for, but she caught on at once and waved it off.

Once the conversation turned to a new subject, the attention on us lessened; Grey grabbed my hand, pulling me towards the door. When we got outside, he lowered the tailgate to his Jeep, where Charlie and I had kept blankets and pillows since the warm days of waiting for him to get out of practice had gone. The chill of winter had finally come. I climbed into the cozy cocoon, watching fireworks explode in the sky above us as the new year ticked near. It was only an hour away.

Standing instead of joining me in the Jeep, Grey leaned against it. He kicked at the ground nervously, scuffing his converses.

"What are you thinking?" I asked.

He smiled deviously like he had been caught. "I'm thinking I want to kiss you at midnight, but I don't want our first kiss to be in a room full of people. Sooooo, I was kind of hoping I could kiss you now, if that's okay." He said, half-turning to face me.

My heart skipped. I was hoping things would happen as they did in the rom-coms I stayed up watching with Charlie. I'd hoped it would be natural, but this wasn't, which made it awkward. I was too nervous, too sure I'd mess it up somehow.

He came to stand in front of where I was sitting Indian style on the floorboard. Cautiously, he brushed my hair away from my face.

"Have you never been kissed before, Ally?" He asked tenderly.

I shook my head no.

"You don't have to be nervous. You can't do it wrong." He reaffirmed.

"I'm not nervous." I lied.

"Liar."

"You're nervous." I retorted. In truth, I had no idea if he was nervous.

"You're right." He agreed, leaning closer.

He shifted his hands from my hair to my chin, holding me steady. I thought about pulling away. The anticipation was too much like anxiety, making me feel like I might implode. But then again, it was *Grey*. He was pure and kind. Even if I did manage to do it wrong, it'd still mean I had my first kiss with the boy I loved. I stopped overthinking it and tilted my chin up, pursing my lips.

"No, Ally. Not yet." He chuckled lightly.

I felt embarrassed at my inexperience, but he shushed me as if he could hear my feelings screaming at him.

Lightly, he pressed his lips to my cheek. Then, the skin next to the corner of my mouth. Our hands found each other and intertwined in the air beside us. His nose touched mine as he hovered in the space above my lips.

"This is the moment before everything changes." He whispered.

Then, I was kissing him, and it was more than I ever could have imagined. I saw the rest of my life in that kiss.

now, august

RILEY LIVES off-campus in a relic of an apartment building. The walls are stone, and the windows have iron bars inside the glass. The concrete floor adds to the place's chill, but his decorating has warmed it up. He greets me into a living room with an opening on either side for the bedrooms. 90s grunge band posters and more current band tour memorabilia have been neatly framed and arranged to provide a gallery wall behind the sofa.

There is lamp lighting, and his couch is a worn gray tweed. The chairs on either side of it are an outdated orange and unmistakably hand-me-downs, judging by the condition of the fabric. He has plaid blankets strewn everywhere. The entire set faces a wall with a grand fireplace, the only valuable attribute original to the building. I am shocked that a flat in England is big enough to house this much furniture.

The collection of guitars in the corner is what catches my attention, though.

"Do you play?" He asks.

"I do." I nod.

"Here." He hands me a guitar, and we go to work on the song. Me on the couch, and him lounged back in one of the gaudy terracotta chairs with his feet on the coffee table. I look over the lyrics he's scooted across to me.

Hold out for the liars, the hiders, the cheaters crying under their beds.
No one's laughing when they're dead.
Ha ha ha ha.
No one's laughing when they're dead.

"I love that!" I exclaim. "Do you mind if I try something?"

He gestures, telling me I have the floor.

"Hold out for the liars, the hiders, the pretenders who feed you hope instead. No one's laughing when it ends." I sing as I strum, then pause to think out loud. "Then maybe, like the ha ha ha ha ha coming in from the background," I say before returning to the vocals. "No one's laughing when it ends. Maybe you should think this through again before I finish what you started."

I trail off. Riley gapes at me and appears speechless, something I can't imagine happens often.

"What?" I ask, suddenly self-conscious.

"One:" He holds up his pointer finger. "I love those changes." Up comes the second finger. "Two: I did not know you could sing like that! Your voice is fucking brilliant." He awes.

I ignore the embarrassment beginning to flush my cheeks, and look away. I'm saved by flashing lights and an incessant buzzing. His phone is about to fall off the arm of the chair, where it vibrates. Someone named MATT is calling. He glances at it quickly before flipping it over fast. It begins buzzing again seconds later.

He seems concerned, this time getting up briskly from the chair and standing awkwardly before waving his phone.

"Sorry, a friend. I have to take this." He announces before excusing himself to the bedrooms on the left, where he shuts the door behind him.

Mollified by the distraction, I scribble more lines in his composition book while attempting to figure out who will sing which part. I haven't heard him sing yet, so I'm not sure where he will sound strongest.

He renters the room after a short while, seemingly recovered from whatever was troubling him. Plummeting back into his seat, he grabs his guitar from where he left it.

"Where were we?" He questions nervously.

I shake my head with a smile, hoping he understands he doesn't need to put on a front or feel embarrassed about the interruption. Whoever was on the phone, I'm not going to pry. Lord knows I have plenty I'd rather not share. I play him through what I've started, and we bounce chord progressions back and forth until they evolve into the right sound.

"You know, what if— " I hesitate while I work to figure out how to vocalize the idea. "What if this wasn't a battle song so much as a love song? Maybe two people who have been fighting their feelings for each other? The first verse could be her calling him out. The second, him to her."

"Should we call these people Rivera and Ally?" He asks in amusement. I'm learning Riley is way too observant.

"How about something less inappropriate?" I try.

"Less accurate?" He sticks his guitar pick between his lips to keep from laughing at my face. I throw the pen I was using to write with at him. I miss.

"Alright, alright." He uses his best "compromise" voice. "What shall we call these avoidant lovers?"

"We'll call her August," I say, using my birth month.

He nods, switching from biting his guitar pick to the pen I threw at him. "I like it. We'll call him Noah."

"Noah?" I ask, laughing. "Like Noah's arc?"

"Noah, like the first boy I fell in love with." He says it casually through closed teeth as he clicks the pen with his tongue.

I understand now why he was irritated when I accused him of flirting. The "Trust me, you're not my type." The phone call from MATT, who I am now sure is not just "a friend."

"You're not out," I state tepidly.

"Matt's not. The parents of my football captain have skewed views on who he should love. Since we spend a lot of time together, I can't be out either. Appearances and all." He must decide he's done talking about him because he shifts the focus of our conversation back to the song. "So what would August have to say?"

The night passes quickly from there, both of us getting wrapped up in our personas and their inner conflicts. As I'm leaving, I pause in the hallway outside his apartment.

"Tomorrow, we can meet again and work through our stage arrangement. Maybe add some choreography?" I ask, hopeful.

"Careful, Virginia. Don't go getting attached to me. You just might fulfill the prophecy and become my best friend." He winks, hanging on to the half-closed door.

* * *

I feel giddy on the short drive back to my dorm. I had made friends at the pub, but it hadn't occurred to me that we never saw each other outside of that setting. We never hung out in *their* space. It's a different kind of connection, somehow.

I'm still processing this when I enter the room and see my dorm mate has decided to spend another night away. I'm enjoying having the space to myself, but where the hell does she go? I noticed that the Ouija board and the candles usually lining the top of her bookcase were missing. I tell myself not to read into it. The important thing is she's not fucking around with the spirits here. I have enough ghosts.

I shoot Libby a quick update and check in on how her show is going. It's then that I see Derek's name in my recent messages and remember the audio file he'd sent. I press play, then abruptly pause it before a note can escape from the speaker. If I listen to this, I won't be able to unhear it. It won't change anything. It could, however, further complicate my feelings. I close my messages without deleting the song. I still want the choice to listen to it later.

I consider googling him, the curiosity eating away at me to know more about who he is, especially now that I can no longer ask him. I don't. If my name had been published in the articles written after the fire, I wouldn't want him googling me, either. It felt like an invasion of privacy deeper than invading his journals. If he wanted me to know his secrets, he would have told me just as I would have told him mine. I have to respect that.

Closing my eyes, I force myself to lay in silence, listening to the drunken laughter of girls below enjoying their college experience. I lay there until, eventually, I fell asleep, fading back into my nightmares.

now, september

RILEY and I spend the next week revolving around our piece.

Between our Tuesday classes, which is luckily a light load, we rendezvous in the courtyard by the vending machines and work through our composition. Since the lyrics were solidified last night, we're down to fine-tuning the music.

After classes finish, I meet him by the auditorium dressed in all black as he'd insisted. I had thought it was an idea for our performance, but when I rounded the corner, he waved me over impatiently before shoving a beanie over my head and blacking out my eyes to mimic a raccoon's with a cream he's pulled from his pack.

"Riley, we're sneaking in, not robbing the joint." I remind him.

"Shhh. Don't ruin it." He accuses, keeping his voice low, before pulling the door open.

"Look at that. You didn't even need to pick the lock." I taunt sarcastically, rolling my eyes. He glances back at me before shoving something into his pocket. There's almost an aura of disappointment surrounding him. I question whether he had actually planned, or been hoping really, to break in after all.

The disappointment disappears as we enter the auditorium. Riley makes his way down the aisle, flinging himself into the same seat from our first class, and passes me a bag of popcorn that is mysteriously still hot.

"Did you just pop this?" I wonder aloud. Waving his hand dismissively, he throws a few pieces into his mouth before he begins discussing our performance. Seeing the stage, we can visualize what we want it to look like.

"I should enter from the right and start that guitar riff. August should enter from the left when it's your cue to sing." He points to the side of the stage.

"August?" I laugh at his casual use of my song character's name. The theater is mostly dark outside a couple of spotlights still illuminating the stage.

"Just hear me out. We wrote this as their story. We could carry that storyline to our performance on stage. It won't be you and I up there, but August," He talks with his hands, motioning to the left, "and Noah." Then, the right. He envisions how the dynamic of our two characters will play out in front of an audience; when I look at the stage, I can see it, too. He's earnest when he turns back to me, and I tell him I love it.

On Wednesday, Riley and I work twice as hard in dance. We're both trying to determine what moves we can recycle for August and Noah. I'm trying not to stare at Chambers with questions in my eyes, trying not to be obvious about my desire to untangle Derek's past. Riley is my favorite distraction and keeps me focused on the task at hand for the most part.

Midweek performance class isn't so much a class as a

time slot. Each group gets an hour today or tomorrow to work through their arrangement with Derek. Our time slot isn't until later in the afternoon, so we have time to kill while waiting.

Riley heads out to meet Matt while I grab a bite to eat, and when we regroup in the auditorium, it's only the band. Jane, who introduces herself as the stage manager, informs us that "Mr. Rivera" had something come up and couldn't join us. As much as Derek has fought to keep the "Mr." unattached from his name, his position has required a level of formality that hasn't been easy to shake. *Had something come up, my ass.* Derek is avoiding me. Then, I think of Duke, and guilt replaces my annoyance. I *hope* he is avoiding me. I can't bear to think of the alternative. I settle into that idea instead.

Once Riley and I begin to talk to the band, describing what we want to do and what sound we want to achieve, Derek's absence is forgotten.

We're heading to Riley's after our session when I tell him I need to stop by my dorm to grab my laptop. There is someone in my room as we enter, and I realize I am finally about to meet my roommate. I'm thankful I don't have to do so alone.

From the back, she is a small but stocky girl with a black pixie cut that stands up wildly as if she had just been in a mosh pit. She's dressed in combat boots, fishnet stockings, and what I can only describe as a cape. She folds her clothes messily on her bed, not bothering to acknowledge our entry. I make an effort to introduce myself, but she says nothing in return. I'd think her style was cool if her attitude wasn't so off-putting, if I didn't find her absence disturbing these past few days.

Riley hops up on my bed like he lives here and starts rolling around on my comforter like a dog trying to get comfortable while I grab my things.

"I didn't get your name," I say to my roommate, hoping to break the ice. I'd hate to spend the year in awkward tension with the girl who could be sleeping five feet away. If she sleeps at all.

"Ally, *please*," Riley interjects, frozen mid-roll. His palm has swung out to grasp my arm in warning; his expression clouded with worry. "Don't antagonize *it*." He whispers loud enough for her to hear.

My eyes go wide, and I drop what I was holding. I swing around, ready to apologize for his rudeness. Facing her was a bad idea.

"My name is Morticia." She growls. Her hooked nose is less than an inch from mine. Her black lipstick makes her teeth appear more yellow than white when she speaks. There is an odor, like something rotting, coming from her mouth. I can't tell if it's real or if I'm imagining it based on all I'm taking in. What I hope is costume blood has dried in a line from the corner of her mouth to her chin.

"Ahh!" Riley jumps behind me.

"Yes." She leers at him. "Be afraid. Be very afraid."

"*Fuck me*, Morty. You are one terrifying lass." He antagonizes further.

I'm looking between them with horror when she shrieks, "IT'S MORTICIA!" and runs out of the room. If you can call what she does running. It's more of a crouch and spring. She makes a show of flaring out her cape behind her at the door.

"WHAT THE FUCK" He spins his head towards the doorway. "WAS THAT?"

"Are you trying to get me killed?" I yell at him. I wave towards her books. "She studies this stuff. She could do it."

He falls back on the bed, laughing before getting up to help. He makes quick work of opening my dresser and throwing a ton of clothes that don't match into my bag. "Probably best not to stay here tonight."

As we're walking out the door, he says, "Ally. Ally." When I hesitantly give him my attention, he asks: "Who am I?" and crouches, flaring out his imaginary cape. I can't keep a straight face all the way back to his apartment.

now, september

MY PULSE IS RINGING in my ears on Friday as we sit, waiting for our turn to perform. We've rehearsed enough times in Riley's living room that he seems cool as a cucumber while I'm freaking out. Shouldn't it be the other way around? Riley is supposed to be the one with stage fright, while I'm the girl who spent weeks performing for drunken crowds, and they're not always the easiest audience to please.

I watched our classmates sing their anthems, power ballads, and duets. Most stumble through trying to do too much with their set production or barely move around. The best parts of each song wear Derek's influence like a stamp. I catch a glimpse of his sandy brown hair, and my heart quickens, thudding louder. The source of my anxiety becomes clear.

Today, he was dressed in a dark royal blue button-up with a gray vest. Were those boxes in his bedroom full of this new wardrobe he seems to have acquired? Seeing him when I walked in crafted that same summer buzz beneath my skin. He was sitting on the edge of the stage talking to the nasty blonde and her friend who had sat in front of us on Monday.

Noticing where my focus was, Riley leaned in and whispered, "Her name is Macey, and she's no one you need to be worried about. She's been trying to get with me for years. Her type is the unattainable, which, right now, seems to be him." I had started to tell him I wasn't bothered but Riley already knew me too well.

After staying over Wednesday, I returned to my dorm in the morning to find a dead bird in my bed. That was pretty much the deciding factor for moving out. Riley's flatmate had decided to take a gap year, leaving the second bedroom open. It seemed fated for me to move in.

He and Matt, whom I finally had the pleasure of meeting, helped me move my things last night. We spent the rest of the evening turning board games into drinking games, and I felt like, at last, I was getting the college experience I had dreamed of.

I hadn't had a chance to warn Riley about the nightmares, and I was grateful that I hadn't managed to wake him yet. As much as I already trusted him, I wasn't ready to have the "dead friends" conversation. He nudges me, letting me know we're up next.

From backstage we watch as the current act plays and bites his instrument at the same time. He's clothed in black from head to toe. I'm trying to place him when Riley says: "When did Morticia join our class?" I push him and concede a smile. That's exactly who he'd reminded me of.

His set begins to wrap, and Jane gives us our 30-second warning. Riley turns white. "Why am I suddenly terrified?" He laughs like it will calm him down. Quickly, it fades, telling me it didn't work.

I take hold of both of his hands and repeat what Derek told me my first night singing to a live crowd.

"It's not about the people. It's about the music. It's about soul. When you get out there, it's just you and me in your living room. It's August and Noah. Can you be that guy?" I ask him.

His panic spell seems to break and subside. "Yeah. I can be that guy." He kisses my cheek. "See you out there, August." He departs to his side of the stage, his prophecy fulfilled in record time. My pep talk has also worked on me, and I'm ready.

The stage clears. It's time. Riley enters from the left as planned and begins playing the electric guitar. I close my eyes, and when I open them, I only see Noah.

"*Ah ah ah ah.*" I sing over the rift twirling into view. The music stalls and picks up as I start the verse.

"Back of the bar, I don't think,
I touch your face like it's a saving grace."

I touch Noah's chin, only it isn't Noah anymore. It isn't Riley. I imagine it's Derek I'm touching. I tilt his head toward the light, searching his eyes. It's the wrong eyes. Too blue like mine and not the cover of pine trees I was aching for. I must look as desperate and defeated as I feel because Riley's face responds to mine with one of concern. To the audience, it must seem so real. I pull away, walking to the edge to address the crowd. I avoid looking at Derek, instead pushing those emotions into the words.

"I can't stay, but I can't seem to change my mind.
What if, even after all this time, some of the ashes of the old me survived?

Am I really a phoenix or a ghost posing as a girl just trying to get by?"

I start to move as I sing. Noah falls into step behind me. We're sinking into a familiar rhythm of what we'd rehearsed. It becomes easy, choreographed, and muscle memory takes over. I sing the first chorus alone. Noah moves his guitar behind his back to take my hand, preventing me from walking away from him as he sings to me.

"Everybody's looking at me, but nobody knows,
How I feel when you're near like I might implode.
Baby, you can run, but we're all broken hearts,
Rattling when we walk from all our broken parts,
Just trying to survive in the dark."

We get through the next chorus together, and in the final verse, Noah and August finally confront each other about their feelings. Each line is a back-and-forth, a pull to and a pull away from. I let go vocally and hit some high notes while he stays shallow and breathy. The final line is his, and he kills it.

"But it doesn't have to end." He cuts through the silence after the music has tapered off.

When we wrap, the crowd goes wild for the first time today as Riley and I come back into ourselves. His arms wrap around me, and he lifts me off my feet. The spotlights are so blindingly bright, the white splits refracting into so many colors I feel like I've been neglecting. There's purple, fuchsia, royal blue. There's so much more than the *gray* I've been living in.

Riley glimmers and the lapel off his pressed collar glistens. He is full of that performance high and so am I. The pads of Riley's fingers press into the back of my hand as he pulls me backstage. My eyes finally lock with Derek's as I go.

It's my fault, really. I couldn't resist searching out his assessment. Where I'd imagined praise, there is only resentment. His jaw is clenched so tightly it appears as though his bone might shatter from the tension. My skin becomes bumpy; I have too many goosebumps to maintain my smoothness.

Derek has held the weight of his emotions in his jaw since I've known him. How it's set is a revelation of everything he is feeling. Relaxed, happy, sad— all defined by that curve of cheek into chin. In this second, I can't determine if it is anger or destruction that most wish to rage.

Derek claps his hands, the sound like breaking glass. We're in the car crash phase now. I'm in shock, too confused by his reaction to know what to do. He nods once towards the back and disappears into the sea of students. The slow-motion blur, the silence, subsides. Thud. Thud. Thud. Buzz. Buzz. Buzz.

Riley is still raving about how it felt up there when we step behind the curtain. He heads in the direction of the door that will lead us back to our seats. I send him along without me, making an excuse about needing to use the restroom. He steps out the door into the auditorium. At the same time, the door down the hall opens, and Derek steps in. He pauses in front of a small office and waits with his back stiff.

I approach cautiously, less like I'm about to interact with a teacher and more like I'm coming face-to-face with a wild animal. What does it say that the animal thrills me more?

I step into the office, the door scraping closed behind me. Carefully, he puts space between us, barring himself behind the desk—his nameplate glints derisively like an exhibit tag at the zoo.

"Back of the bar, I don't think. I touch your face like it's a saving grace." He growls, bitterness clinging to each lyric he recites. "So, it's not that you only touch me in the back of bars; it's that I'm not the only one you touch." He scowls.

I laugh. The noise wicked, unstable, the accumulation of a woman gone mad. Derek seems less human than snake. At last, I feel like I recognize the guy I met this summer. I like him venomous, unapproachable, like at the bar. The world has stolen from me, and now it's dirty dipped its grimy hands back into the cookie jar to steal this, too. I'm fucking fuming, and it's *nice* not to be the only one upset.

"I don't remember you being this dense," I say, adding more poison to the potion.

"*Dense*?" It comes out a hollow hiss.

"Dense, avoidant, downright rude. Am I missing anything?"

"Well, if we're throwing around labels, how about prissy, obnoxious, and blind? You were so wrapped up in your little act out there that you missed the point of the assignment, and lyrically, the song fell flat. You skated by because you put on a show, but truthfully, the song wasn't any good, Ally. I expect more next week." He spits, leaning forward with both hands planted firmly on the desk. His knuckles are turning white from the pressure.

Under normal circumstances, I'd be taken aback at his cruel feedback. I'd feel devastated that I wasn't good enough to meet the standard. But this isn't normal. We were fantastic out there. Being the only pair to get a standing ovation, it was damn sure merited by more than 'our little skit.' Thankfully, the class is graded by those people, not by him. Another surge of laughter spews out of my mouth.

"The song wasn't any good because the subject matter wasn't any good." I rationalize.

"The subject was to write a song that got people amped up, and your little playboy wrote a love song with no heart." His nasty words spin aggressively in my head, fueling my annoyance.

"The subject matter that *'heartless'* song was based on was you. So, you're right. Next time, I'll write about Riley instead, and then maybe it'll have enough passion behind it to move you!" I exclaim. I wish I could scream at him.

His eyes close in frustration, seemingly with himself this time.

"I thought..." He starts and trails off quietly.

"I know." I snap, still vexed.

It's unexpected when he steps out from behind the cage of his desk and dips his head low so we are level. Stupefied, I act like an immature, insolent child, extending my fingers to touch the tiger. He bows further as if to let me. I graze the stubble on his chin and trail upwards to the pandora's box of his face. The tiger, the snake, the man look back like he's waited his whole life for me to find him and touch him like this.

"Ally." He sighs pleasantly. More goosebumps tingle to life on my skin.

He leans into my warmth, the predator fading to the bird with a broken wing I saw on the balcony that night in the gardens. In the distance, the crowd applauds.

The sound reaches us through the walls from where it had been muted. The rest of the world that had been under-water now amplifies. It stirs us out of our private oasis enough to remember where we are. *Who* we are. We both understand we are playing the wrong roles in this setting. Like the wild animal, the sound startles him back to being rigid, untamed. The tension reappears in his face. I step forward, trying to change the laws of nature, and he retreats as if to teach me some laws are absolute.

We separate, and my head becomes cloudy, the air heavy instead of clearer.

"Things have to be different now," Derek says, defeated.

My heart lunges, shifts, shatters. I don't know if he's talking to me or himself, but the words have stolen the moment. Everything dulls, less lustrous, as the setting coats itself under the film of our new tone. His office was now just an office and not the magical place it had seemed moments earlier.

There is nothing left to say that won't add to the ruin. We are standing in the aftermath of Pompeii. Neither of us seemed to notice the blow, only the devastation left in its wake.

I nod once and leave the room, leave Derek, behind. When I see Riley waiting for me, I smile. I pretend I'm not carrying around the ruins of so many lost cities and futures inside of me.

then, january

I WAS in English class with Mr. Walsh. It was January, and he had been spastic about the school running the AC in his classroom this time of year. He had filed numerous complaints, but the school kept denying the air was on.

"They're trying to freeze me out, so I'll quit." He mumbled to himself.

We were taking a test on *Of Mice and Men* by John Steinbeck, trying to tune him out so we could focus. He slammed down the book he'd been reading, making it impossible to concentrate, and climbed on top of his desk, extending his hands to the vent.

"Unbelievable." He said. "You." He pointed to some jock sitting in the front row. "Yes. *You.* Hand me that tape from my desk." The jock looked down at the paper in front of him and then back to our manic teacher. "Don't worry about the test. Look at that; you got an A. Now, hand me that tape."

The jock shrugged like that settled it and moved to hand him the tape and some paper. None of us were answering questions anymore, too captivated by the scene playing out. Walsh taped a paper to the ceiling next to the vent. Sure enough, the paper began to ripple as it flapped in the breeze. "I knew it." He whispered to himself.

Stepping down, he pulled out his phone to video the evidence. "This will show them." He said after a beat, tucking the phone back into his pocket.

The door to the classroom sat open, and Walsh's least favorite student, Urie, strolled by outside. Urie was an exchange student who didn't understand the concept of being restricted to a classroom. He often interrupted Walsh's lectures to ask questions like when lunch was and if he could borrow a pencil. When he actually showed up for class at all, he would randomly get up and walk out without permission—sometimes to go to the bathroom, sometimes for no other reason than he was bored.

Walsh was not a teacher you wanted to antagonize, though. Since he and his wife, another teacher a few doors down, separated earlier that year, his patience had worn thin. What he had once viewed as an important role in teaching, in shaping the minds of the next generation, now seemed like his life's greatest joke.

Urie, realizing his mistake in planning, tried to move casually and quickly, hoping to go unnoticed. It didn't work. Like a guard dog, Walsh was at the door barking at him in an instant.

"Urie!" He yelled, snapping the attention of the few who had returned to the assignment before them. The few hoping to somehow get a passing grade in this class.

Urie paused outside the door, meeting Walsh's glare, before breaking into a sprint down the corridor outside. Walsh ran into the hallway and screamed after him. "If you want to skip my class, don't hang out by my door, you idiot!"

Returning, Walsh paced back and forth in front of the

whiteboard before finally throwing his hands up in the air. "Who the hell can blame him? Who wants to freeze to death in here with you soul suckers. He should tell the office about the damn air in here while he's loitering the halls."

Then again, he walked out. He gave no explanation. Offered no time at which he'd return. Everyone stared at the space he left, his now empty desk, and finally each other.

There was a tap on the window behind me. Grey was standing outside in a puffer coat, laughing, swirling around a ring of at least a dozen keys. I flipped the ancient latch and slid open the glass panel.

"What are you doing here?" I asked wide-eyed.

I glanced back to the door. Walsh could be back any second. Grey's ever-present smile was illuminating and didn't fade even in light of the tension seeping off me. I could only imagine Walsh going off on Grey like he had Urie.

"Is that how you thank me for breaking you out?" He put on a wounded act.

"Oh yes." I nodded sarcastically. "Getting detention is exactly what I want to do right before I graduate!" I hissed.

"Come on, Ally. Live a little! We're going to get ice cream." He said as Charlie appeared behind him. She was bouncing up and down like a little bunny rabbit in excitement.

"What's with the keys?" I prodded. Our untraditional conversation had attracted an audience. My classmates stared. I should have been used to it by then. Being with Grey warranted a lot of attention, but still, I wouldn't say I liked the feeling of so many eyes on me.

"I had to get you out somehow." His smile turned

wicked, and the fat JANITOR tag on the keys flashed brightly in the overcast sun.

"No way." The jock from earlier behind me began snorting. I pieced it together.

"The AC. It was you." I accused and awed at once.

His expression was devious. "You can adore me and all my cleverness in the car. Now toss me your bag and get out here!"

My excitement grew. I looked back at the class. A few girls were sizing up Grey appreciatively and nodding eagerly for me to go. *They* would go in my position. Some shrugged. Most appeared as bored as they had five minutes ago. Not even a jailbreak was enough to break them from the curse of another mundane high school day. I didn't want to be like them. Lifeless, missing out. I tossed my bag to Grey, who grunted as it slugged him in the chest.

"Jesus. You keep bricks in here?" He huffed before handing it to Charlie and holding his arms to assist me next. My foot was on the ledge when I heard it.

"Unbelievable," Walsh said from the hallway. "Lousy excuse for a principal." His string of complaints grew louder the closer he got to the classroom.

"I've got this." The jock grinned cockily. "At least one of us deserves to get out of here." He said as he slipped behind the door.

"Shit." Grey's voice rang from outside, followed by a gust of wind as he ducked out of sight. I slid back into my seat just in time for Walsh to reenter the room.

Nothing ever escaped his notice. "Parrish!" Walsh zeroed in on me. "As if it weren't already cold enough in here, you thought— what? You'd open a window to let some snowflakes in? Where's Justin?" His eyes came to rest on the jock's vacant seat.

From his hiding spot, Justin-the-jock tiptoed out and around the door. Walsh caught onto the movement and swung around. They met each other's eyes, and like Urie, Justin sprinted down the hall. This time, Walsh ran after him, which was something none of us had expected. I would have been worried for Justin if I hadn't been certain that, as the star of the track team, he could easily outrun him.

Having a small window of time, I stood quickly and swung my leg over the center block and out the window. I listened for reapproaching footsteps as I worked my other leg through the opening before plopping to the ground below. Grey takes my hand.

"Great. Now, where the hell did Parrish go?" I heard Walsh pant from the classroom.

"Run." Grey mouthed. And I did.

We had to stop before we made it to the Jeep. The three of us doubled over in laughter, unable to catch enough air to run any longer.

"Damn, girl. When you go bad, you go all out." Grey joked.

"Says the delinquent with the janitor's keys." I quipped back.

"What can I say? I'm trained in espionage. Being an excellent thief is just a perk of the trade." He said. Charlie stared at him in shock before she bubbled out in hysterics again. They both roared to life, attracting the attention of several students who had just shown up for their final class. I took a mental snapshot of the three of us. So free. So alive.

THIRTY-FOUR

now, september

I STILL WAKE up searching for Grey, my hands floating like feathers over the sheets. The nightmares are getting bad again. The memories were too realistic, as if I wasn't dreaming but traveling back in time as a spectator of my own life. I know I will have to fight a few rounds, endure a few weeks of this, before I can have another reprieve. It's not remembering them I have an issue with; it's how much it hurts to.

I use another tool my therapist gave me: for every bad thought, follow up with a good one.

I feel the emptiness of that first night at college. I follow it up with the joy I felt the night I moved in here.

The grief swims in my stomach, my lungs full of smoke, as I visualize Charlie's picture up on the altar at her memorial. I follow it up with August and Noah, the rush of Riley and I on stage.

I remember Grey's fingers playing with the ends of my hair, making my scalp tingle. I can feel his phantom touch even now. When I look at the blank walls, all I see are the empty spaces that should be filled with string lights, with

235

cork boards cluttered edge to edge with photos of my friends from home. All I see is the hollow void.

I feel like I woke up living a life I didn't go to sleep in. I've felt this for a year. The bad dreams, the melting faces, make my skin feel like it will rip itself apart. The good dreams, the memories, are almost worse. It's the good dreams that turn being awake into a nightmare.

So, I try to find good thoughts to treat the bad ones. I try to drown myself in the wonder I felt with Derek in the gardens. The magic and the awe. That was the first time I lost my identity as a zombie and felt human again. In every moment with Derek, I was living for the next. Finally, *now* and not *then*. But, this, too, has been taken.

For every drop of poison, I eventually find the antidote. It takes time. It takes energy I don't have to pull me out of bed. So, I don't. I stay.

I miss my first class. I watch the clouds go through their transformations. The rainy sky pales as the sun shines beyond the clouds. Then, the air thickens, and the sky darkens once more. It's a metaphor, I think—a parallel to my moods. I'm curled up into a ball. My fuzzy pajamas and cozy socks do nothing to warm me. The chill is coming from inside me, and I know I will not make it to any of my classes today.

My antidotes only work so many times until the poison builds up a resistance. It blocks. It spreads. Then, I have to start the process over and find new antidotes. It's exhausting.

The door to the apartment unlocks, and Riley begins to whistle as he rustles to his bedroom. "Als!" he yells. I hear his keys spin around and imagine them twirling through the air as the ring keeps them secured to his finger.

I don't answer. It's better if he thinks I already left.

Better to not see him until this part of me turns over. The next chapter of me will be better. More like the Ally he thinks I am. The Ally I *should* be, am *supposed* to be.

I run my fingers over the skin on my shoulder. The feeling makes me shudder. It is a reminder that I am irreparable. How did I think I could do this? I'm alone. I have people: Riley, Libby, my mother, and my friends from the bar— but there is a film over our interactions—an ignorance. There are too many things I can't find a place for in our conversations. The only people who have ever truly understood me are gone. I'm aware that I need to have more patience. My connections will strengthen as new memories are formed until there is enough to create that sense of safety, of familiarity.

"Yo Virginia!" Riley bangs on the door. "Give it up. Your keys are still on the hook, and your shoes are by the door."

"I'm sick. I don't think I'm going to make it to class." I yell as loud as I can through the door. It isn't very loud. I do sound horrible. I sound *convincing*. My throat is dry and raspy from all my tearless crying.

He doesn't reply, so I think he's left. Then, the doorknob rattles before Riley lets himself in. "What? You think I don't know how to pick the locks in my own home? *Right*." He lies on the end of my bed. "I know the difference between sick and sad." His tone is still full of sass, but I see the concern when he places his chin on my knee.

"You're right. I don't want to go out there today." I rub my nose with the sleeve of my shirt.

"So, we'll stay in instead." He smiles sideways, and my heart grows in my chest. "But not in here," he adds, pulling me to the couch. He shoots a final look around my space. "I'd be depressed if my room looked like this too. I thought for someone so creative, you'd be better at decorating."

I push him hard.

"There she is." His energy is infectious. It helps.

We're halfway through our second movie and sharing what he calls "a slice" versus just calling it pizza. The candle flickering on the table smells like rain, reminding me of home—my phone chimes, sabotaging my state of escapism.

Our new assignment, along with our individual rehearsal and set times, has been posted to the Performance board page. This week's assignment is a solo assignment, meaning my rehearsal will be without Riley. I placate myself by knowing I will still not be alone with Derek. At least the band will be there to minimize the angst I feel in his presence. I switch my gears over to the subject. The prompt is missing something you never had. I read too much into it before cutting my phone off for the night.

Once Riley goes to bed, the assignment creeps back into my head. I borrow one of his guitars; by two am, I have the skeleton of a song.

now, september

MY REHEARSAL SLOT this week is on Thursday. Time passes in a blur, and soon enough, it's 7. Still so early into autumn, the sun clings to the sky outside before I walk into the side door Riley and I had used to sneak in. I enter the auditorium and move onto the stage where Derek is sitting, facing away from me at the piano.

It's been nearly a week since I've seen him, and it hasn't lessened his effect on my nervous system. He presents no sign of hearing me approach; his mind vanished into the symphony. It's a beautiful tune, light and dreamy before turning dark and nefarious.

"I'm red like your coat, like your oath, like your big wide eyes,
It's okay; we're both safe, wearing our disguises.
Welcome to the new storyline,
Where I don't walk the girl home, I just tell her to go.
I don't hunt for the kill, just the thrill of getting too close.

I'm just a man dressed in wolves' clothes,
Beatin' down your door.

Little Red, Little Red,
Let me in.
I swear I'm nearly innocent."

I remain silent, transfixed, until he finishes. A sigh escapes his throat. He looks out over the empty seats where his audience should be cheering for him, demanding an encore. He checks his watch before turning to leave. When he spots me, he quells. We always go from motion to stillness around one another, from chaos to calm. I feel like a clock being reset. I don't have time to process that thought.

"How long?" He asks, and I understand without him clarifying the question.

"A while," I admit. "I was hoping to practice one more time. When you began to play, I couldn't bring myself to leave." I should feel nervous saying this, but outside of the anticipated buzz, I feel all too comfortable in his presence. I feel like I can say anything. That's what makes this so dangerous.

"Again, with the honesty." He looks down like he wishes I had said anything else.

"Do you want me to start lying to you now, Rivera?" I ask in genuine curiosity. I can't bring myself to add the "Mr." the rest of the class has adopted. His eyes flash, and his face goes hard before softening again. "That was beautiful." I wave towards the piano.

"Thank you." He says modestly. Neither one of us speaks for a while, both studying the other. After a beat, he clears his throat. "Are you ready to work on your song, Miss Parish?"

I hate it when he calls me by my last name. It's too formal. It was better when he thought my name was Rebecca. I debated asking him to call me that instead. I don't. It will be easier if I go along with how things are meant to be. My life is always dictated by whatever the easier choice is.

I answer by grabbing a guitar. I decide after class to pick up my own. Again, I make the easier decision. In no longer having to ask or borrow, I cut out another point of interaction. No, this will be better for me, I rationalize. I'll be able to create freely, in my room or on the go.

I sit at the edge of the stage and look up at him, waiting. He comes to sit beside me while leaving a safe distance between us. We don't talk about the arrangement or what I plan to do to perform it. I play, and he listens.

"The arsonist has come back to town,
he's burning everything in sight starting with you and I.
Some people call it dreaming,
I call it dying while I'm sleeping.
There's nothing peaceful about waking up in pieces.

Do you think, do you think, do you think love could heal us?
Because I don't think, I don't think there's enough to fix what's
wrong.
Only confessions I make come out, come out in song.

Break another branch off the family tree.
Start a little house fire
Watch it take what's left of me.
And I wanna curse God, tell him that he got it wrong.
They were meant to grow up, they were meant to be loved.
I was never meant to lose them then."

It's a dark, folksy song, catching country influences in certain parts. I have tears in my eyes when I finish. Derek sits still for a long time before moving to the piano, asking me to play the chorus again. I sit beside him on the bench as he adds a piano overlay to the guitar. As expected, I love the change. It deepens the song somehow, adding a lighter tone over the darkness like a nightmare set to the stage of a lullaby.

"What else?" I ask.

"That's it. The song's already exactly what it's supposed to be. Anything more would tamper with the heart of it." He says, staring at the keys instead of me. Only twenty minutes of our scheduled hour together has passed. There isn't anything left to do, but it feels good to make music with him again. He hits a few more keys, and I strum along, hoping to latch onto more time.

"When you didn't show up Monday, I thought you had dropped the class." He admits, repeating the same notes. I like to think he sounds glum. I want to believe this is torturing him like it's torturing me. Derek is the best antidote of them all.

"Would you have preferred if I had?" My curiosity wins out.

There won't be a wrong answer. Dropping it would be easier. Maybe if I did, I wouldn't need to fight so hard to stay away from him. But not dropping the class meant I got to perform, to be on stage with adrenaline coursing through my veins. Everything faded there, and I felt I was exactly where I was supposed to be. Staying meant I got to continue experiencing that. Plus, I wouldn't have to invent ways to see him. I regurgitate the same argument in my head from the first class.

He ponders my question, appearing to be having the same internal struggle. I'm curious about what his advantages and disadvantages would be. I'm hesitant to ask, as I really want to hear his explanation. The fact that I want to know is exactly why I shouldn't ask.

"No." He finally answers. "No, I wouldn't have preferred that."

I hope he will say more. In his silence, I can only *assume* what he is feeling. I want to *know*. Any second now, he will announce that it's a wrap on our session. To drag it out a little longer, I open my mouth to tell him what the song is about. Then I close it. Letting him in would only cause my feelings to deepen.

Derek can't be who I confide in. It would be cruel to both of us. I play with the idea of telling Riley about the Kingsleys. I really should let *someone* in. Maybe that is what Duke meant about pain being a connector. The more you hold in, the more you create a divider between you and everything else. Only by letting it out can you break down those walls.

Thinking of Duke makes me want to ask about him. I want to know if he's added to his creation. I want to see how he is. I wonder if Derek has told him about our situation. But everything leads us back to what I've labeled 'The Lion's Den.'

"I guess that's all for us today. I'll see you tomorrow, Miss Parrish." Derek decides for me—the easier decision.

"Mr. Rivera," I say with a departing nod.

He leaves me on the stage as I left him in his office. Always less and less like we're leaving the room and more like we're leaving each other. I lay my elbows on the keys, letting disjointed notes fill the room. I rest my head in my palms.

"Ally?" Derek calls. He stands awkwardly at the edge of the stage as if something is nagging him. His fitted shirt tugs at his muscles, quickening the rhythm in my chest.

"What was the song about?" He asks.

"I'll tell you mine if you tell me yours," I say, smiling gently. I like the way we talk out of each other. My voice, his thoughts. His words, my soul.

"Do you have to ask?"

I nod, still wanting him to admit it, yet knowing he won't.

"You. Your turn."

I glance around the room in shock that he finally gave way to a fraction of the truth here, in such an open space.

"I scheduled you this late because I knew no one else would be around at this hour. I don't always trust what I'm going to say around you. Like now, for example." He closes his eyes and shakes his head like he can't believe how stupid he's being.

"It was about death," I admit.

"Will you clarify?" He asks, opening his eyes into mine. The light catches them naturally. Honeycombs again. I haven't seen this shade since the yellowed streetlights when he walked me home. Maybe that's where the bees come from that always seem to form in my stomach around him.

"Will you?"

Derek sighs. "Do I *need* to? Do you think I wanted this, Ally? I couldn't get you out of my head. I had just hit send to text you that song. Next thing I know, I'm looking up and there you are in *my* classroom. You weren't supposed to be a fucking *student*."

"So, I'm Little Red, and you're The Wolf? You're interpreting yourself as a predator?" I laugh as though it's ridiculous. As if I hadn't considered him a caged tiger the last time we were alone together. It seems our perception is the same. Our metaphors, our meanings, different.

Derek's careful composure crumbles and his straight-lined lips turn to grimace, to snarl.

"Let's just say it's number one on a list of a hundred other things, Ally. Even before *this*," he gestures around the room, to the school, to his title on the auditorium door. "I was never good for you." He scoffs.

"Why?" I ask, point blank. I don't care that he's frustrated. Derek has always had this look, though I'd never interpreted it as anger as much as function. How his brows dip low instead of high, his eyes narrowed—a surge warning to all he's built up.

"Because I'm damaged! Okay? I'm too messed up to be good for you, Ally. My position here isn't ill-fated; it's a saving grace. You have to let this go. We can't go back, and I don't *want* to." He spits.

I find the most inappropriate things humorous. A moment ago, he was telling me he couldn't get me out of his head, and now he's telling me he doesn't want me. His reasons aren't *good enough*. If he had held steady to not wanting to lose his job or disregard his ethical code, maybe I could have respected that.

"You're *lying*. I thought we didn't do that. You're not a wolf. You're just a coward." I say in a quiet accusation.

He takes a step back, stunned. I don't want to be here anymore. It isn't morals driving his decisions; it's fear. And it isn't that I can't stand to be around him; it's that he's become a mirror. I see my behavior in his actions. He's picking the easier path, as I have countless times, but I don't want to live like that anymore. I'm still *alive,* and what is the point of it all if I'm robbing myself of the experiences I have left? How much time have I wasted?

I vow also to pick up paint on the way home. Riley and I

are going to paint our rooms, streak campus, and do anything else I can think of to make up for my lost youth.

Standing, I begin for the door, passing Derek along the way. Derek, who still appears horrorstruck as if my words have riddled him with bullet holes. His buoyancy has gone; he drudges to stay afloat. I've been shipwrecked by his cliffs enough times that I experience no guilt. This is his to weather alone.

I almost make it out. I almost convince myself that a scared man is not a man worth wanting. I *almost* do. Our shoulders brush, and it disintegrates the costume of the girl who doesn't care. It resurrects the season of the bees. *It fucks everything*.

We both stare forward, touching but not talking. We both lean in, a little more weightless against the other's supporting frame.

"For the record, I couldn't get you out of my head either. I still can't, and *I miss you*." I exhale more than speak. Freed by my confession, I can go now without the shackles that had chained me.

Suddenly, I'm against the wall behind the stage curtains. Derek's chest is pressed to mine, his skin radiating heat, so much heat that I feel feverish. His hands on my waist are cementing us together. Mine find his neck so right in my grasp that it almost sears my skin. Our mouths are parted as he holds my gaze. Derek leans in slowly, and I think he might kiss me. I tilt my head up, practically begging him to.

We've played with the idea for too many weeks. Fuck my revelations, my epiphanies, fuck anything that isn't him. I don't want to leave this room until I know what he tastes like. Both of us are shaking, frenzied. We're as pathetic as two addicts finally getting our fix.

At the last second, he dips his head low. His nose brushes the space in front of my ear before his lips find my collarbone and drag across it, his tongue leaving a trail of cold air in its wake. I'm delirious as I pull him closer, tangling my fingers in his tousled hair.

Derek grips the fabric covering my back, twisting it into bunches as if he wished he could shred it to pieces so there was nothing separating us at all. His forehead rests on my shoulder, and I'm scared to move when he breathes me in. I'm scared the moment is too fragile, and any sudden shift could startle him into retreating.

"What are you doing to me?" He asks, his words vibrating against my skin.

I pull his hair, wanting his lips on mine, forcing a groan from his throat. Lust fills his eyes when he looks at me, and I feel I'll never get that look out of my head if he doesn't kiss me right now. I bite my lip, mustering the courage to ask.

"Do you still want me to touch you?" I ask the wrong question. He laughs like I've told him the world's cruelest joke.

"I *always* want you to touch me." He echoes his words from that night by the garden gate, leaving out the 'pretty much.' I notice.

"Stay," I warn, and he stills completely.

I ran my hand across his jaw, savoring the feel before planting my lips on every spot I'd been dying to touch for weeks now that I'd been prohibited from doing so. Brushing his lips with my fingertips, I part them slightly before taking his bottom lip between my teeth and run my tongue across it. *Fucking hell.*

A door opens at the end of the hall, and he instantly separates us, backing away from me. I silently scream at the universe.

"You've got to be fucking kidding." He mutters under his breath, fuming.

"Thank you for the feedback, Mr. Rivera." I cover as the footsteps grow closer. We've both returned to open spaces again, but it feels closed off, as if we abandoned parts of ourselves back in the corner.

A beautiful brunette stops in the hallway outside. With her pencil skirt and Instagram-worthy cheekbones, I envy her poise. She eyes Derek with a sort of familiarity, a kind of ownership, and my prejudice against her grows.

"Derek." Her lips spread into a pageant-winning smile. "Are you almost done here? We said eight. I've been waiting."

"Margot." He says breathily. I hate the sound of her name coming from his mouth. "I'm sorry. I was finishing up." To me, he nods. "Miss Parrish." They depart together.

I watch as they exit the hallway through a door leading outside. This time, when he leaves, he takes me with him. He leaves the zombie standing in my place, feeling oh so used. I was about to make out with someone's boyfriend, and the thought makes me sick. Or maybe it's the thought of Derek having a girlfriend that makes me feel ill.

After five minutes or so, I recover enough to move.

* * *

I followed through on my plans and found a music store near campus. Inside, I brush my fingers across all the acoustic guitars. I don't know what I'm looking for, but they all seem so common. Redwood this, black framed that. I anticipated spending five hundred or less if I could find a deal. A clearance rack towards the front of the store had a few beaters that should get the job done.

I spot a beautiful wood-paneled electric acoustic. The wood is light, but it looks like someone poured acid on it, creating a dark, marbled effect. It's stunning, but it's three thousand dollars. I pass. I don't feel the connection I hoped for to drop that kind of cash. I'm about to give up and settle for one of the beaters when a glass case catches my attention in the back. In it, a guitar sits on a stand for display. I'm propelled forward as if gravity had centered around it.

The guitar is made from Brazilian rosewood, a rare piece to own as the trees have become endangered, making them illegal to harvest. The guitar is vintage and preowned by an artist who took creative liberties with the sound-board. Half of the wood grain has been dyed black, and the original spider web graining of the rosewood still shines through. The other half has been bleached and stained pale. They merge in the middle like a moon connecting with the night sky. Small birds have been painted flying across from one side to the other. The yin and yang of the piece, the contrast, calls to me in a way none of the other pieces have. The price tag is a hefty five thousand, but if Grey could have chosen how I spent the money he left me, this would be it.

The man at the counter was skeptical when I asked to hold it, clearly afraid I would damage it. When I ask him to ring up the guitar, stand, and case, he seems shocked. I feel like I just bought back a part of myself and drive home with a smile. Riley whistles when he comes in for the night and sees me playing what is now my only prized possession.

now, october

"TELL me how you went from having zero decorating skills to now— you're what? Trying to get me to repaint my bedroom? Really? Who are you, and what have you done with my Ally?" Riley pokes my nose at "my Ally." His expressions are unique, overdone, and something I have come to look forward to. I haven't been able to memorize his face completely. It changes too much. He walks backward down the aisle to our spot in the auditorium.

Today, he wore a jean jacket, freeing up the usual green leather one for me to steal. He keeps telling me I need to amp up my apparel, so he's forcing me to borrow his until I get my "own look." I feel eyes boring into me as we walk and take note of all the female stares declaring their animosity. Riley was insanely attractive with his high cheekbones, his unique style, and his charismatic—dare I say annoying—personality.

For reasons obvious only to me, Riley has not reciprocated their interest. I show up out of nowhere and singularly commandeer his attention. The elusive punk suddenly connected at the hip to the new American girl. I understand their envy and feel lucky not to have to share in it. I feel grateful that I get to know the *real* Riley.

"What bullshit color were you thinking anyways? Cum white or something? How is that different from regular white?" He asks, taking his seat and throwing his feet up on the chair in front of him. The class is just starting to fill in, and Riley is loud, so I'm acutely aware that everyone just heard him say, "cum white."

"It was cream white, and can you try not to say 'cum' so loud?" I scold under my breath.

He grins to provoke me, but it doesn't work. I'm excited about painting, even if he isn't.

"You are not allowed to get cum paint on my jacket." He says just as loudly. I sink in my seat and cover my face. Now he's trying to embarrass me, and it *is* working.

"Parasons, Parrish!" Derek barks from the front of the room. "Can you try to maintain some respect for boundaries in public spaces?"

I see Riley's face transform into a look I've come to learn over the past few weeks. There is a difference in the slow uptick of his smile. How his tongue traces over his bottom teeth in anticipation. It's the look of a challenge. I already sense that this will not end well for me.

"I'm just trying to teach her some respect for my bedroom *and* my clothing." At that, he lifts my arm in his jacket and lets it drop. "Sir," Riley smirks, adding the final blow.

He did not just fucking say that.

Derek steps forward involuntarily. His jaw does its tightening thing, and he glares at Riley in a way that makes me nervous. The situation is escalating too quickly. I bear witness to Riley's murder in Derek's thoughts before his attention turns to me, fading into complete and utter disgust. His fists, which had come to clench at his sides, straighten out, and he turns so he can rub away the tension from his face without notice. *I* notice. He steps backstage in what I assume is an effort to restrain himself. I have never seen Derek so affected before.

I know how it looks. A week ago, I was confessing my feelings behind the curtains, and now I'm wearing Riley's clothes and talking about cum and bedroom walls. Considering no one here knows he is gay, it definitely looks like we are screwing. When I start to worry, this is the conclusion Derek has come to. I remember *her*, his stunning Margot. He's lost the right to be upset.

Riley tips across the armrest into my seat, and *now* he chooses to whisper. "I really thought he was about to hit me, Als. I didn't realize you two were that serious." He sounds way too pleased with himself.

I aim for the target patch he's got on his shoulder; I don't miss.

"OW! Where are all these muscles coming from? You keep a punching bag hidden in your room, or do you reserve them all for me?" He rubs his "wound" and regards me with the defiant pout of a small child.

"I swear to God, I would bend you over my knee if you wouldn't find a way to make it kinky." I snark causing him to roar in laughter.

Riley knows better than anyone that Derek and I are not seeing each other. When I'm not in class, I'm at home. The only person I'm ever on the phone with is Libby. I don't have enough of a social life to be sneaking around.

"Come on, Al." He whispers in my ear as Derek reenters the room. "The guy was absolutely *seething*. You can't tell me there is nothing there."

"Riley," I warn.

The corner of his lip tugs up, and he knows he's got me.

"You can tell him the truth about me when you guys fight about this later. Might make it easier once he understands I'm not a threat to him. Until then, I'm going to play this out. I've never been in a love triangle before. Never been *loathed*." He can't contain his smile and the other side of his lip twitches up. "Oh! We could be each other's beards, Al. How much fun would that be?" He strokes his imaginary beard.

I roll my eyes and steal a Twizzler from his pack, which always seems to have an endless supply. The less talking I do for now, the less trouble I'll get into.

"See? That's exactly the kind of thing a girlfriend would do." He picks fun at me for taking food from his bag. I'm about to tell him to shut up, but Macey, who had just arrived in her seat, spins around to glare at us.

"Did I just hear girlfriend?" She butts in. "No way you two are together." She croaks cynically.

I shoot a warning look at Riley, who wiggles his eyebrows in response. He is not above using show tactics to prove a point. I would not put it past him to shove his tongue down my throat just to rub her nose in it. Luckily, the class has filled out enough for Derek to begin. Macey turns back around.

Derek climbs onto the stage from where he was chatting with a few students in the front row. All signs of his previous aggravation have gone. He assigns us what he calls a "Flash Task." Basically, at the start of every class, he gives us a mini project that is meant to shape us into better performers and influence the style of our next song. This week, he has decided on doing mashups of songs from different genres. He gives us time to work some ideas out.

Riley writes his ideas on a notecard and holds it up

between his two fingers for me to take. I read it and bust out laughing. I see Derek tense and crack his neck to the side. I watch him out of the corner of my eye. Even with the line drawn and the arrival of the mysterious Margot, I can't shake the habit of watching him now that I've grown into it.

I write back and hand the note to Riley in the same fashion. Derek shakes his head from where he sits. Riley shoots forward with laughter, and I giggle. I can feel the annoyance from across the room. We were supposed to have ten minutes, but he called it at seven and walked to center stage.

"Alright, lots of great things are happening out there, but how about a little challenge?"

He shows a video of a YouTuber on the projector. The vlogger plays a track in the background and then sings a clip of a song while his guest jumps in and sings a clip of another song until one of them runs out of ideas and loses, or they get to the end of the song together. It's a twist from what he had us working on.

"Let's call this game Improv. Who wants to go first?" His eyes land on Riley.

"I'll go." Riley half raises his hand and volunteers readily.

"And to compete against him?" Derek asks. I know he is secretly hoping no one volunteers so he can compete.

"I volunteer." I raise my hand. There's no need to make this uglier. Riley offers me a hand out of my chair. Derek grinds his teeth.

"Alright. Let's do it." He does his best to sound casual, and I almost believe him. He plays music in the background as we walk to the stage. "So, I'm going to play a song in the background. You sing over it, whatever song pops into your head. A couple of lines and then switch. At the end the audience will decide who sang best, or like the video, if you run out of ideas— you lose."

I nod my acknowledgment and take a mic. Riley tilts his head arrogantly and grins. Oh, it's on. The lights flash, and it's time.

Riley starts by singing 3oh3's *Don't Trust Me.*

"Tell your boyfriend,
If he says he's got beef
That I'm a vegetarian
And I ain't fucking scared of him."
He sings, and I bite back laughter.

"Why men great
Till they gotta be great?
I just took a DNA test turns out,
I'm 100% that bitch.
Yeah, I got boy problems
That's the human in me."
I quip back with Lizzo.

"The way you look at me
I just can't pretend
I know you ain't in love with him
Break up with him."
He smirks, the Old Dominion lyrics spilling from his mouth.

"Last night, I came to a realization.
And I hope you can take it.
I'm too good to you
I'm way too good to you."
I him him with *Too Good* by Drake.

"One sip
Bad for me
One hit
Bad for me
One kiss bad for me.
But I give in so easily."
Charlie Puth. Bold move, Riles.

"Baby, this is what you came for."
"Lightning strikes every time she moves."
"Everybody's watching her."
"But she's looking at you."

The final Rhianna song ends us off, the crowd cheering wildly. We made it through to the end, which is more than Derek or anyone was expecting. The secret is we were having fun. The scary things aren't so scary when you're not afraid to fail. I waited for myself to fall off a note, miss a beat, or lose the words to every song I had ever heard. I was looking forward to the moment I lost, knowing it would become just another thing for us to laugh at. But, as soon as Riley would sing a line or make a face, the words would pop into my head.

Derek claps and offers us a clipped "Good job." but I can read him well enough to know he wants to smack Riley around. I can't imagine him ever talking to me again.

We head back to our seats. Riley takes his place beside me and says, "Loathed at last."

"Would you stop it already? He's our TA." I laugh and throw the last bite of my newly acquired Twizzler at him. He catches it in his mouth.

When he finishes chewing, he leans over. "Ally. Don't play me a fool."

"I'm sorry, Riles. Am I gushing over him, or are you?" I wink.

He glares at me. "Low blow."

I raise my eyebrows suggestively, and he laughs. "Alright. I set myself up there."

"How's Matt?" I ask him, and he fills me in on the latest drama. I try to work with him through the ins and outs of his relationship. With Matt being the school's central midfielder and Riley being the guy in a band, they're both panty droppers. I can see how it would cause a lot of problems. I admire how strong their relationship is to survive it.

My phone buzzes.

I SHOULDN'T HIT A STUDENT, RIGHT? SO PLEASE, STOP TESTING ME.

Derek. My heart skips a beat. My eyes flash to him, but he is watching the next battle start on stage, showing no indicator that he knows what he's just done. He's ruined me. He's ruined any chance of me believing the façade, ruined any respect I had regarding his relationship. He can't seriously be upset about Riley when he has *Margot.* The way he said her name rings in my head, and I am angry about it. Furious.

now, october

ONCE CLASS HAS ENDED, Riley takes a painstaking hour to finally leave and meet Matt at their usual place. I wait by the window, watching his car pull away, before grabbing my keys off the hook. A note I had scrawled about meeting with Libby has been posted on the fridge in case he deviates from his usual routine.

Traditionally, on Monday, the pair grab a pint at the local pub before spending the night at Matt's. If things go as planned, he won't be back until classes end tomorrow, and the note will be long gone by then. With all my bases covered, I stop overthinking and drive.

I'm so angry, I can't see straight. I had been suppressing my feelings for Riley's benefit, but here, in my own space, they fizzle, ready to pop off. Derek's behavior was entirely unacceptable. From his public display of annoyance to his over-the-line text message. How can he expect me to remain professional when he's consistently been anything but?

This thing between us has gotten too big. It's only a matter of time before one of us causes irreparable damage to our reputations. We need to put a stop to it and soon. When I arrive at the conservatory, I hit the red buzzer stationed beside the gate.

Derek's voice rings out rich over the intercom. "Yes?"

"We need to talk."

"Ally, you shouldn't be here." He sighs.

"So, you're not going to let me in?" I ask, not bothering to shield him from my irritation. I sized up the fence and wondered if I could climb it. I've decided he's getting a piece of my mind, even if I have to put my athletic ability to the test.

I wait silently for his response, my fingers thrumming impatiently on the steering wheel. A nasty pit of nerves has taken root in my stomach and begun to grow. I can't continue taking Performance if he doesn't let me in. It's an old argument, too exhausted to have again, but I'm confident after today, I will do something stupid if I stay. I can't rationalize us away anymore, not with Riley, or Margot, or his title as my *advisor*— and that makes it hurt. The hurt makes me furious. As soon as my temper diminishes, I cycle back through all the moments that led me here, and my progress is lost again.

After an exaggerated minute, the gate opens. When I pull up and get out of my car, Derek's waiting on the steps. Seeing me, he stands, running his long fingers through his hair as if it will help him escape the situation.

"This is wildly inappropriate." He begins.

"Are you kidding me?" My vision blurs. "Are you actually fucking kidding me?"

"*Bloody hell, Ally.*" He looks at me like a deranged animal about to pounce. *Like hell, I am.*

"You." My face grows warm. "You, Rivera, have the nerve to kiss my neck in the classroom but feel justified saying *I'm* being inappropriate?" I scold, my voice louder than I'd intended.

"I never kissed you. Just say what you have to say, Miss Parrish." He slumps against the stone wall, disinterested despite my rising volume.

He never kissed me? Seriously? He practically gave my neck a tongue bath, and he's trying to dodge accountability based on a *technicality*? It would have been less intimate if he *had* kissed me! The closeness, the desire behind that touch, has haunted my skin. I can't fall asleep without feeling how his lips grazed me.

Glancing out over the yard, the sun catches his hair, making the chestnut brown glow gold in the afternoon light. He's fucking gorgeous. I remind myself that Lucifer, too, was once an angel. Now I'm upset with him for what? Being pretty? I forget all the words to the speech I had memorized on the way over.

I retreat. It's not even worth it to yell at him anymore. I'll surely sound like a blithering idiot if I try to speak now. Composed was the plan. Outraged but organized. My attraction has caused me to become scattered. I need to calm down.

"That was the end of your tirade?" He asks, following after me.

It's tougher to ignore him when his long legs help him keep pace easily. I spin to face him, ready for round two when his thumb flicks under my eye.

"Hey, talk to me. You're crying." Derek implores tenderly.

To prove him wrong, I reach for my cheek, surprised when my fingers pull away damp. I substitute shock for outrage. He doesn't get to be nice after all he's pulled. I jerk my hand away.

"*Do not* touch me." I sneer.

"Ally." His eyes are wide. Alarmed. It's *me* who is the wild animal.

"*Don't.* You don't get to go back and forth, Mr. Rivera. Am I Ally or Miss Parrish? Should I drop your class or stay in it? You can't get me out of your head or you've already forgotten about me? Clearly, all lingering questions for you." It felt good to get that out. *What the hell was I thinking coming here?* I play through the cycle again. *Oh, yeah.* "You know what I think?" I don't wait for him to answer. "I think you *texting me* was wildly inappropriate." I mimic his accent on the last words.

"You're right." He maintains his distance. "Look, just come upstairs where we can talk." His tone is calm and collected, but there is an instability in his eyes, threatening to crack my resolve.

"You literally just told me I shouldn't be here five seconds ago." My heart hammers in my chest as I turn back to my car—anything to not have to look at those eyes.

"I did. And you shouldn't. It *is* inappropriate for you to be here, *and* it was inappropriate for me to text you. Stay anyway." He pleas from behind me. I see him lingering a few feet away in the window, hands in his pockets.

What was it Taylor Swift had said? *A figment of my worst intentions?* His features are as shadowed as the forest in the dimming sun, his heat even more sweltering. He waits for my answer while I study his distorted reflection. This whole thing is distorted. The familiar buzz thrums under my skin right where he touched me, preventing me from walking away.

"Five minutes," I say superiorly, strutting past him into the conservatory. He cruises in front of me, leading the way through a shortcut to his room. When we reach the stairs and I climb them two at a time, thinking I can beat him to the top. It is a lost cause. His frame carries him swiftly past, and he waits with the door open when I reach the last step. I let out a huff.

His living room now has a couch. It is the oversized leather one I recommended weeks ago, one night in the bar after he first brought me here. The burgundy rug and light gray walls blend with his newly unpacked belongings creating a small, eclectic space. It reminds me of Libby's, and I feel a pang of homesickness.

"Nice couch." I snark, taking a seat. He smirked, and I reminded him that he had five minutes.

"Why are you here, Ally?" He inquires, moving to the chair beside me where he rests his elbows atop his knees. I find it irritating how even that small action is endearing.

"I came to yell at you for your message," I admit, glum in my admiration that somehow continues to build.

"I'm sorry. I was out of line." He shakes his head in agreement.

I think this over and nod. I had wanted him to take accountability for his actions, and now he has. What more is there to say? *Everything,* my subconscious answers for me.

"I'm sorry, too. I know how I would have felt if the situation had been reversed. Riley just likes to provoke people." I take a path I hadn't intended, saying words I hadn't chosen. I still can't lie to him.

"Does he know?" He presses after a moment. He's not looking at me; he's looking past me straight through to the wall.

"No." I kick at the floor. "But he suspects. Your reactions certainly don't help. He's too perceptive." I smile, thinking I would never take a bet against Riley. He's been right about everything since I met him.

He nods bleakly, taking in the new information. His jaw tenses as his teeth grind together. "So. You two?"

"No." I snort. "Long story, but we're sort of roommates. I told him his room was ugly and he should paint it cream or white, and somehow, he heard cum white and got stuck on it. That's what you overheard today."

"You're wearing *his clothes*, Ally." He continues to look past me, and I wonder if that is the reason why. He can't stand the sight of me in someone else's clothes?

"Margot?" I ask in disbelief. He can't be upset and not expect me to be as well.

He throws his head back, laughing. I forget I am mad at him and want to see him do it again. I love his laugh and begin to smile before I know what is happening to my face.

He leaves the room, returning moments later with what looks to be a family photo. Derek stands beside Margot and two other men. I was right about his brother being a giant. Based on the way Derek is hugging Margot tight to him but leaning away from the older man in the center of the photo, I assume it's his father. That would make my guesses that they don't get along right as well.

"My sister. She's very punctual and does not appreciate when I keep her waiting. However, I had a bit of an unexpected distraction. I was drilled with about a million questions about you when we left."

"She knows?" I gasp. I can't imagine his sister thinking he is having a relationship with a student and being okay with it.

"She saw the way I looked at you. She suspects." He offers a halfhearted grin. I don't hear anything after how he "*looks at me*." How does he look at me? Maybe we're not kidding anyone, only ourselves. How obvious have we been? Nothing has happened between us. I mean, *not really.*

"His clothes." Derek gestures in a caviler wave, indicating that he has not forgotten our earlier subject of conversation. I'm still wearing the jacket, so I see why it would be hard to ignore. I shrug it off, and he gazes over appreciatively.

"His *jacket.*" I correct. "I left mine on a cafeteria bench, and someone else got to take it home with them. It's on loan until I get a new one. Plus, Riley claims I haven't come into my style yet. Whatever the hell that means."

He looks relieved, so relieved. It was a productive five minutes, anymore though, and things will turn very unproductive for me. I force myself to stand.

"Friday—why didn't you sing what we had rehearsed?" He quickly poses another question, prompting me to stay longer so I'll answer.

"It wasn't ready." I had forgotten how I had changed the song at the last minute. I couldn't bring myself to confess my grief to everyone openly. It was blatantly about losing the Kingsleys. Admitting it felt like losing my fresh start here, too.

"That's the first time you've ever lied to me." He says, grievous.

"I don't know," I confess. I close my eyes so his built-in polygraph machine won't pick up on my cues. I don't *want* to lie, but the truth is the song was always ready. *I'm* not.

"You still don't trust. You didn't trust the audience." He makes a heavy assumption—a *right* one. I say nothing, and he continues. "You can trust people, you know."

"I'm sure." I laugh.

"You can trust *me.*" He says, taking a step forward. His stare conveys that he is being genuine. *I did, Derek. I did. But you keep breaking my heart.* I give a quick shake of my head to acknowledge the statement, remembering I was heading to the stairs.

"I'll see you Thursday, Miss Parrish." He purrs, and I want to growl, actually growl, at him. I try, and a strangled sound comes out instead. He struggles to withhold his amusement.

Get it together, Ally.

"See you Monday, *Mr.* Rivera." I am proud of how calm my voice is when I say it. Straightening out immediately, he lets out a frustrated huff. It's a small acknowledgement that I am not alone in this and now *I* am relieved, so relieved.

I hold up a finger, indicating to him to wait, as I walk over to the bookshelf, grab a journal I know is only half finished, and turn to a clean page. Grabbing one of the pens left on the coffee table, I begin to write.

"What—" He begins.

"Shhhh." I cut him off.

I make a list:

1. Only ever call me Miss Parrish.

2. Keep your hands to yourself.

3. Always try to explain what you mean. I will trust what I can believe in.

Signed: Allyson Parrish

I rip out the page. Folding it, I pass the parchment. He reads while I return the pen to its spot on the table.

"Rules?" He chirps pleasantly, breaking my heart a little bit more at how cute it sounds. He's not a wolf at all, but a puppy that's been abused. Scared of what people can do, he bites instead of nuzzles. Except me. He nuzzles me. Or at least he did. Once.

"Yes," I confirm, crossing my arms. Glancing around the room, I think back to *Doctor Who*, wearing his shirt to sleep, and dancing to Elvis. I want to do more of those things. I want to do them under different circumstances.

"Ally." He says gently. He breaks rule one.

"One," I warn.

I won't look at him, feeling too incredibly stupid to provide any further acknowledgment. It's unfair how he teases me, how he makes me want something I can never have. Stepping forward, he uncrosses my arms before placing his fingers in mine.

"Rule two," I say, somehow out of breath.

"I don't like your rules." He says gravelly.

"You have to stop confusing me. You can't tell me you want a strictly educational relationship one day and look at me with 'fuck me' eyes the next." I take a step back, though I don't unhook our fingers.

"Fuck me eyes?" He laughs but continues to bat his lashes. My hand tingles. My toes tingle. I feel the anger amping up at his cruelty. He's giving me another forbidden moment he will soon take away.

"I'm pretty sure the last time we were in this room, *you* were the one taking your clothes off, if I remember correctly." He recounts with complete accuracy but none of the context. I had taken my shirt off due to my scar, not some dirty agenda the way he seems to recall.

Releasing him, I recoil before scowling. I poke his chest with all my might. "That was not some seduction tactic. God, Derek!" I yell. The ache in my chest is growing the more we fight.

His hands were in my hair as if he could sense it, and

suddenly, his lips were pressed to mine. Every single inch of my skin is static; I am being electrocuted. The rules float to the floor. I moan into his mouth, hungry, unwilling to admit how desperately I've craved him.

"Say it again." He growls with his lips against my own.

"Derek, say wh—" I start.

He quiets me by pressing his mouth to mine. His hands hook beneath my knees, lifting me so my legs wrap around his waist. Gently, he backs me against the wall. Adrenaline shoots from my lips straight into my stomach, and at last, I taste him uninterrupted, running my tongue along his bottom lip. He tastes like mint and faintly of cigarettes. It mixes with his scent of orange and bergamot, like resort soap and hotel sheets. It was the scent I remember hanging on to his shirt the last time I was here before I could distinguish what it was. It was as if someone had found the perfect combination of things that would appeal to me and put them into this man.

"You said *my* name. Not this Mr. Rivera bullshit." He rasps, holding my gaze.

"I thought you preferred Mr. Rivera?" I test.

"No." He whispers against my lips. "I fucking despise it, Ally." His tongue flicks against mine.

"Derek." I love saying his name. His smile is radiant, absorbing me before reality hits and mine starts to falter.

"What is it?" he asks, brushing his thumb across my cheek. I had been thin, pressed, dehydrated. Every second I've spent here in this transparency has rejuvenated me, and I don't want it to end.

"You can't use damage as an excuse to stay away from me. Not anymore." I say into his mouth. "However fucked up you think you are, it doesn't make me want you any less."

He scoffs. Unwrapping my legs from his waist, he places my feet back on the ground before brushing the hair away from my face, like I'm some fragile doll he doesn't want to break.

"However fucked up I *think* I am?" He repeats inconsolably. His tone doesn't match the mercy of the moment. He rejects me once more, turning his back. "What do you know of pain, Ally? Lifelong, soul-bruising pain— do you know what it does to someone's character?" He scrutinizes, backing into the arm of the sofa where he can lean instead of stand.

"I might be the only person that does," I admit in an exhale.

His trauma room eyes are tinted green like mine in the dying light of the quiet room. He shifts, fishing for evidence that I'm giving him the truth. When he finds it, he speaks again.

"Okay." He nods contemptuously. "You want my confession then, Ally? Since you're so sure you can handle it." He asks, his tone crude.

"Yes," I confirm without wavering.

"When I was young, my mum got really sick while my dad looked after her. She died of an insulin overdose, but she wasn't diabetic. Every month, I sit across from him at the dinner table and smile when he asks me to pass the salt like I don't want to smash everything in sight because I seem to be the only one who believes he murdered her." He says, hatred seeping back into his voice.

"That's a lot to unpack." I ponder, refusing to let empathy raid my tone. He'd mistake it for pity, and he's too proud to accept anyone feeling remorseful on his behalf. Follow-up questions obstruct my thought patterns, and I let the sentence linger.

"Obviously." He retorts, entertained by my response. A smirk has taken over his jaw, angling his features upwards. He's shaking his head like I'm insane. His admission was heavy, but did he think that would stop me from wanting him? At this point, I'm not sure anything could.

"What else?" I prompt.

"Oh, my dad killing my mum wasn't enough of a secret for you?" He snickers.

"That's not what I meant. What else is keeping you away from me?"

His eyes bore into me, less like pine trees than scalpels trying to dissect my brain, attempting to figure out how it works. Sighing, I stand between his legs, resting my forehead against his own.

"Derek, I want you." I breathe. He shifts me closer, holding my hips to his. The sparks in my tummy ripple out to everything. I'm becoming dependent on the feeling of his hands on my waist. I run my own over them as evidence. "I feel this. You touch me, you look at me, and I feel *everything*. Tell me what you're so afraid of so you can understand I'm not going to run."

He nods timidly before he begins his second confession.

"A year ago, I put this guy in hospital for grabbing my arm. Just for grabbing me, I struck him so hard that he went into a coma for a month. Maybe you think you can fix me, but you can't. Please get that. You're looking at me like you're in heat, like you want me so badly to be that guy you met in the bar over the summer, but I'm not him. You used to think I never got angry, but like I told you, I operate on anger, Ally. Is that what you want out of a man?" His words are harsh and ripping, but he delivers them delicately in a plea. The only thing I was wrong about was him being a coward. It took a great deal of courage to share that with me—courage I certainly haven't had.

"Are you going to put me in the hospital?" I ask pointedly. I know the answer already.

"What? Ally, no." He stutters, shaken by the question. This is good. I want him to be off guard, so he answers my next one.

"Why did you hit him? He didn't just grab you. What happened?"

He flinches. He had to know this was coming, but he can't tell me it doesn't matter, not when he needs me to know my safety isn't at risk. I'm being incredibly manipulative, but I need him to understand I'm not scared, and he has to let go of all his walls and his reasons before he can believe it.

"I grew up with Zach and Jace. We were all into music, and when we were sixteen, we started a band. No one knows who started it. We kind of always *were* a band, but suddenly, we had a name for it, and things began to change. I'd write the songs, Zach would perform them, Jace would come up with choreography. We were really, really good, and we started booking gigs. We even recorded an album together, which we were about to head out on tour for." He explains.

"Then, I found out Duke was sick. I had worked my whole life towards an opportunity like that, and it was over before it even started. Just like that, my dream disintegrated before my eyes.

Duke, of course, told me to stay, but I couldn't. Losing time with him was worse than losing the tour, but what did it matter when it was inevitable I was going to lose them both anyway?"

"So, I was about to go on stage when Jace grabbed me,

telling me not to. I was too wound up to be out there, and he could sense it. He put his hands on me, and I just snapped. I *wanted* someone to give me a reason to be angry. I don't even remember hitting him until Zach was pulling me off. Naturally, the band fell apart. I don't know. Maybe I wanted to take the opportunity from them, too. Then I didn't have to suffer alone."

"*Wait*—Jace? Chambers was the one you hit?"

He nods, hanging his head in shame. My stomach knots, and I feel gross about his confession, yet somehow, I understand completely. Didn't I make my mother suffer along with me? And if it had been me about to go on tour when the Kingsleys died, I surely would have lost my mind just the same. On one hand, music was the only thing that could have gotten me through it. On the other, I was barely capable of getting out of bed. I know what the pain of losing someone does to a person. Derek wasn't alone. We both almost killed someone last year.

"How often did you visit him?" I dig.

"Every day. When his mom asked me to stop coming, I wanted to respect her wishes, so I'd sit in the chapel instead and pray. I don't even believe in God." He admits, laughing softly.

"Did he ever forgive you?" I continue to pry, aware that he must have.

"He claims to, but it was his first tour too. He'd choreographed the whole damn thing and never got to see a single dance. For weeks, they weren't sure if the concussion had caused brain damage. I ruined his career, Ally. He teaches instead of tours because too much stress could put him at risk. I put my best friend in the hospital, and he repays me by getting me a job." There is so much shame in his voice. "He's remarkable. You know what Jace said when he woke up? 'Is *Derek* okay? Tell him *I forgive him.*'" He chokes out, his lids red-rimmed as they begin to water. Hastily, he wipes at them with the back of his hand.

"Guilt has this funny way of changing how we see ourselves, but you're not a monster, Derek. Jace doesn't think so, and neither do I."

He eyes me skeptically, unconvinced. I rest my palm on his cheek, hoping it will communicate what I cannot. He leans into it for a second before burying his face in my stomach.

"How are you real?" He wonders aloud; his words muffled in my belly as his tears soak my shirt. I run my fingers through his hair, attempting to comfort him. I feel ill at ease, not by these revelations, but by the idea that even after this, I might somehow be restricted from touching him freely again. Only then, it won't be his secrets keeping us apart—it will be mine.

"My stepdad is a cop," I whisper.

"Ally, I would never hurt you like that." He sputters, straightening his spine to ogle me in horror.

"You didn't let me finish. You gave me your confessions; don't you want to know mine?" I ask attempting to break away. He holds me in place, shaking his head no with a stubborn pout on his lips.

"Yes, I want to know. No, you can't leave. I'm not... *comfortable* when I can't touch you." He clarifies. Up close, his devastatingly handsome edges appear both soft and hard at the same time. "Stay."

He is the opposite end of my magnet, and I could not pull away even if I had wanted to. I have to tell him now while I have guts. While I have the responsibility weighing on me. I won't be able to give him the same courtesy of truth later.

"With my stepdad's profession, he keeps a gun in the house. About a year ago, I picked it up." I try, the words sounding even more unpleasant out loud. "I didn't want to live anymore. I was about to pull the trigger when my mother walked in."

"You tried to kill *yourself? Why?*" Anguished, he holds me away for closer examination.

"I lost some people, this family I lived with during high school died in a freak accident. My stepdad had me committed for a couple of weeks while I got some help. It was a dark time for me."

"Al." Derek's brows furrow together, his lips forming into a deep frown.

"Oh, I'm not done," I say, holding my hand to stop him before he can say more. It's better just to rip off the Band-Aid now that the worst is out of the way. "Before that, I lost my dad. He had promised to pick up Oreos on the way home, but he forgot. It was the only time he had ever broken a promise, and I wouldn't let him live it down." I laugh manically.

"So, he went back out. On his way home from the store, he died in a car crash. All because he forgot some fucking Oreos. I was eleven. I haven't touched the cookies in nine years. They actually make me sick now." I sniffle, wiping my eyes with the back of my sleeve.

I force a smile, which produces an awkward, self-depre-cating giggle. I pray it comes across as charming and not unstable. I try to appear bubbly beneath the grief so it's not all he sees. I attempt to prove how I'm damaged enough to understand him but not too damaged that it drives him away— it feels like the curse of being a woman. So charming is a broken man, but us, we balance on such a fine line. The only relief in the room comes from him not looking at me like I'm a total mess.

"Jesus Christ, Ally. Come here." He wraps me in his arms. The tightness with which he holds me makes me feel secure, as if nothing bad could ever happen in his embrace.

"I know a lot about pain, Derek. You were so worried it was going to change my mind about you. Did it change yours about me?"

He leans back, his shoulders stiffening as they flex to support his shifting weight. We return to the moment before the confessions, where he was brushing back my hair. He kisses me tenderly.

"Not even a little." He whispers against my lips. Then, I know it's not just his shadow I feel comfortable in but my own in his presence. I tangle my fingers back into his hair and ask what this means.

"It means we're proper fucked then, yeah?" he answers, jubilantly.

"Without a doubt," I confirm. We don't make each other promises. I don't want us to. It's enough for now that we have chosen each other, honestly. There's nothing else I can think of to ask. Except...

"Is it wrong that I want to touch you?" I ask timidly.

"You're asking if it's sick that trauma bonding turns us on?" He jokes. "No, I feel closer to you without the secrets, Al. I wanted you before, but I felt too much like I was deceiving you. I wanted you to want *me*, not the mask, but I couldn't picture a world where that was possible." Derek explains, pressing his mouth to mine once more.

He stands without hesitation, removing his shirt and discarding it on the floor. Moving a few feet away, he remains perfectly still. Like on the stairs outside, the last of the sun streams through the window in a way that makes him glow.

"I want this to be on your terms, Ally. You decide how much you take, how much you give."

With Derek, it isn't a choice so much as a compulsion. My body would respond to his with or without my mind's permission. I already tell him enough of my thoughts without meaning to. I step closer; he inhales sharply. I observe every freckle on his shoulders, the moles splattered like constellations across his back.

The blackout tattoo circling his wrist and trailing up his left arm contains two halves of an anatomical heart being sewn back together by a pair of pale hands. An albatross flies through the dark landscape, carrying the sun in its claws. He exhales staggered breaths while I trace his body art until I have the patterns memorized. I follow the perfectly bronzed trail of hair that disappears below his pants. God, he's phenomenal. Beautiful seems too weak a phrase.

His eyes are closed, his chest rising and falling rhythmically. I stand before him, pulled to him like I am pulled to the piano. His tempo plays like music beneath my skin, derailing me whenever he walks into a room, or stands too close, or says my name.

"Keep your eyes closed," I warn. He nods his confirmation.

I unzip my pants and step out of them. I follow it by discarding my shirt on the ground. I reach for the zipper on his jeans. His fingers find mine and free the clasp so he can step out of them. The light from the window is fading.

"I'm opening my eyes now, Ally." He commands the quiet.

"Okay."

He opens them and drinks me in. His gaze flickers over every inch of my body before speaking. His tongue draws over his lips to wet them, stirring a heat between my legs.

"May I?" He asks.

I nod.

He reaches for my face and cups the back of my head. His thumb skates down my cheek and across my lips before landing on my chin. He roughly tilts it up, tracing back down my jawline. He outlines my collarbone with two fingers before dropping his hand down the center of my chest. I've lost control of my senses. My body is in a state of emergency; everything is going haywire.

At my waistline, he uses his palms to glide upwards, stopping at my breast. He looks to me for permission. For someone who considers himself a monster, he's showing me complete respect. Men don't understand that's the formula for making a woman fall in love. I nod my consent. I've been reduced to a ping-pong machine reacting to his touch.

Shaking his head, a look I don't understand flits across his face. Derek's breathing grows unsteady. A need unfurls inside me, and I reach out to touch him. Carefully, he catches my wrists and places them back at my sides.

"It's my turn." He whispers in my ear.

He spins me around so my back rests against his chest. Unclasping my bra, Derek lets it fall into the waste pile with our other clothes. Kicking them away, he grazes his fingers across my skin until my nipple falls between them. My chest rises and falls heavily, pressing my breast further into his hand. Squeezing the pink buds slightly, a whimper rises to my lips.

He pulls me tighter against him, his hardness landing

against my ass, which does nothing to help control the situation. The hair falling down my spine is brushed into place over my shoulder before his lips press to my neck. His hand on my waist does not waver, never letting me get more than an inch of space between us before he slams me back, securing my hips to his. I grip his arm to steady myself. It's all a bit dizzying.

"I am going to touch you now." He says into my hair. He waits a moment for me to object. I don't. I am entirely his.

His free hand begins to fall down my waist, tickling the skin just above the waistband of my panties. Slowly, deviously, his fingers dip down until they quickly find what is most sensitive, what makes me *react*. I can't contain my gasp. I can't remember basic things like how to swallow or stand. My knees buckle, causing me to fall against him. He shifts us, leaning back against the arm of the sofa. A grounder to keep us steady while he teases me mercilessly. He plays with me until I'm right on the brink, then slows his pace. I think he enjoys watching me lose my mind.

"You're so wet." He muses in a low voice. He *definitely* enjoys watching me lose my mind.

I am arching my back against his chest, grinding into his lap. The culmination of pressure hitting from front and back threatens to tip me over the edge.

"Fuck, Ally. Your hips." Derek is groaning in my ear, and everything inside me is wound up by his fingers. I have started to work his boxers down with my grinding. I can feel him pressed between my cheeks through the thin material.

"Bloody hell." He pulls my panties down roughly. "I want to see you come *like this*." His words push me over the edge, and I lose all control. My legs spasm and shake, and he holds me in place while pressing down with his fingers. When it overtakes me, he pushes his fingers into me, and I scream his name.

Lifting the fingers he had used to fuck me, he places them into his mouth. I stare at him, transfixed. I turn and press my lips to his. I want to taste myself on him.

"Stay." He says between kisses.

"Did you think I was capable of going anywhere?" I laugh.

"No, stay the night." He chuckles.

"Sleep with you?" I ask, surprised.

"Yes." He smiles. "Do you want to shower?"

"You don't want to...?" I trail off, staring down at the rather large bulge in his boxers. I feel confused and rejected again somehow, but mostly relieved. I am shocked thinking of how intimate that was, and all he did was touch me. *No one* has ever touched me like that except... I don't dare think his name. When I flinch, Derek misreads it.

"*More than anything*." He explains, cradling my face in his palms. "Ally, I'm rock hard over here." He shifts my hand to rest over him as evidence. "*I want you*." Sighing, he goes on. "But I want you in *every* way. I've gotten too ahead of myself already. I didn't mean for things to go that far, not this fast. God, I'm fucking this up. I just... I never want anything you do with me to be something you regret." Derek says, shifting my hand once more, this time to rest on his heart.

His expression is so genuine that trust blooms in my chest at once. Despite his rejection, I've never felt so confident that someone wanted me fully. His explanation alone somehow created a deeper bond and a heightened respect, more even than before. Truthfully, I wasn't ready to have sex. A truth that Derek picked up on before I had. Wrapping my arms around him in gratitude, I nod into his neck.

* * *

Shortly after, he's leading me through his bedroom to the attached bath. I drink in his space. Now furnished, his room is surprisingly tidy, and his bed is coated in a thick white comforter. Resting beside it is a chest acting as a nightstand and a lamp. A few pictures are scattered, and I make a note to check them out later. The entire upper story of this area has been converted to suit him. The sloping ceiling and skylights above the bed are beautiful. I hadn't noticed last time.

When he leaves, I find the towels folded neatly beneath the sink. The water is hot, and his shampoo smells like him, like ginger and bergamot. So, *this* is part of what makes up his intoxicating scent. I wonder where the rest comes from. When I step out, the room is filled with steam. Quickly, it dissipates, circulating up into the vent so I can breathe easily. I wrap the terrycloth around me, realizing I have nothing to wear. A quick glance at the counter, where a sweatshirt has materialized, tells me Derek has thought this through.

Slipping it over my head, I towel-dry my hair quickly and squeeze some toothpaste on my finger to brush my teeth. I open the door and step out.

"It looks better on you." He says.

Derek is stretched across the bed with a tray in front of him. A show is playing in the background, but I can't make out the words. He pulls a grape off the stem and pops it in his mouth.

"What is this?" I laugh, climbing on the opposite side of the bed.

"I ran over to Duke's and grabbed whatever looked good." He shrugs. "This is my grandfather's favorite appetizer. It's a cheese tray with fruit. There are also Steak and Ale pies. The recipe was passed down through the generations back home. I swear they are the best in England."

"Ice!" I exclaim, grabbing a glass of water and sipping it furiously. It's not purified like I'd hoped. I *miss* purified water. I miss the taste of the added minerals. I doubt England even has any, but at least it's cold. It still might be the most refreshing drink I've ever had, even without the flavor I've been craving. My sip turns to an unapologetic chug.

"Americans." He laughs.

I pick over the tray. The fruit is ripe and sweet.

"This is amazing." I bite into the cheese. "Do you always treat your students like this?" I poke fun but really, I'm prying.

"Ally." His eyes are hard now. His expression is serious. "Now, do you understand why I wanted to take things slow? I want you to remain sure of me, of my character. I don't *do* this. This is my first year in any teaching role, ever. In fact, before you, I hadn't 'dated' in a long time. I told you that this goes against everything I am ethically, and I meant it. I knew you before this, and that is the only reason why. It is a piss poor excuse, but I wanted you long before you stepped foot in that classroom."

Summer flashes in my memory. I've slept here before and explored this space when he was only Derek. Before I ever knew "Mr. Rivera." I couldn't stay away from him even then. It was never just the music pulling me into that bar that first night; it's always been more. This may be a sick twist of fate, but at least it's not me playing out some fantasy. I am drawn to him. I have always been drawn to him.

I climb over the tray and straddle him. The buzz grows deep in my body. I don't think I'll ever get used to the heat of him beneath me, the exquisite feel of his skin on mine.

I kiss him hard.

"Derek." I tug at the ends of his hair.

His hands travel my back and reach down to slip under the hoodie. I curse it for being there. He gropes my ass, and surprise comes over his face.

"You're not wearing panties." His eyes darkened, and it became my favorite look.

"Mine were damp." I shrug.

"*Allyson!* Not wearing panties in my bed is really trying my resolve." He jokes.

"I wouldn't want to do that." I reach down and stroke him through his pants. Jesus Christ. Who the hell am I right now? Suggestive. Seductive. I've transformed into an insatiable woman.

Cocking his head to the side, he raises his eyebrows which looks both devious and adorable. He lifts me off and lays me on the bed so he can move the tray. I kneel on the edge of the bed and wait for him to return impatiently. When he does, his shirt goes first. It's an obstacle in my warpath. He possesses me. The need takes over. I press my fingers against his skin, and it's like I can't be close enough. He lifts his sweatshirt off my body and inhales sharply. We're entirely bare before one another. I can't find a single flaw.

I push his hair out of his face. His dark eyebrows bring out the melting chocolate in his eyes. His lips part, and I will lose it if I sit here another second without tasting him.

Our lips press together exquisitely. He tastes like grapes and apples.

My lips want to explore him like my hands did. I kiss his chin, his jaw, the nape of his neck. My hands slide down his sides, and he shivers. I look up at him as I gently lower myself. His eyes widen, but I'm sure. His cock is hard and thick. I try to bite back my gasp as it twitches upwards and hits my cheek. He laughs lightly. I touch him, and his laughter abruptly stops. My fingers trace his length gently before gripping him.

"Fuck, Ally." It is the sexiest sound in the world. I continue to stroke him with my palm, and our eyes hold steady. The intensity makes me look away, but his hand tangles in my hair, forcing my eyes back to his.

"I *want* you to look at me." It comes out in a low rasp. I obliged, and now I couldn't look away if I tried. The heat rises in my hand. He twitches again, and I gasp. His head tilts back in a groan. I take the opportunity to lean forward and kiss his neck down to his chest.

"I'm going to come if you keep doing that." He presses his forehead to mine.

This is so hot. I feel completely connected to him as I press my nipples against his pecs. I don't stop. Every few strokes, I lift his cock to graze the head against my clit. I'm getting wet again watching him. Massaging his precum into myself, I could finish again just from the contact every few seconds. I have never been this bold. I don't let myself become shy. I explore his length without fear, touching and massaging every inch of him. I let my passion continue to guide me blindly.

His breaths are coming out in heavy pants, and he moans in my mouth when he kisses me. My thighs are covered in warmth as he climaxes. I have to actively focus on slowing my pace to nothing while my legs clench together, my second orgasm overtaking me. I'm amazed that it happened at all. I've always been so mental when it came to sex. It took months of learning my body before I was able to come before, yet with Derek, he hasn't even been inside of me, and I've practically erupted twice. Then again, so has he.

"Wow." He says, mesmerized. "That was…"

"Groundbreaking? Earth-shattering?" I tease.

"Yes." He confirms. "Let me get you a towel." He looks over the liquid on my thighs that is now dripping down to his duvet. "On second thought, you might need another shower."

I laugh, catching the towel he tosses me from the bathroom and dab at the comforter before wiping myself clean.

He materialized beside me, offering the sweatshirt we had discarded and a pair of his boxers. "Both optional." He declares.

I roll my eyes and pull it over my head. He dresses only in his boxers before climbing back into bed. I look at him, unsure of what to do. I've been so comfortable around him that I forgot this was new. Forgot that we don't have that couple dynamic to fall back on. I don't know if he likes to be cuddled or prefers just to hang out. I bite my lip in uncertainty.

"Get over here, " he smirks, pulling me against his side. I snuggle closer, burying my nose into his chest where I can breathe him in. He hands me the remote, and we settle on the Discovery Channel, where an Australian man searches for monsters.

Everything is light and airy. "Never hesitate, Al. How many times do I have to tell you? I literally *always* want you to touch me, " he whispers in my hair. Once again, he sees right through me. My arm rests low on his chest, and my fingers, which have been exploring his stomach, now trail over his boxers.

"There's a big snake in the water, " the guy on TV says, and we laugh.

now, october

WHEN MORNING COMES, I expect to feel awkward, immediately freaking out as I jolt awake in a state of panic—confined by sheets that aren't my own, as they constricted like a noose around my neck, reducing my oxygen.

I've thought about this moment a million times. Pushing my nose into Grey's back, only to discover it was someone else's. I've thought about the dread that would come with that realization. Of becoming lucid in the wrong bed. As these worries begin to fester, Derek rolls over. His tattooed arm skims the blanket, lost until it finds me and settles. His scarred fingers barely make contact with my thigh, yet somehow, it's enough to appease him. He exhales as if assuaged, his chest rising and falling gently. I become transfixed in watching him breathe. None of the feelings I had expected come to fruition. Only fear. I am afraid of how well I fit here.

I didn't think I'd ever be able to look at someone the way I looked at Grey. I knew one day, enough time would pass, and I'd grow through my grief enough to have a physical connection with someone. It was a long shot, but still, I saw it as possible. But never did I think I could be mentally linked to another like I was to Grey. Obsessed as I was with every mannerism he had, every minute curve of his body, every thought that crossed his mind. No one was ever going to fit me like that again. Derek surely doesn't.

If I had to find a metaphor, I'd say Grey was an allied country. We were like-minded. I knew we'd never run out of things to talk about, and he'd always have my back. But, Derek. Derek is the ocean, and I'm a sea. We flow into one another without trying.

The old alarm clock ticks to 7 am. My first class isn't until 1. I think of returning to an empty apartment, and my stomach drops. I imagine how I'd sneak down the stairs and out the side door to my car, how I'd arrive at the flat in the same clothes as yesterday and turn the lock. Our cozy Potter living room feeling darker, daft even, after the warmth I've been encased in here. I wouldn't be able to talk this through with Riley. Should he be home, which I doubt, the details of last night would have to remain quiet, unable to be shared. It's another secret, but I've grown used to my secrets, and this is one worth keeping.

Riley's first class is at 9, and he likes to sleep in until the last possible moment, always hustling out the door to make it on time. I've grown into the habit of shoving granola bars into all his jacket pockets so he'll at least have something to eat in his hurry.

I have no new messages, no string of missed calls proving that he must have spent the night at Matt's. If he had been home, I'm certain my inboxes would all be full. Regardless, somehow, he will sense that I have changed, and he will know. One way or another, a conversation will be coming that I will need to prepare for at some point in the day. How will I explain what's caused my dark and gloomy to wane, how my mood has shifted so dramatically?

I decide not to think about it and enjoy the moment I'm in. I let myself drift into what a morning with Derek would look like instead. I haven't ever given myself the luxury of thinking about it, but now that I have, it feels *exciting*.

Derek's hair is so much shorter now than in the summer. Then, he had let it fall messily across his forehead. Now, it's trimmed and styled to always be pushed back. I'm not sure if he cut it to be more professional or if he had tired of having to move it. I battle the desire to run my fingers through it, to kiss his cheek and see his morning eyes open into mine. He stayed up so late talking with me that the desire to let him sleep is greater.

I look around the room for things to busy myself with until he wakes. Like Grey, Derek keeps a stack of books on his bedside table. It's funny how alike they are in some ways. Both studious, creatives. Maybe that's my type: mysterious cocky bookworms. I shake the thought. I had promised not to compare them anymore. Though, this thought feels like it's guiding me down a different path. Grey feels safe to think about here, welcome even. I'm too shielded by Derek's warmth for the cold to find me.

It's nice, in a way, to be able to remember him without the ache. In the past, one negative comparison would have kept me from engaging. A positive one would stand as too much of a reminder that someone else was only Grey in part—a carryover. Like everything else, Derek supersedes all my expectations. My rules don't apply to him.

Of all the titles he has, only one I recognize by name. A

book called *Ender's Game* has a receipt sticking out the top, bookmarking a spot somewhere in the middle where he last stopped. I pick it up, not because it's the one I recognize, but because it appears to be what he is currently reading. It's an opportunity to try to figure him out further. What made him pick this book? Are there things in these pages that can tell me more about the man who has so deeply consumed my thoughts?

I crack the spine to the first page, where a coffee ring sits, staining a circle around a caption in the first chapter. I imagine him at breakfast, how Duke may have walked in, and absentmindedly, Derek would have set down his cup to save his place, not realizing it would leave a blemish. I follow the outline with the pad of my index finger before reading the words.

Before long an hour has gone by, and I'm well absorbed in the story of this incredibly intelligent and empathetic boy. Forced to fight as a child, Ender is sent off to win a war no one really understands.

When the clock is about to tick to 8, I get out of bed, careful not to make noise. I snatch the book from atop the puffy covers and easily locate the kitchen door. Derek's coffee maker is effortlessly discovered, the only appliance on his otherwise empty countertops. I plug it in and start a pot. Lifting myself onto the counter beside the machine, I wait for it to brew, flipping through the pages quickly.

Ender is trying to beat the giant, and I'm obsessed with how the author describes each scene in such detail. No thought is cloudy, and no action is half done, causing me to assess what I would do in the same situation, if I would think as logically. I contemplate if Derek would notice if I snuck it into my bag when I left.

A window at the end of the cabinetry looks over the

hedge maze, just as the window in the living room had. Cracked, the breeze topples over the windowpane, dancing through the small space until it ruffles my curls. Derek's shampoo must be good because today, they actually look like curls and not the frizz I've resigned myself to expect. Sunlight stretches across the pages, mingling with my good mood, and I feel further saturated. I startle when a voice interrupts the room.

"You've made yourself at home," Derek says.

It doesn't come out like an accusation but as praise. His features, soft in the morning light, have abandoned the strain that's caused them to stiffen these past few weeks. It seems both our tensions have melted away with last night's confessions.

I feel my lips turn up at the corners. I'm enjoying our looks being unfiltered. I'm not fighting my feelings like I was at the bar or urging myself away from him like at school. Laying the book on the counter, I marvel, finally able to admire him without restraint. Derek supports himself against the frame for a beat longer before the gravity's too much, and he ventures across the space dividing us.

He pauses a few tiles away. The tiles are large, checkered stones, dated, a foot or more wide. A few tiles are unacceptable when I ache to have him closer. I study the distance. Leaning forward, he peers up at me playfully. The sandy color in his hair left from summer is fading already, giving way to something darker, messier. I lift my hand slowly, his fingers finding mine in the air, our grips catching for only seconds before he gives in. His hands fall to my waist, shifting me against him so the distance disappears. Gently, he presses his lips to my temple.

"Ah, I love being able to do this." He whispers into my hair.

Goosebumps form on the top of my legs. I giggle under my breath. It comes out like a laugh, a moan, and a grunt all at once. His eyebrows go up as the sound catches him off guard. Embarrassment flushes my cheeks. I can't even *laugh* coherently around him. I'm not used to being nervous around him or anyone anymore. Then, nothing had mattered. Now, *everything* does. My brain becomes so full that it goes blank, feeling overtaking any space for thought. I begin to panic. *Act normal. Act normal.*

Derek's palms press to my cheeks before rearranging my hair to tuck the strands behind my ears. When he finishes he lets them come to rest on my shoulders.

"I love that you're nervous. I'm so bloody nervous around you all the time. I forget what to do with my hands." He waves them in the air between us like they're unidentified objects.

"I've watched you. It's annoyed me to no end, how I can't seem to stop watching you. How you walk, these uncontrolled micro-emotions that sort of flit across your face when you talk to someone, and I can tell exactly what you're thinking." He smirks and talks sideways to the floor, glancing up at me every few seconds.

"It's extraordinary how you move through the world, and—and," he stutters, "and you take that and pour it into your work so effortlessly. You treat the music with such care: how you speed up and slow down the same lyric, so it's two feelings in one breath, how you find a beat that's catchy but a cadence to how you sing the words that is absolutely gut-wrenching. Every time you sing, for three minutes, I watch all the people in the room become as captivated with you as I am." His gaze is steady on me now, gauging my reactions. "You don't have to be nervous around me, Ally. I'm already done for." He laughs, shaking his head in disbelief.

I am in awe. I feel like I have never truly been seen before this moment. It's endearing how he leads with his vulnerability. I adore the big, clunky hands that he doesn't know what to do with. Even now, he rests them on his hips before scratching his face before shoving them into his pockets. I'm looking at him through another lens. My admiration has turned to appreciation, and there is such a heavy force in that difference. Admiration breeds desire, lust. Appreciation breeds value, love.

"Derek," I say in mock disapproval. Really, I say it because I want to taste his name.

"Ally?" He questions shakily. I can see the worry form in a crease on his forehead. Worry that he's said too much.

I crack, finding no joy in teasing him. "Please stop moving so far away after you give big romantic speeches. It makes it quite difficult to touch you."

His warmth envelops me as he steps back into my space, and every bee buzzes back to life. Where the violinists from the Titanic had been playing beneath my skin, ready to go down with the ship, a whole Goddamn orchestra replaces them, reinflating my lungs with air. I settle his nervous hands with my own.

"These," I tell him, "are my favorite part of your body today." I kiss each finger, touch his chest, stroke his hair. I kiss him like I need his oxygen to breathe. Everything has changed. We will never be able to go back to what we were —I never want us to. The mechanical beep beside us reminds me of the coffee I had long forgotten, breaking us from the kiss.

"Coffee?" I ask breathily, and he laughs. The right laugh. The chuckle that escapes him is so lovely I want to bottle it so I can listen to it over and over. Resting my fore-head against his shoulder, I breathe him in from the source. My hotel sheets. My fresh start.

"Derek?"

"Hmm?" He hums. He's pouring the coffee into two travel mugs. I almost change my question to ask about the mugs. No, no, this is important.

"What happens now?" I ask. I'm asking about when we leave here. What comes next for us? Was this a one-time thing? I look up to see how the question affects his mood.

He tilts my chin up to level, his face so serious, I begin to worry he is about to break my heart.

"I was thinking—" He hesitates. "breakfast?" He finishes, the creases in his face falling into a smile.

"Breakfast?"

"Mhmm." He reassures confidently. "I say we take these thermoses to Duke's and see what Adeline is whipping up for breakfast. She's his live-in caretaker, but she's also an incredible cook. I know Duke would love to see you again. Preferably in more clothes." He sizes up my one-piece outfit. In my defense, his shirt hangs almost down to my knees.

I kiss his cheek slowly because I can and hop off the counter. He tops off our mugs while I redress in yester-day's jeans. I'll need to leave early to shower and change before class. He passes my cup as we head down the stairs. When we reach the bottom, he takes my free hand in his.

"What time is your first class?" He asks.

"Not until one. Yours?" I raise my eyebrows.

"Ha-ha. Clever Ally." He rolls his eyes at me. I keep star-ing. It was a serious question. "Yeah, okay." He continues. "My first session is at one as well. Need a ride?" He jokes.

"Ha-ha. Funny Derek." I imitate him. He bites his lip to keep it from revealing his humor.

I asked Derek if we could take the long way. I want to see the rest of the gardens. I feel like I've only seen such a small amount of what's been built here. My hand is entwined in his, and I feel like I've traveled back to simpler days. There is no anguish hanging over me. These moments with him feel like a gift I don't want to let slip away.

We stroll through the main conservatory building. He had pulled me along when I attempted to grab my shoes; understanding filled me when we began to walk across the grass. Grass that feels like feathers caressing my bare feet. I tag him, running off. He catches up quickly, throwing me over his shoulder as we head into a hallway of windows and mirrors. In some, I find myself looking into another room or out over the yard; in others, I see only my reflection looking back. Planters are hung like chandeliers holding boughs of ivy, flowers stemming from them that I can't identify.

Duke has thought of everything in his dream world—rooms of exhibitions and unparalleled beauty and rooms like this distorted funhouse. "The Reflection Hall," Derek informs me. It is fitting, as it has forced me to reexamine the world and think of the place I want to hold within it. I decide any place is fine so long as I'm with Derek.

The hall leads to a room with a giant wisteria tree at the center. The ceiling goes up to a glass dome, but the tree is so vast and full that you can barely make out the glass from under it. Lavender hues coat the space in dusty light as if it had been lit by fairy dust. A couple of swings hang from the branches, swinging softly over fallen petals that cover the floor in purple.

"Whoa," I muse.

"I'll let Duke tell you about this one. If everything had to be torn down and only one room could remain, this is the one he'd keep. It's very special to him." Derek hums poetically.

I resist my urge to sit on one of the swings. I want a full tour before I have to return to class this afternoon, so regretfully, we move along. The wisteria room acts as a hub with five hallways branching out from it. He lets me pick, and I choose the darkest path.

The hall is more of a tunnel; the overhead rounded like a U. Derek explains that it's a terrarium built collaboratively by an artist and herpetologist who wanted to highlight all that was being lost in deforestation. Walking through the center of it feels like being in a 100-layer dirt cake. Instead of pudding between the layers, there are a series of tunnels, each housing a species of tropical frog or lizard. Blacklights have been set in the hall to catch their colors, making them glow vibrantly as they travel throughout their home.

Again, I feel astounded. It's inspiring all he has done. Every room holds a vision, a story to be told, a different way to capture a person's heart.

"Derek," I laugh, covering my mouth. My eyes are like fireworks, venturing out in many directions, lighting up at each new thing I see. "It's endless. I think I've fallen completely in love with it already, and then I discover another part, and I fall even deeper." I spin into the rainforest room; my dance class with Chambers demonstrated my newfound grace.

"Me too." He says. He has this look about him. It's how I've seen parents look at their children on Christmas morning, full of adoration. Only, he's looking at me.

I stop spinning and cross the room back to where he

stands. I touch his face in the same fashion I always touch his face, without fear or filter. "You got your sparkle back," I tell him.

"Wha—" he starts to speak, but I cut him off as I press my lips to his. My skin feels like it's being held up by the force of the hive. I'm part of the exhibit, too. A collection of bees turned into a girl who likes a boy.

then, october

I HAD WOKEN EARLY, around five thirty or so in the morning. This was a day I had been dreading for weeks. I had hoped it would flit by without recognition, without cognizance. It had not. It blared at me, the date shifting from black to screaming red from where my calendar sat across the room.

I'd tried to take it down more than once, but my mother would only rehang it, restating the necessity for keeping track of my therapy appointments. I think she liked it there to serve as a reminder that time was passing, whether I chose to acknowledge it or not.

Unable to fall back asleep, I slinked over to the window and propped it open. Usually, I'd venture out to the deck to get high, but today was an exception.

The idea of stepping out of my room felt forlorn. The sky had begun to grow from a blackened night into a dusty blue. I let the drugs fill my lungs as I blew the smoke out through the screen. Under the influence, it was barely tolerable. A step up from the intolerable it had been moments before.

The birds whistled from the barren limbs of trees. With the lightening atmosphere, I was just starting to make out the details of the branches on which they were perched. The crisp autumn air filtered back to me, the smell of fallen leaves painfully reminiscent of seasons past. In my altered state of mind, I was unable to purge the memories, and one by one, they phosphoresced across my mind, playing back.

This time, a year prior, I had been in New York with Grey and Charlie for their birthday. Nothing felt okay. I was too tired, too absent, to want to go on any longer. The calendar mocked me, not the way my mother had intended as a symbol of the time already passed, but as a reminder of the time that would come to pass. The weeks that would still be empty, void of them.

Mike wouldn't be rising for his shift for another half hour. I had a limited window if I wanted to escape, and I so desperately did. Tip-toeing into his office, I fiddled with the lock on his drawer where he kept his gun. This is where guns belonged, in secured boxes kept in closets and under beds, left in nightstands to protect against intruders. It didn't belong in my hands, somehow too heavy even though it was smaller than I remembered. My fingers didn't belong near the trigger; they belonged still entwined in his.

These were the thoughts ringing in my head as I slipped back into my room, quieter than a mouse. I didn't bother locking the door like I usually did. I reasoned that it'd be better, less traumatic if they found me quickly. They would carry no memory of having to beat it down, terrified of what they would discover on the other side.

I knew my mother loved me, but I was determined that she had never experienced loss like this. She had never reacted to my father's death the way I had. She had nothing to compare it to when I'd lost the Kingsleys. It was a disturbing thought, at best, but at least this way— she might be able to understand the pain. This wasn't a plan built from resentment; I had no wish to make her suffer. I tried to rationalize my decision however I could so I wouldn't chicken out. My escape plan didn't involve a return.

I toyed with leaving her a note, but I had lost my words. Nothing I could say would portray the gravity of my betrayal. She had given me life, and I was throwing it away. What words could I leave her to convey my most profound apology? There weren't any. So, I didn't leave a note. No letter. No goodbye.

I sat back by the window, balancing the gun in my lap. I didn't remember the textured grip feeling abrasive in my small, pale hands. Hands that had never tanned despite being drowned in poolside sun just a few months ago when they were still alive, back when I was more than a phantom, too. I was already haunting my mother's house. The girl I was is already dead. So what difference would it make, really? Yet, I felt a sense of fear. I was not afraid to die, but I *was* scared I wouldn't do it right. That, like the fire, I'd somehow live through this too. Allyson Parrish, the invincible girl.

It wasn't as if I'd never shot a gun. In his way of bonding, Mike had taken me to the range plenty of times over the years for "defensive training." As if I'd had anything I needed to defend myself against in our small town. A town that had been rated as one of the safest places to live in America. I scoffed. It hadn't been so safe for the Kingsleys, but I guess gas leaks didn't rank high on the traditional list of dangers.

It was time to quit contemplating, quit worrying. I'd had plenty of target practice, and this target was closer than any I'd tried to hit in the past. I placed the barrel against the soft spot under my jaw and closed my eyes. I whispered goodbye to the saddened room and simultaneously to everyone left who loved me. To Libby. To my mom. I began to count backward from ten.

Ten seconds before I pulled the trigger, I thought of my dad. My moral compass. The best man, the one who every man had to live up to. I wondered if there was a heaven, if this act meant I'd be banned, or if I'd finally get to see him again. How I'd tell him to forget the damn Oreos and that Heaven was so much better as a place and not a name spelled backward. I imagined he'd laugh at that.

Nine seconds before I pulled the trigger, I was still stuck on heaven. Hell was something I was familiar with; I'd been living in hell on and off my whole life. The sickness, my dad, the Kingsleys— they made whatever demon bound to torture me for the rest of eternity look like child's play. Heaven, though. Heaven, I could not imagine. Surely, if there was such a place, the Kingsleys were the kind of people deserving enough to get in. If I were allowed past the pearly gates, then I wouldn't miss their birthday after all. My attendance record would remain flawless.

Eight seconds before I pulled the trigger, I thought of the first birthday we'd spent together— mine barbecuing over the summer when James had accidentally flung one of those mini hot dogs into the pool and the kid from next door had cried, thinking his penis had fallen off from being in the water too long. I recalled Grey's laugh perfectly, open-mouthed, leaving his face in an array of joy. Only a couple of months later, their birthday was held further back at the edge of the fields. Seemingly every kid from our school surrounded the fire pit as cars lined the street, blocking driveways, pissing off the neighbors.

Seven seconds before I pulled the trigger, I thought of the second birthday. How long after the cake and the candles, Grey and I had gotten locked out of the house and taken the Jeep into the field. We'd lined the tailgate with lanterns stolen from the porch. It was the first time I gave myself to him. Like a horror movie, I'd gotten my period but he didn't seem to mind. He didn't crack jokes or let me feel ashamed. His bloody handprints stained my body, and I felt then that I'd become a woman in every way. He whispered over the crickets and frog songs that he'd love me forever.

Six seconds before I pulled the trigger, I remembered the third birthday, the trip we'd taken to Myrtle Beach. Grey, Charlie, and I were high off caffeine, sipping the best sweet tea I'd ever had from the arcade café. The arcade we'd spent hours in every night, winning every game. We filled plastic bags with our prizes: finger traps, plastic poppers, and too much candy we'd never eat. We walked the beach past midnight, stepping over all the jellyfish that had washed up on shore while Grey stopped to pick up each one and throw it back in. Even with the pain they'd caused, Grey swore passionately they didn't deserve to be left for dead.

Five seconds before, I thought of the last birthday. Grey's energy as he woke me up at 5 a.m. to leave. The car ride with Charlie swerving across the road to the airport, Starbucks in hand, playing the alphabet game over our playlist. Central Park Zoo, where Grey had made up narratives for each of the animals. He and Charlie spitballed their imagined dialog back and forth. I can feel the railing of the exhibit, the cold painted metal, like the cold metal of the gun in my hands.

Four seconds, I thought of how they would never have another birthday. They would never grow up. I'd never see

Grey's novels on the best sellers list or Charlie's designs featured in the magazines she used to read.

Three, I thought of how I would never have another birthday. I thought of the things I'd never accomplish. The songs I'd never write.

Two, I grew annoyed with my tears. Annoyed at how my hand shook without permission. How the trigger depressed slowly, too slowly.

One-

I turned towards the sound of the creaking door, and I saw my mother's features change from concerned to horrified.

She dropped the plate of cupcakes she had made, one for each of the people I'd lost, and covered her mouth. Her sobs drowned out the sound of the gun falling from my hands and clattering to the floor. Drowned out the sound of her knees hitting the floor until she screamed "Michael!" and he ran in, dressed in his uniform. All but complete, minus the weapon gleaming in the sunlight as it streamed through the glass.

now, october

CAUGHT up in conversation with Duke and Adaline, Derek and I were both late leaving for campus, so I hadn't had time to stop by my room to change. I showed up to my Harmony and Ear Training class in my two-day unwashed jeans with Derek's shirt tucked in, the sleeves rolled to look as stylish as possible. It's almost too intimate wearing his clothes in public, too much like I'm wearing our secret openly. However, the scent radiating off it, so distinctly him, adds a layer of comfort to my day.

This class has also become one of my favorites. Mrs. Reeves has challenged me to hit notes I didn't think I was capable of. Today, she has paired us off to practice harmonizing with opposing tones. Mine is lighter and more melodic, so I've been matched with a blonde boy named Cooper, who has a deeper baritone.

We jump straight into the assignment. For the next hour, we sing notes in different keys, trying to mimic each other's sound. I'm amused as he attempts to hit my high notes. Sucking in an absurd amount of air, he tries to push it out the way I had instructed. Cooper struggles while I quickly develop his lower keys. Seeing the process behind how he bends his voice clicks in my brain. Despite enjoying the project, I've been watching the clock tick down the minutes. 2:30 is so close. I have a 3 o'clock session with none other than Mr. Derek Rivera. It's only been a few hours, yet I'm already eager to see him again.

I rush to my apartment as soon as class lets out, swinging into my usual spot in the car park. I take the stairs two at a time, pleased to see Riley with his bare feet on the coffee table when I burst through the door. He extends the Post-it I'd left on the fridge in my direction, and my pleasure fades to panic. Offering no explanation, I flee to change. I have less than fifteen minutes to get back to campus.

"Alley-Cat, that shirt is *so* not a part of your wardrobe," Riley yells distastefully.

Ignoring him, I scramble, preparing to throw on the first thing I find. The clothes in my drawers are not my clothes. They're my sizes, but I definitely did not buy them. I'm not sure where *my* clothes have gone.

"Riley!" I scream in sheer annoyance. His laugh trails through the crack under the door. I end up in a sweater, fleece-lined tights, and a leather skirt. It only slightly alleviates my anger that he arranged my drawers by outfit. Thankfully, my underwear hadn't changed spots or style. I think I may have murdered him if they had. I run a brush through my hair before speeding out to grab my keys. I'm down to ten minutes, the exact amount of time it will take me to drive to the auditorium

"We'll talk about this," I gesture to my outfit. "later," I growl at Riley.

"I'll pick you up after class, Al. We can grab a pint and discuss this intriguing note you left since I know for *a fact*

Libby is still in Rome." Riley snarks with his signature grin. Groaning, I jet out the door.

Derek is at the piano when I enter the auditorium sometime later. In my haste, I do not make a quiet entrance. The doors clatter closed loudly behind me. The last session must have wrapped early because the band appears restless. An impatient Jane glares, flipping her attention between me and the clock.

"You're tardy." She accuses when I'm close enough to the stage.

"I know. I'm sorry." I apologize. It isn't worth pointing out that I'm exactly two minutes late. Her reaction makes it seem more like an hour. She's right, though. If I were late to a job by two minutes, I'd still be recorded as late. If I had an audience waiting for me, wasting their time would have been disrespectful. I should have stayed in yesterday's gunky outfit. I try to focus on now and be here instead of letting something small work itself into a spiral.

"What have you prepared?" Derek asks.

His phone lights up on top of the piano by his notebook, and I see the date for the first time today. It's October 14th. Grey and Charlie's birthday. Did I fool around with Derek on Grey's birthday? Was it after twelve when we did things? I think I might be sick. I picture Grey's scar falling into his dimples the first time *he* touched me on this very same day. The simple combination of letters and numbers on that tiny screen is all it takes to make my world flip upside down again. I'd thought I'd moved forward, but time no longer feels linear. It's in a loop, caving in on itself.

Last year, Grey and Charlie's birthday was the day I was committed. After I'd dropped the gun, Michael had called the hospital. An hour later, two men in matching mint polos arrived, putting me in the back of a medi-van to a facility somewhere in the mountains. I had no visitors. For a week, I was more drugged up than I had ever been in my life.

When the pills weren't acting as a sedative, they acted as a truth serum, forcing me to relive my trauma while the other patients screamed about theirs in the halls. I'd listen to them yelling into the night from behind doors that were always cracked open, doors that could not lock regardless. There was a lack of security then, the way there is a lack of security now. I feel like nothing is keeping me safe from the outside world. All my demons bubble to the surface.

"Miss Parrish? Have you prepared anything?" Derek asks again.

I shake my head no. I don't think I'm answering his question. I think I'm trying to defy the universe. *No, they're not dead.* I reach for my phone while Derek steps away to speak to Jane and the band. I don't listen to what he says, no longer caring. I dial Charlie. If it had all been a lie, I'd forgive her if she were somehow alive enough to answer. I'd take the deceit if it meant I somehow got a miracle. I pray. I believe so hard that it's possible that I recoil when I get her voicemail.

"Hey, it's Charlie. Leave a voicemail, loser." Her voice rings out clearly as if she had just recorded it yesterday. I remember the day she did record it. She was scrolling through Twitter with one hand and painting her toenails pink with the other when she decided she needed a bigger change. The bigger change was rerecording her voicemail. So typically Charlie. I see her as if she is four feet away and not four months and a year.

It's as though I've melted into the earth, into the under-world. There's so much ash, I can taste it. I can't breathe or hear and everything everywhere, it hurts. My dreams flash behind my eyes, Charlie screaming as she burns. Screaming like she only ever does in my subconscious. The night of the fire, investigators said she would have been dead before I even made it inside. What if I had followed him home instead of waiting? I knew something was off. Did he know he was going to die that night?

I think through how odd he was acting for the billionth time. Grey was rarely reserved or in a bad mood. He was always affectionate. That night was so different. He seemed detached at dinner. I had thought something was going on with us, but what if he knew somehow that he had reached the end?

There are stories out there about things like that. Accounts of loved ones acting strange on the day they died. Adults who had stopped showing their parents affection suddenly hugged them goodbye and told them they loved them before getting into a car accident on the way home.

The day my dad died, he had popped into my room to hug me before he left. Usually, he just said it from the door. It could be possible that we get a warning before we die or perhaps a gut feeling. But even if Grey did know, even if he had confided it to me, would I have been able to stop it?

Images flip through my brain of different outcomes. Outcomes where I show up early and ask them out for ice cream. Where I ask Charlie to sleep over that morning. Where Grey doesn't leave my front porch. Or where I urged Marilyn to let Gigi go to her friend's sleepover even though it was a school night. Would one of them being alive be better than all of them dead? I imagine their suffering at being the only survivor and decide it's pointless to consider. It only hurts more to imagine any one of them in that much pain. It'd be triple what I feel. Their whole lives were entwined. I only had four years.

The piano, the people, they've all disappeared. I redial Charlie so I can hear her again. And again. She says the same thing every time. Not even a syllable of variation. I haven't called in months. Her voice is so alive and whole. I push the phone away tersely. I think my heart might explode in my chest. I shouldn't be here. I should be in my room covered in fuzzy things, staring out at the sky, a wall, or anything else that can't tell me it's all going to be okay. It's not. Nothing will ever be okay again.

"Ally."

The room is hot. It's too hot. I hiss as my shoulder begins to burn—the crack of the beam thunders before weighing me down. I collapse under the weight. I need to get it off.

"Hey, not here. Come on."

I navigate through the burning hallway. Marilyn and James are on this floor. Last door on the right. I could never make it up the stairs. Maybe I was trying to save the wrong people. The door opens by itself, and I step back into the foyer. *No!* They need to have another birthday. They're too young.

I'm choking on the smoke. There's too much of it. I feel like I'm still carrying the beam on my back. It is excruciating. I feel for the molten wood, trying to shake it off. My shirt lifts over my head as something cold rests against my shoulder, and the pain begins to subside.

"There we go," Derek says.

He sits on the ground across from me in the burning living room. I'm leaning against the Kingsley's couch. I want to scream at him to run and get out. He can't burn here, too. But my throat is too sore. I've inhaled too much. I try to speak and croak instead. He shakes his head for me not to talk.

"Did you know Scotland's national animal is a unicorn? My mum told me that when I was only a boy, it always sort of stuck with me." He's leaning against the bricks of the fireplace. The flames are everywhere but the confined space where they should be. "It fits in with all the other legends, I suppose. The Loch Ness monster, kelpies, selkies... the ghost pipers." He trails off ominously. I feel my eyes widen, and he leans in, sure he's captured my attention.

"The ghost pipers were my version of the boogeyman, Al. They haunted my dreams. I'd wake up to the sound of bagpipes in my bedroom, too scared to go back to sleep. Scottish legends aren't just fairies and lake monsters. No, they go deeper, more firmly rooted in history than that.

Back in the sixteen hundreds, the English Civil War exasperated a bitter rivalry between two clans: the Campbells and the MacDonalds. The MacDonalds stormed Duntrune, the castle that had been home to the Campbells. They took it overnight, and while they sieged control, a piper played, who had been gifted to them by a warlord they'd encountered along their journey. Pipers were sacred to the clans, superstitious even. They kept spirits high, often bringing victory with their songs. It was deemed bad luck to kill a piper, which is why when the rest of the Campbell clan returned, they killed all of the MacDonalds, keeping only the piper alive to play for them.

Alas, after some time, the warlord came to meet the MacDonalds, who he still believed to reside in the castle. The Campbells had planned for this, preparing the piper to play a song of welcome to trick them into an ambush. But pipers are strong-willed, spirited, and loyal. Instead of a song of welcome, he played a song of warning, causing the warlord to turn his ships around. Enraged, the Campbells punished the piper by cutting off his hands so he could never play again. Still today, his warning can be heard through the walls of Duntrune.

During a renovation in the 1800s, the skeleton of a man was found without his hands. In another part of the castle, years later, during another excavation, they discovered his severed hands. Needless to say, learning my ghost story was based in truth had me mental." Derek retells.

"Your mom told you that story?" I ask, floored. I can't imagine a mother telling her small child that legend.

"God, no." He laughs. "I saw it on the History Channel. She only ever told me about the unicorn and the selkies." Selkies?

"Now you're just making up words." I protest.

"Oh, come on, Al! Selkies!" He genuinely acts like I'm going to cave and tell him I've known what he was talking about this whole time. "Seals who turn into beautiful women?" He tries again. Whatever fundamental memory he is trying to trigger does not exist.

"No?" He asks.

"No." I shake my head, laughing.

"The selkie and the fisherman?"

"I got nothing, but that sounds more like a story I can see a parent telling their child." I play, gently kicking his leg with my foot. We're sitting on the floor in his living room. Only this isn't his living room. We're in his office at school, and I am panicking. A minute ago, I was convinced this was the conservatory. I feel like I've lost time. I can't remember how I got here. I don't like that feeling.

The mental barriers that normally give me a sense of security evaporate. Did I freak out? Who saw me? Was I onstage performing when it happened? Fuck, dude. I'm not wearing a shirt. If I stripped in front of the school, I don't know how I'll be able to go back out there. Not if I just put on a show of how psychologically broken I am.

"Ally, look at me." Derek has moved to sit in front of me. He brushes my hair away from my face. I can tell it's matted with sweat, the big clumps moving together at one time. He works his fingers through the strands and tucks them away before restarting. I focus on the feeling of him touching me. Even if I did freak out, he still seems to want me if his crossing a million lines is any indication.

What is the last thing I remember? I can work through this. I can't. I don't remember anything before five minutes ago.

"Derek?" I ask. He raises his eyebrows in attention. I let my eyelids fall closed.

"What happened?"

He doesn't answer. I peek up at him. He's waiting.

"You showed up for our session to work on your song. You started to have a panic attack. I told Jane and the band we would do a stripped-down song from scratch so they wouldn't be needed. You were trying to get your shirt off, so I brought you here so you could." He recounts. He doesn't seem upset, or angry, or even concerned.

"This is normal for you?" I push, confused by his reaction. He should be running for the hills, not looking at me like it's still last night.

"I used to get them a lot after my mom died. At first, I didn't want to talk about it." He sighs, falling back to a comfortable sitting position but remaining near enough that he can still touch me. His knees sit on either side of my own, and he drapes his elbows over them lazily. The contact between our legs shares a comfortable heat that radiates through me.

"There didn't seem to be a good time to bring it up in

conversation. By the time I did want to talk about it, time had passed. I learned my grief made people uncomfortable. They had moved on. I didn't understand how they could. I felt angry, resentful." His face scrunches as he recounts the uncomfortable details. "I put all my emotions in a box, but the smallest, most random thing would shake me, and I would explode. The more I tried to hold it in, the worse the panic attacks got." Derek explains, reaching into the floor beside him to offer my sweater back.

That is the closest anyone has gotten to accurately capturing what this has been like. I slip my shirt over my head, immediately placing his palms back against my face. His lips tick up at the corners he leans forward to press them to my forehead. The pounding in my chest has slowed down. I'm starting to regain my barriers, to feel safe again. We're at school violating every boundary in the book, but he doesn't seem to mind like he would have a week ago.

"You were ten?" I pry so I don't overthink. Derek talking about pretty much anything gets me out of my head.

"Yeah. Ten years of sun." He says the words exactly as he's thought them a million times. I'm sure by how confidently he speaks them and how raw his voice is when they come out. My heart melts in my chest. "I used to call her that." He smiles like a little boy and looks down at the ground. "My sun. The guiding light." He emphasizes the 't' in light.

I can't stop smiling despite the subject matter.

"What?" He asks, laughing at my expression. "Are you having a laugh at my pain? You really are a sick one, aren't you?"

"No! No!" I bubble back. "It's just I used to think of my dad as the moon. He made me feel so safe. Better than any night light." I've never told anyone that.

"Ally, *that's* your song." Derek looks at me in awe. I understand immediately.

"One more story, please, don't go so soon,
Stay a while longer, Mr. Moon?
Tuck me in and sing a lullaby before our 'Goodnight.'
You are my favorite night light."

I sing, the lyrics popping in my head as soon as he suggested it. He hops up at once, lifting me to my feet. Running after him down the hallway, we exit onto the stage. He slides onto the piano bench almost comedically and begins to play. The music is exactly right for the song. In the next half hour, we have the verses and the bridge worked out. Derek formulated the music while I worked out the lines. Whenever I'd get stuck, he'd ask me something about my dad, and I'd find the words. I sing it through a final time.

"That's it." Derek sits back. He looks like he just made magic, wonderstruck and dumbfounded. It's a beautiful expression on him.

"Sometimes, I catch myself wondering if I grew up the way he would have wanted. If I would have turned out to be the same person if he had lived longer. Do you think your mom would be proud of you?"

"I don't know." He shrugs. "I hope so. And Al, you may not have grown into the person your father imagined, but you grew into exactly who you're supposed to be. I *know* he'd be proud of that."

He speaks with such conviction that I believe him. We sit staring at each other, our bond unspoken but evident. How can I already love him? This whole time I spent avoiding and desiring, was I falling? His mouth opens like he wants to say more when the door to the auditorium flies open.

Derek has transformed again. His posture straight from relaxed. Rigid feels like a better word, but I get the feeling that only I would see it that way. I'm the only one who's ever seen him in any other fashion.

"Mr. Parasons." Derek addresses in his teacher voice. Even his voice has changed in the presence of others. He keeps so much of himself hidden. Has he always been simply an actor playing his part? Would I have ever known the difference otherwise? I love Derek's anger. In every role, it looks the same on him: hard eyes, tense jaw, apparent restraint.

"Mr. Rivera." Riley taunts, approaching the stage. "Is *my girlfriend* done here? She should have finished up thirty minutes ago, yeah?"

Derek shifts uncomfortably.

"Riley, I never agreed to the girlfriend cover story." I sigh. His eyes widen in surprise, peeking around to where Derek sits beside me, partially eclipsed from Riley's view.

"So, it finally happened," Riley smirks at the two of us.

"I don't know what you're talking about." I lie. I try to sound convincing.

"One day, you're going to admit it to me, Ally. I'll wait outside. My offer stands, though. We'd do great at being each other's beards." He winks before retreating off.

I groan and wait for him to reach the doors before facing Derek. His expression is surprisingly amused. His shoulders shake as he starts to laugh.

"Beards? Riley is gay?" Derek bellows, laughing harder.

"He and his boyfriend helped me move out of my dorm. He's at our place most nights, actually." I admit. "Riley's been pushing for this whole girlfriend beard since our first class."

"Ally, I seriously wanted to punch the kid's face in." He smiles. "I've had to fight every impulse to keep myself in check."

"I know. It wasn't my secret to tell." I shrug. Derek processes this as an array of emotions cross his face.

"Come over?" He asks after a beat.

"Later? Riley switched my wardrobe when I was gone and needs a serious talking to."

"Ah, so that's what's with the skirt. You do not strike me as a skirt kind of girl, Parrish."

I roll my eyes. "I used to be very much a Disney princess, thank you. My attire was filled with pastel sweaters and floral dresses. I even wore heels and makeup." I gasp in mock horror.

"What changed?" Derek pries, seeing through my humorous explanation.

"Me," I admit honestly. "I have to go before my pup gets too impatient and makes another scene."

His warm expression follows me out the door.

then, halloween

THE LAST HALLOWEEN we'd spent together, we went to the annual party at a graveyard near the school. Charlie had been discussing our costumes since summer but had yet to come up with an idea that allowed us to go as a trio.

We were deciding between two options employing our usual way of making decisions back then: Rock, Paper, Scissors. I'm not sure who came up with it, but as soon as I'd made the motion to start the game, someone yelled, "Wait!" and suddenly, a month later, we were walking among the gravestones with Grey dressed as a giant rock, Charlie as a pair of scissors, and I was a blank sheet of paper. It had seemed fitting then; I was always the plainest of the bunch. I liked being paper.

Once we'd reached the crowd, Charlie was hit with a wave of scissoring jokes— a fallout she had not anticipated. Being Charlie, she went along with it, leaning into the persona. Grey got slapped with a rack of "rock hard" jokes, naturally most of which came from his best friends Chris and Ollie. I was paper. Paper didn't get any jokes. I *really liked* being paper.

I'd always loved Halloween. I loved the new Disney Channel original movies that came out every year, the candy corn, and the air of possibility that hung in the night. For the first time, I didn't mind not having a bigger crowd to cling to. This was an event where I'd felt content to fade into the background, hot cider in hand, ready to people-watch. Growing up in the hospital, I'd never gotten to trick-or-treat as a child. These parties were the closest I'd gotten.

Our class had started a small fire down in the grove – a short stretch of bare trees scattered some yards away from the tombstones. Living in a rural town, most people had brought their own lawn chairs, but someone had thought ahead and set up bales of hay. Grey and I had draped a blanket across one and began roasting marshmallows from a bag being passed around. It wasn't long before the scary stories started, fueled by the graves around us.

One girl told a story about her cat being locked in a basement room. She kept hearing scratching and went to investigate. Upon opening the door, she'd seen glowing red eyes dart under a chair in the room. When she'd gotten on her knees to lure him out of hiding, she'd gotten a phone call from her mom stating she was on her way back from the vet with their two cats.

Another spoke of her grandparents' home; she'd always feared this one room where her grandmother kept a collection of antique dolls. There was this one life-sized doll she used to play with that she'd named Betsy. One day, when she was brushing out the doll's hair, her arm had raised straight up in the air. Years later, her grandfather told her they'd bought the house cheap at auction as the previous owner had died in the house— a woman named Betsy. The doll had since disappeared, no one remembering its existence outside of her.

This went on for a while, one ghost story sparking another. As I continued to get spooked, Grey tucked me into his arms, holding me close.

"It's okay, Al. Ghosts can never hurt you like the living can." He'd whispered solemnly. I'm sure it was meant to comfort me, but somehow, that acknowledgment sat with me deeper than any scary story had.

now, halloween

WE ARRIVE in a field nestled between the hills. The first thing I notice when we get out of the Jetta is the layer of trash already littering the ground. There are too many feet, too many rain boots, stomping the articles into the dirt and muck for me to make out what they used to be. The beat of the music courses through the ground like an earthquake. It's louder, thumping harder than my heartbeat until I can't discern which is which. Riley's mouth parts in awe before his signature smirk takes over.

"Let's rock it, poppit!" He leans close, shouting over the music, but his words quickly become whisps, lost in the night. I take the hand he's extended and follow along. I've never felt so much energy in one place. People pass by like neon streaks, all in costume, high off something.

Riley's been talking up "Doomsday" for weeks now. Every year, there's a party like this on Halloween, and he's never missed one. Not since he was thirteen when he would sneak into the back of his older brothers' pick-up truck. There, he'd hide under blankets, waiting until the coast was clear and he could join the party. When they finally caught him, he described it as the worst beating he had ever endured. However, he insists it was worth it.

He'd gotten to snog an upperclassman named Lucy that year. He swears it was Lucy's putrid breath, her glob of not-so-cherry lip gloss that had clung to his lips even hours after the kiss, that had turned him. After that, he didn't fancy ever to kiss another girl again. Regardless of how his tastes had changed, he entered secondary school as a legend.

Dragging me through the parade of people, Riley tripped over the lace of his dress every few steps. We've been on a Pirates of the Caribbean kick lately, which heavily inspired our costumes and matching tattoos. Earlier in the week, he'd dragged me with him to get the iconic Mark of the Sparrow inked on his forearm. Somehow, I entered the shop purely as a support system and exited with the mirror image, my very first tattoo. While he stuck to the original outline, I made a slight modification. I'd asked for a phoenix instead of a sparrow.

Riley was supposed to come dressed as Jack, while I was to be outfitted as Elizabeth Swan. A few nights ago, Drunk Ally thought it would be funny to make Drunk Riley try on her costume. At some point, he'd decided we were not switching back. This is why I was here now, in my beaded mustache, while Riley's scrawny, fit shoulders bulged out of my corset, causing me to erupt in giggles for the millionth time. I begin to lose my nerves as I trail behind him into the center of the chaos.

When we stop, he tosses me one of the airplane bottles he'd stuffed into his bust. Looping our arms, we throw back the contents, discarding the bottles. Normally, I'd be against littering, but he'd informed me earlier that a clean-up crew would sweep the place tomorrow. While I hadn't wanted to come, Riley had piqued my intrigue with the premise of the event.

Doomsday had been going on ever since anyone could remember. Riley's parents, even his parent's parents, had all been in attendance during their youth. It had never been shut down by the police. The theme and the location were kept secret until the week before when The Scavenger took place. Clues were hidden throughout town in the bottom of coffee cups and scrawled along the stalls of club restrooms. All had to be collected in order to string together the GPS coordinates.

The idea of a party untouched by modern methods, clean of social media, had excited me. Truthfully, I missed celebrating Halloween. I missed dressing up and getting lost in the spirit of the holiday.

Derek was wrapped up in one of Duke's parties tonight, a party I would have been attending if Matt had been able to come to this. Unfortunately, the football team had a big game tomorrow, forcing Matt to go to bed early, where he would most likely be fast asleep by now.

Outside of our initial shot, Riley has abstained from alcohol, proclaiming himself as my designated driver. He's been insistent on me having the "full Doomsday experience." We've merged with his old school friends, who have quickly taken to Drunk Ally.

Someone, I'm assuming Riley, presses a cup into my hands, and I tip it back. A girl begins to put some sort of dye in my hair, turning the blonde strands pink. It feels good, tingly almost, so I let her. Riles begins to get peer pressured to perform on stage, and I'm so proud of how far he's come from the boy who had stage fright less than a month ago that I shoo him along. He begs me to sing with him, but I can barely walk a straight line without clinging to his friend Penny for support. I like Penny. Her hair is copper, like her name, and I think there's a song in there somewhere.

I cheer for him with the rest of the group as he mounts the stage, which is really just a bunch of tailgates sat side by side with some plywood ratchet strapped to the tops. It reminds me of home, and my tummy becomes honey, warm, and elated.

"Riley!" we all scream, whooping loudly. The slew of drunken strangers pick up on our calls, and shortly, everyone in the vicinity who is not vomiting or latched onto the mouth of another is screaming with us.

As he sings, the strobes flash wildly, like artificial lightning, and the wind picks up rustling my unicorn hair. I feel epic. Raves are way better than high school parties. The people are so much nicer. Everybody is my friend. I have a thousand friends here. I begin to count them.

Tinkerbell is definitely my friend. Harry Potter is my homie fo' rizzle. *Wolverine might be too spicy to be my friend,* I think to myself as he flashes his blades at me wickedly. I repeat the motion, and he becomes less fierce, breaking into laughter like a bubbling brook. Can streams laugh? Fuck it, they certainly can. Damn it, who am I kidding? Wolverine is, beyond doubt, a buddy.

I'm absolutely jubilant, clinging onto Penny and this other guy to my right. I feel like a little kid squished between two adults, ready to swing into the air. Between the strobes, I catch glimpses of more costumes and more friends when I see *them*— Rock, Paper, Scissors— disappearing into the crowd. Time seems to slow down, the smile slipping from my face. I untangle my arms from other arms and follow in their footsteps. I reach out, latching onto the bicep of the rock, and he swings around, not a rock at all but a stone.

"What the fu—Oh, *hi*." Grandpappie from Frozen winks at me. My stomach churns from mistaking the identity of the man behind the costume.

"Sorry, I thought you were someone else." I stutter quickly, fleeing for the bathroom. I'm quickly coming to the realization that I've allowed myself to drink too much.

A new song takes place of the last, the beat reaching my bones, sending waves of vibration through my body. My achromatic despair fades back to sparkler pink. I stretch to the stars, wondering what it would be like to stir the sky with my fingertips, if it would feel like feathers or like pushing around pebbles underwater.

I sway my hips to the music, losing myself. Arms wrap around my waist, and the smell of cedar wood infiltrates my nose. I should push the hallucination away, but it's so nice to feel *him* again. I've *missed* him so much.

"I've been looking for you, Ally." His suede voice is better than the song, better than any song. Instead of retreating, I lean into the delusion.

"Grey," I whisper, turning to bury my face in his neck. His tanned fingers push the hair away from my shoulder and lean into whisper.

"Are you writing poetry again, Als? What is it tonight?" He muses softly, rocking my hips in time with his own.

"The stars. What do you think it would feel like to touch them?" I ask, and he laughs, open-mouthed like he can't get enough oxygen.

The thought picks away at me like a hungry crow. I run my fingers through his thick curls when someone yells,

"Fireworks!" The word *fire* sticks in my mind as the explosions start. Then the smell comes, that retched sulfur. It's too similar, paralleling the smell *that* night, the night I can't seem to put together in more than a collage of flashes right now.

Things feel wrong. I need to see Grey. I need his apple eyes to reassure me, but there's only coal sitting in their place—only the ruminants of a charred man.

Finally, I push him off. His hands are made of flames, leaving burns on my skin. Someone is screaming. I cover my ears to block it out. I think it's Charlie. Charlie's always the one screaming. Riley appears out of nowhere, his dress ripping as he throws Grey to the ground and begins to hit him.

"What the fuck did you do to her?" He yells, throwing punches in too quick a succession for an answer to be plausible. Coming to my senses, I run into the commotion. I'm always running in instead of out. Maybe that's my problem.

"Grey!" I shriek. "Grey, no! Riley, stop! Please stop." I sob, tugging at his arm. Riley stares back at me apprehensively. "Can't you see he's burning, Riles? Please get off!" I plead. Grey laughs, but it's the wrong laugh. It's Not Grey.

"Man, it's hitting her hard." The guy says. Stepping off, Riley picks him up by the collar of his Gaston costume.

"What did you give her, Harry?" Riley asks angrier than I've ever seen him. His voice comes out too high, as if he's inhaled helium. I flashback to the Alvin and the Chipmunks VHS tapes I watched religiously as a kid. I become paranoid that the chipmunks are trapped inside Riley's throat, trying to escape. He's so upset, it seems like the wrong time to check.

"Just a little liquid E, mate." Not Grey says with a

twisted smile before spitting a glob of blood into the grass. I shudder.

"Wait—Not Grey drugged me?" I ask in confusion. "Not Grey sucks," I exclaim. Then I giggle for no reason in particular. Riley rolls his eyes at my commentary, shoves the guy back to the ground, and drags me back to the car by the arm.

"I don't really want to go. Things aren't so terrible now that I know it's the drugs. No one's actually burning, Riles. Isn't that great?"

"No, Al, it's really not great."

"Don't be grumpy. Hey, have your hands always been so soft? What kind of miracle lotion do you use on these puppies?" I ponder, examining his hands when we get to the car. Even the callouses he's built up from playing are soft.

"Lube."

"Ew. Gross." I drop his hands, rubbing mine on my pants hard enough to create friction. I can only see Matt's jizz like particles under a UV light as if Riley somehow transferred it over, and now I can't get off, no matter how I try.

"Get in the car." He laughs.

* * *

On the drive home, I'm incredibly bored. I explore the center console, then the glove box. When he's not paying attention, I slide the bag of joints into my pocket from his stash.

"Ally, I saw that. I'm supposed to be the obnoxious one, remember?" He sighs, falling back heavily against the aged gray cloth of the Jetta's seating.

"Rats! You caught me. Does that mean I can't keep your weed?" I tilt my head curiously.

"No, put it back." He demands, unable to hide his humor.

"No way to treat your best friend, but okay." I snark sarcastically.

The headlights bounce off the road and reflect onto his face, highlighting the youth of his smile. He subtly raps his fingers on the steering wheel in time with the song playing quietly over the radio. An overwhelming sadness comes over me.

"Riles, Charlie would have really liked you, you know?" Tears spill onto my cheeks. "Don't die, okay? I don't want to lose another best friend."

Riley turns to me with a serious expression. It's probably the first time I've ever seen him serious. Taking my hand in his, he starts to say something when my phone begins to buzz. He nods for me to answer.

"Hello?" I squawk into the receiver, my voice mimicking a parrot, which I find hilarious, and I snicker uncontrollably. Riley muffles a *"bloody hell"* from the driver's seat, forcing me to stick out my tongue in retaliation.

"Ally?" Derek asks over the receiver, capturing my attention.

"Derek." I sigh pleasantly.

"Are you drunk?" It's hard to hear over the chatter in the background. It dies down the further he moves away from the commotion. When it falters off, he repeats the question.

"Surprisingly, no. Well, maybe a little. Or I was. I don't really know. The drugs have made that part fuzzy. Not Grey 454? 478? Not Grey Four-hundred-and-something drugged me. Riley gave him a knuckle sandwich, and now he's taking me home, so I probably shouldn't be talking to you. Shhh." I explain, giggling.

"Ally, send me your address." He demands.

"Negative. I'm drugged, not stupid. That's a bad career move, Chief."

"Ally." He warns.

"Fine." I sulk, sending him the address.

now, october

SOMETIME AFTER WE arrive back at the flat, there's a knock at the door. Toweling my hair from the shower, I bound over to open it.

Derek is waiting outside, looking crisp in an expensive tux. Before now, I could never picture him standing in my hall, let alone visiting me at my flat. It had seemed too extraordinary to imagine. I glance around nervously, worried about the implications of being seen, but he doesn't seem aware of anything outside of me.

His attention is overwhelming. I've never been the center of anyone's universe before, but here and now, I seem to be the center of his. The angry set of his jaw eases the further I prop open the door. His face breaks into a genuine smile as he begins to laugh. I don't care what he's laughing at; I'm just happy to see him. Pulling him in from the hall by his sleeve, I step into his arms.

"What are you doing here?" I question, happily encased in his scent. It's more defined tonight, the left-over smells of the party lingering on his clothes. Encased in the florals from the garden, I'm picking up a more pronounced tangerine, juniper, clove. I want to make a candle out of it.

"You sent me the address a half hour ago. You don't remember?" He asks, gently tugging the mustache from my upper lip. I must have forgotten to take it off. Pushing up onto my tiptoes, I press my lips to his, relieved that I *had* remembered to brush my teeth while in the bathroom. He tastes like he smells, strengthening my addiction. I question how his mouth has already learned mine so well, the two moving in complete synchrony.

"Al! Don't fuck up the food!" Riley yells from the kitchen. Breaking the kiss, I furrow my brows, confused at how I could "fuck up" accepting takeout.

"I don't remember ordering food either," I explain breathily to Derek, shrugging as he chuckles at my clueless state.

Riley teeters in from the kitchen, his costume soaked and muddy as it drips on the rug. He stalls completely when he spots Derek and looks between the two of us awkwardly, his mouth hanging open. I stare at the puddle forming beneath his feet. I can't recall what the hell happened the past few hours or how my best friend ended up looking like such a mess.

"Shit, dude. I thought you were kidding about Rivera. Fucking hell." Riley shakes his head in disbelief. "So, I was right the whole time?"

"Why are you wet?" I wonder aloud, ignoring his questions.

"You can't be serious," Riley states, fully appalled to the point he staggers backward. "I've been cleaning up the flood your drugged ass left in our kitchen."

"What are you talking about?"

As an afterthought, I glance over at Derek, expecting

him to put some distance between us with Riley in the room. I suppose I'm anticipating the formality he usually carries around others, but it does not come. He keeps his proximity to my side, his fingers finding mine as Riley speaks.

Riley proceeded to explain how he unlocked the door, and I began to chant, "Time to be clean." as I proceeded to strip in the kitchen, confusing the sink hose for the shower head. When he attempted to stop me, I threw a nasty right hook and accused him of being a pervert for spying on me in the bath. Once he'd wrangled me to the *actual* bath, he'd returned to mop up the mess I left on the floor.

Derek tries to remain irritated with him for leaving me unattended at the party, but the growing bruise around Riley's eye from the punch I'd landed has helped to soften the tension. Perhaps it's the drugs still in my system, but I begin to laugh, finding the whole thing rather funny.

After reenacting our homecoming events, Riley showers, and I show Derek to my room so he can change out of his tux. I fight the growing urge to strip him out of it myself, but I'm too put off by the mess scattered about my room. I hadn't been anticipating company, or I'd have tidied up. With a final glance at the dirty clothes piled in the corner, I leave him be, departing to throw the towels in the wash Riley had used to dry the floor.

When Derek returns, he looks like my Derek in his plain white tee. He's wearing a pair of sweats I've never seen before, and I try not to ogle him as he kneels to start a fire in the hearth. Once the food arrives, I start up a movie and shuffle a deck of cards while we wait for Riley to begin eating.

Soon enough, the three of us are gathered around the coffee table, shoveling ramen into our mouths while Derek drills Riley on how I got drugged in the first place. Once Derek's curiosity is satisfied and he decides he's pleased with how things were handled, the night becomes easier. We get into a spirited game of cards, and I dare say the boys are even having fun together.

"Rivera, it's freaking me out seeing you in normal clothes, mate." Riley jokes.

"Stop trying to distract me. You're not winning this round." Derek fires back.

I'm almost happy things played out the way they did, drugs and all, as it brought me to this moment, watching the two of the most influential people in my life bond together. I feel completely content, entirely at home— until Derek steals the game out from under me.

"No!" I shout, slamming my hand down on the coffee table. Derek tosses his head back in laughter.

"I told you. I am champion." He smiles triumphantly.

"Ugh." I groan. This is my third losing hand. At this point, it is after 2 a.m., and I'm feeling deeply nostalgic for my old sleepovers with Grey and Charlie. I always lost then, too. Cards were Grey's forte, not mine.

"Grey?" Derek asks warily.

My eyes go wide in alarm. "*What?*"

"You said 'Cards were Grey's forte.' Who is Grey?" His face is arduous. He was agitated enough with everything else tonight; this is the last thing I want to bring up now that the three of us are in a good spot. I deal another hand.

"Your go." I propose, hoping this will be one of those times he lets it go.

"Are you avoiding my question?" He asks, eyebrows raised. *No such luck, kid,* I think to myself.

I sit in silence for a moment, picking at the tassels of the blanket I've wrapped myself in. Riley's on the floor surrounded by pillows he's spread out. *Harry Potter and the Philosopher's Stone* is playing in the background. Combined with the candles and friendly fire, the room is warmly illuminated. It starkly contrasts the cold I feel seeping out from me, the cold that always comes with the reminder of what has died.

"Yes," I say at last. I *am* avoiding the question.

"Why?" Derek cocks his head to the side. His pine tree eyes are piercing, but his body language opposes their seriousness. I am always delighted at his juxtapositions, amused at his ability to be so many people. Right now, he is young and curious. He is not acting jealous like I would have expected.

I look to Riley for a way out, but he stares at me with the same morbid curiosity. I can't find an excuse that doesn't involve lying to them. It makes the cozy room suddenly too small, too claustrophobic.

"I don't want to talk about this," I tell them, hoping it's enough.

"With all due respect, Als, you haven't *stopped* talking about this. Earlier, you pulled me off of that asshole screaming '*Grey*,' then it was '*Not Grey drugged me*,' now '*Cards were Grey's forte*.' I think you might *need* to talk about this." Riley interjects. "Who's Grey?" He prompts again.

Even in the light of the uncomfortable inquisition, I am drawn to them. These are *my* boys. I want the topic to shift. I want to lie on the floor in the sea of pillows and watch the movie, or climb into Derek's lap, or laugh with them for hours about impossible things. As much as I want to live in a thousand other scenarios, these are the people I want a future with, which means I have to tell them the truth.

"My boyfriend back home." I start. Derek's gaze shoots

up from the cards in his hand to meet mine. His spine corrects itself, becoming taut.

"Your boyfriend?" Riley sputters, beer leaving his mouth and spilling onto the table. The look on Derek's face is disgusted. He hates the sound of the words, hates the idea of anyone else in that role.

"He *was*," I say calmly, though I feel nothing of the sort.

"Was," Derek repeats, settling. "So, you talk about your old boyfriend when you play cards with your new boyfriend?" He asks as the new thought overlaps the last. Now, I see the jealousy, but by his comical tone, he's trying hard not to let it get to him.

"Is that what you are? My boyfriend?" I tease.

Riley scoffs, annoyed at the shift in conversation. He knows my tactics for getting off-topic firsthand. Derek is obviously my boyfriend. However, with our situation, I've never had to define it. Before tonight, no one outside of Duke has known enough to question it. I wonder if that's how he thinks of me, as his *girlfriend*. I've never referred to him by the title, even in my head. He's always just been Derek—the person I most want to be around.

"Yes," Derek answers without further discussion. "You loved him?" He pushes, steering the subject matter back.

"More than anything," I admit softly, closing my eyes. "He was my first."

"First love?"

"First everything," I answer, opening my eyes. Riley listens intently, looking between us as Derek absorbs the new information. I can visibly see the internal battle play out in his features: the stubborn, jealous man versus the intrigued one.

Flashes of every first I shared with Grey circulate through my brain. The first time I ever slept in his bed, in any boy's bed. Our first kiss on New Year's. When he became my first boyfriend. The first time we made love outside in the rain when we got locked out of the house that summer. I see his laugh and his scar and his always-there smile. It hurts so much I have to wrap my arms around my stomach to keep it from caving in.

"How did you meet?" Derek asks, the intrigue winning out.

"My friend, Charlie, was his sister," I admit. Recognition dawns in Riley's eyes, and I know, somehow, he's already figured out how the story ends.

"That's convenient," Derek mutters, seemingly more annoyed. From his perspective, I see the sleepover crossovers, all the times Grey would have been around while Charlie and I were together. I can't speak against it, he'd be right. "She was a good friend?"

"My *best* friend," I confess, feeling sad momentarily before I remember all the reasons *why* she was my best friend, all the good she brought into my life. I tell them what she was like, her designs, and how she'd market them with my songs, always encouraging me. Derek lights up as I talk about her, and then his eyebrows crease. "But Riley is your best friend now?"

"Yes. Riley is my best friend now." I laugh, reaching across the table to ruffle Riley's hair.

We've switched games. We're playing twenty questions on my life's biggest tragedy, and I might actually be enjoying it. Or perhaps it's like that first morning waking up at Derek's. I'm enjoying getting to talk about the Kingsleys instead of keeping them locked away like my dirty little secret, like something I've been too ashamed to speak of.

"No more Charlie?" Derek asks playfully, sipping his beer.

"No. No more Charlie." The sadness creeps back in. I hear it tearing at the edges of my voice.

"Did he break up with you?" The gears spin in Derek's head, searching to find reason for the pain I'm in. It would make sense if Grey had broken my heart and Charlie and I had lost touch.

"No." *I think he would have loved me forever.*

"So, you broke up with him?" Derek tries.

"No."

"Charlie broke you guys up?" He gasps in mock horror, lifting his tattooed arm to cover his mouth delicately. The contrast is amusing.

"No." I laugh, nudging him lightly.

"Do you have any guesses? Because I'm out." Derek refers the question to Riley, making a final attempt. Riley's gaze bores into me, full of empathy. Biting my lip, I stare at the ceiling to keep the tears from coming.

After a moment, I stand, waving Derek off to keep him from following me to my room. I return seconds later with an article. I'm not sure why I cut it out or why I've kept it all this time, other than I felt like I needed proof that they were actually gone. The parchment, trimmed from our local paper, is faded and worn, creased too many times from me opening and refolding it, tucking it into pockets or between the pages of whatever I was reading at the time. I lay it on the table and wait for one of them to make the first move.

Riley's fingers find it, his eyes raking over the words. Derek is too busy examining me, looking for clues into what the article could possibly convey.

"We can skip class whenever you want." Riley drops the paper back on the table and stands, motioning for me to do the same before folding me into one of his bear hugs.

"You've earned it, okay?" He jokes. I laugh, pushing him back onto the floor.

"Ally," Derek says from the couch. His face is green, nauseated. "The family you told me about that died in a freak accident, this is them?" Then, before I can answer: "The scar on your shoulder, it's a burn."

I sigh to keep from crying and slide back down to the couch beside him.

"It was a support beam. I didn't even make it through the foyer."

The article had detailed the gas leak, the death of the promising football star and his family. Out of respect for my privacy, Michael had talked to his contact at the paper, ensuring they'd leave my presence out. Word had still spread locally. Too many people had family members who were doctors and nurses in our small town, but at least I wouldn't have my name listed in the articles. At least the tragedy wouldn't have to follow me to college. Back when Michael assumed I'd still be going to college that fall. I've let go of a lot of my bitterness; I like where I've ended up.

"The nightmares, they're not about your dad— they're about the fire? And the panic attacks?" He assesses out loud, putting all the pieces together. "It's why you couldn't call him Grayson. Sonnie." He adds as an afterthought. I stare at the floor. I hate hearing the many ways this loss has impacted my life.

"Look at me." Derek's voice is demanding but tender. I do what he asks.

The green flecks in his eyes pull at something inside of me as they flash between both of my own. It requires focus to track which one he is looking at, so I give up, tracing the freckles on his nose instead. They're left over from the summer sun that must have kissed him months ago. I reach up to touch them, and my fingers end up on his jaw, as always. Derek grins widely.

"What?" I ask in my best British accent. It's shit.

"Are you doing a British accent?" He chokes out. "Ally, *no*, you're really, *really* bad at it. Keep your American accent. I love your American accent."

"Excuse me? My accent is quite proper. Yours is bad. I am not amused!" I protest.

"I like how I can do that." He says quietly, leaning into my touch.

"What?" I ask again, in my normal voice.

"Distract you."

We stare at each other for a while before Riley clears his throat, reminding us that we are not alone.

Things settle back to easy again, and the three of us fall asleep on the couch, our paper towel-rolled wands ending up on the floor. When we wake, Derek helps me swing Riley's feet onto the sofa while I tuck him in. For the first time, I fall asleep in *my* bed, wrapped up in Derek's arms. I don't suffer from the nightmares, another confession releasing their hold for the night.

* * *

The next day, we *finally* painted our rooms. Matt came over after his game, and Derek invited Jace, who'd not been surprised by our relationship as Derek had been confiding in him since I showed up at school. He'd brought more beer, which made the boys instantly content with his presence in the group.

In the end, Riley's wall ended up a dark green, like Derek's eyes, and mine was painted a dusty blue, like the sky in England. We'd painted five small white birds flying out of the corner, one for each of the people there. When everyone had retired to the kitchen for pizza, Derek added two more.

"One for Grey and Charlie." He whispered.

"Derek?" I said softly, tearing up.

"Hmm?" Admiring his art, he hadn't turned to face me, giving me enough courage to speak my next words.

"I love you. I love you, and it scares me because it's the strongest thing I've ever felt."

Derek looked at me then, his expression conveying his feelings without needing to speak them. He pulled me close and kissed my nose.

"Al, I've loved you this whole time."

then, november

I'D LEFT Charlie after she'd fallen asleep, *Mean Girls* still playing from the TV down the hall in her room. I'd learned how to balance my time over the past few years. I knocked twice on Grey's door; from inside, he knocked twice on the wall above his headboard, inviting me in. Noiselessly pushing the door closed behind me, I crept under his sheets to the spot he'd cleared for me. He had been leaning against a stack of pillows, dipping cookies into milk. He offered me one, but I refused.

"Already brushed my teeth," I explained.

"Un-uh. That's not it." He'd commented, tilting his chin up in defiance.

I pushed the pack of Oreos off to the side and wrapped myself around his bare frame. I planted kisses along his chest, inhaling the chocolate and cedar wood lifting off his skin. I'd hoped to distract him, but it didn't work.

"It wasn't your fault, Ally. Don't blame the Oreos." He said in his silly voice, pulling my face between his palms.

"I like the way they taste on you. That's the extent of my

love for Oreos." I laughed, pressing my lips to his. They were soft like marshmallows.

"Why did your dad stop being a doctor?" He asked sometime later after we'd snuggled in, watching a rerun of *Futurama*.

I spied my guitar in the corner of the room, left from earlier in the week, where I'd been playing by his window, waiting for him to return from dinner with the boys. My hands itched for it, wanting something to fiddle with. Detaching from him, I climbed out of bed and pulled it into my arms. It comforted me the way a pet would, purring to life as I quietly plucked its strings awake.

We had talked quite a bit about our childhood. Grey had grown up in the system, bouncing around foster care before bouncing around Air Force bases once James had adopted them. James retired from active duty the year they moved to Virginia, switching over to independent contracting, which had freed up more time to spend with his family. While Grey had no trouble talking about his father, I still struggled to talk about mine, at least anything that happened near the end.

I carried a great deal of regret over how he'd ended his career once I'd gotten better. It was evident he missed it by the stints of depression he'd spiral into whenever Empyrean was brought up. While I knew there was more to his decision to leave than just my betterment, I blamed myself. The facility had been in Canada and far away from my mother and me. It hadn't been sensible for him to stay on. Still, I felt responsible for his unhappiness. Not to mention the guilt I was harboring over sending him on the errand that led to his death.

"Are you hoping a song will make me forget my question?" Grey asked, moving to the floor across from me after he'd tucked a pillow behind my back so I could lean against the wall without pain. Always so considerate. "Because you're right. I'd love to hear you sing. You've never sang for me, Al. Only Charlie. Why not me?" He pouted.

"Because your opinion means too much." I smiled, strumming lazily.

"My opinion, ma'am, is that I love you, so I know I'll love the fuck out of you serenading me. Dammit, Ally, I want to be serenaded! I read *my* words to you all the time. This can't be a one-sided relationship, you know. It simply isn't healthy." He teased.

I rolled my eyes, knowing he'd won.

"I've got my hands out, and I've been collecting tears of angels
for a while now,
But the Fountain of Youth wasn't all that they claimed,
And all of Rome wasn't built in a day,
Happy endings make you wait, which is how I know it's okay
to age.
I love going 'Grey' with you.
Cause when they said your name, I recognized you.
Before I knew your face, I knew I'd love you one day.
So, babe, don't make me talk about my dead dad."

I sang shyly at first before trailing off in giggles at the end.

"That was almost incredible." He roared, crawling across the floor before pulling the guitar from my hands and tickling me until I thought I might pee.

now, november

DEREK and I are in the main kitchen, surrounded by century-old appliances that somehow still work like a charm. Duke has refused to have them upgraded over the years, scoffing every time Adaline proposed such a thing, stating it would be like throwing a piece of history out with the rubbish. Duke and Adaline have been out of town for the past few weeks, leaving Derek and me alone in the estate, sharing it only with the gardeners.

Without Adaline here to spoil us with her cooking, Derek and I have started to fend for ourselves, rummaging through his mother's old recipes for inspiration. The gazpacho, the paella, and the tapas have become my favorite meals. He swears he isn't half the cook she was, but I'm afraid I have to disagree. The food has been phenomenal. However, I've been craving good ol' American cupcakes for dessert, which is how things have quickly gotten out of hand. Derek seems to carry the philosophy that everything should be iced but the actual cakes.

It had started with my cheek, with him palming my ass while he leaned over my shoulder to lick it off. He was attempting to get a rise out of me, and oh, how it was working. I'd pushed back into him seductively before spinning out of his grasp and resuming my work. He groaned in frustration. Sauntering over playfully, he'd *acted* like he was there to help, but his rouse was short-lived as he 'accidentally' got icing on my tee.

"Get it off," I warned, not understanding the implications of what I was asking.

"*With pleasure.*" He grinned, dimples and all. Taking a seat, he'd pulled me into his lap so I was straddling him. I smiled, shaking my head.

"You're bad..." I accuse, now in a delightfully precarious situation.

"Shall I get you off?" He smiles widely, twisting my words. He grips my hips, lifting slightly so my pelvis drags down his torso, stirring the want inside me.

We've been close countless times, but he always stops things before they go too far. It's been frustrating, having his fingers, his tongue inside of me, but never the appendage I most wanted. We've been close enough that he can read the desire on my face, dripping off of me like wax off a candle. He knows how he's toyed with me, how he's worked my body up to orgasm most nights I've spent in his bed. But I wanted more. I ached to be full of him, to absorb every part of him into me as wholly as I could.

I'd made love before; I knew the reward it came with. The closeness that followed. The sweet nothings that would reverberate through the night whispered across pillowcases. I loved Derek, but I didn't want to make love to him—I wanted to fuck him. I didn't want him to be gentle with me. I wanted his dirty words and his dirty looks and everything in between.

I felt a deep pull toward escapism. Toward his calloused

hands that wouldn't coddle me. I was unafraid of bruising. I was attracted to the fingerprints he left on my thighs from where he'd secured my squirming hips, holding me to his mouth. I pictured those marks, those badges of honor on my waist, hoisting me into the wall, pushing himself deeper. My panties grew wet at the thought, and I nodded eagerly in response to his question. I hoped today would be the day he'd lose his hero complex and stop trying to save me from him. I didn't want to be saved. *Yes,* my body begged. *Get me off.*

He leans forward, tauntingly slow. The anticipation was enough to drive *any* woman mad. *But me?* I was absolutely mental. At last, his mouth closes over my nipple, his teeth plucking at my skin even through the layers of clothing, stretching my nipples away from my body. I gasp as his fingers find their familiar holds, and his nipping turns to sucking. The blue confection seeped through the dainty cloth of my white blouse. I think it looks better this way.

He pauses, smirking up at me, my face red hot—flushed with need. *Are you going to let him get away with this, Ally? No. I'm certainly not.* I scoop a handful of icing from the bowl on the table and raise my hand deviously.

"Ally. Ally. ALLY! Come on, there's no need to be childish. It's just a bit of cake." He attempts to deter my motives, but it's a lost cause. I pretend he's right, lowering my hand momentarily so he doesn't expect it when my finger trails a sugary streak down the side of his neck. His cock strains against the fabric beneath me, jumping in his pants as I begin to work in slow circles, licking the icing off.

"I must admit, I was mistaken." He rasps and begins removing my shirt. Discarding it on the tile, he draws sprinkle specked patterns across my chest. "I rather like this, after all." His tongue flicks over my skin. My back reaches new levels of acrobatics, arching to previously unachievable angles. *Holy fuck.*

A moan escapes my lips, my body reacting to his touch, shifting me forward on his lap once more.

"Fuck." He groans, matching my dry thrusts in pace with his. Every bit of friction is delicious, and I find fault with the material still separating me from *feeling* him. I run my hands across his abdomen, working up the fabric of his top, muttering a silent prayer that the rest of his clothes will soon follow.

"Come to dinner with me next week. Margot hasn't stopped asking about you." He begs as I fight to get his shirt off, the two of us laughing as we struggle. "I want my family to meet the girl I've fallen in love with." He says once the obstacle has been removed, my face held between his two hands.

"You're asking me this now?" I giggle. "Right now?"

"I was going to ask you earlier, but I was a wee distracted, and I plan on being more distracted as soon as you say yes." He chuckles.

"Say yes." He whispers, brushing his lips across my clavicle and to my ear. My breathing becomes heavy before his teasing comes to an abrupt halt. Suddenly, he moves his arms behind his back and leans against the chair's frame.

"I'm not touching you again until you agree," Derek states, making a bold play. I will say yes, of course, but I'm curious if I can break his resolve. I press my lips slowly to his, then more open, urgently.

"*Derek.*" I moan.

"You know what? Fuck 'em'." He cracks. Standing, he wraps my legs around his waist before grabbing the bin we've spent hours preparing from scratch and lowers me to the floor. The penny road tiles are freezing and knock the wind from my lungs.

"A simple yes could have spared you that, you absolute devil." His shoulders shake in amusement. I become transfixed by how his laugh ripples through his body, his muscles gyrating as he hovers over me. Reaching for his hand, I lower it into the waistband of my jeans. His fingers respond instantly, knowing the exact path to trace that drives me wild. I push further into his hand, and he forgets his question, forgets his objections.

I don't recognize myself. I've always been the nice girl, the quiet girl, but more recently, the don't-talk-to-me girl. I've never been a sex-crazed girl, but I'm lying on the kitchen floor like I'm depraved—every breath courses through me like it's my last. Like I can't get enough air to sustain the pleasure.

"These need to come off." He huffs in annoyance. I agree and raise my hips to help the endeavor.

I can't hide my disappointment when he lowers himself onto me, his jeans still in place. Derek gives me a scornful look, and repeats his favorite line as of late. "Not today, Al."

"Why?" I plead.

"You *know* why." He retorts, grazing his mouth around the edges of my small breasts protruding from the bralette I chose this morning. In the past, I was self-conscious about their size. I was self-conscious about *my* size in general. Not feeling skinny enough to compete with the models and not curvy enough to compensate for it elsewhere.

When I brought this up, Derek had found it hilarious. "It's not the size of the breasts that matter, Ally. It's the ripple that goes through them when you're close to the edge. It's the nipples. And yours are fucking *perfect*." He'd said. Now, he tries to steer my thoughts elsewhere in toying with them, but it isn't enough.

"I love you. All of you. Your past, your mistakes, your right fucking now. What more of me do I have to give to convince you I could never regret this?"

Sighing, he shifts further down, letting his cheek rest on my chest. His fingers follow the patterns of the lace.

"I don't know." He admits quietly. "I want you. You have to know how much I want you. I'm about to drill a hole in my trousers; you've got me so wound up. But it has to feel right for *both* of us. Yeah?"

I hate when he makes sense, and my guilt overtakes my desire to pressure him.

"Of course," I tell him, running my fingers through his hair. "But *that*," I say, moving his fingers from my nipple to my waist. "That makes me want to fuck you. *This*. This is safe."

He laughs, breaking whatever lingering tension was left between us. He shifts down until his mouth is level with my soaked panties and stares up at me in question. "And this? Is this safe?"

His index finger slides alongside the silky material and down my opening before circling and looking back at me.

"*Definitely not*." I joke. "But I'll allow it."

He moves the soaked fabric to the side. The exposure to the air in the room breaks my skin out in goosebumps. Tantalizingly, in slow motion, he works over every inch of my skin. My back contorts as his tongue flicks. This is the closest I've ever come to being baptized. I can't rationalize why something so dirty makes me feel so pure, but I want more of it. It feels like he spends forever working me up, and when he finally reaches the spot I want him, I can't hold on to it.

"I want you to come for me now, Ally. Come on my tongue so I can taste you, baby." His words vibrate. As soon as he reapplies pressure, my orgasm rips through me, rolling my eyes back in my head. His dirty words send me to a level I have never experienced before.

He looks too pleased with himself as he offers a hand to help me. I use it to drag him onto the floor and work him into my mouth. I trace the vein from base to tip, gargling my saliva around his length until he's vibrating with the need to release. His hands tangle in my hair, pulling himself deeper into my throat. When he's close, I swallow as much of him as possible. It's something I have never had the desire or urge to do before this moment.

I fall into a pile beside his body on the tile. Our hands find each other on the floor, our fingers intertwining.

"Yes," I tell him.

"Yes?" He laughs incredulously. "You're agreeing to meet my family with my come still dripping down your throat?"

"Well... Yes." I state, most assured, as we fall into hysterics. We really are proper fucked, as he put it.

now, november

THANKSGIVING IS NOT a celebrated English holiday, as there were never any recognized Indians here who had once taught the pilgrims how to survive. There was no famous day when they broke bread together. While the Harvest Festival aligns with the date, they do not get the day off work, and schools do not close. However, it was my father's favorite holiday, and it felt wrong not to celebrate it.

We'd spoken with Duke over the phone days ago, who was all too eager to tie the occasion into the family dinner Derek had conspired me into attending. Never missing an opportunity to celebrate, Duke had called around and found probably the only pub in London that serves turkey.

I had classes until the afternoon, while Derek had only had one in the morning, so I'd made the two-hour drive back to London alone. I didn't mind. Being around people so often now, I rarely had moments alone, and I was enjoying the silence, as it gave me space to reflect.

Growing up, Thanksgiving was the only big celebration we had at the hospital. Christmas was a sadder occasion, as everyone was glum and missing their families. Most of them, like mine, lived too far from Empyrean to make the drive. So, it was Thanksgiving we looked forward to throughout the year. The holiday was constructed to be thankful for those around us and not those who weren't.

Libby knows how special the day was to my father and me. Initially, she had planned to join us for dinner, but her flight from Morocco had been delayed, so I would meet her at the house afterward.

I'm in love with British pubs. I love how each one that serves food in the country always seems to have an old stove-turned fireplace and leather booths with too many tiny tables scattered around. I love the walls that you can never see because they're covered in too many framed paintings, artifacts, and flags—an entire gallery of where the place's character is derived. I love the history seeping out of every pore. This is what I think about when I arrive and push through the crowd, searching for Derek.

It's close to kick-off for football tonight, and the crowd is especially lively. The local team is playing Liverpool, which is a tremendous honor. Many consider Liverpool to be the best next to Manchester, a fact I only know thanks to Matt, who has planned a whole night around this evening's game. It appears everyone who supports the local team is in this building; it's so crowded. Every hand is attached to a pint.

I slide through all the bodies gathered around the bar to see a man towering over the other heads. I assume it's Derek's until I get close enough to recognize his brother from the pictures. Margot notices me first, waving me over eagerly. Duke follows her attention, and his face breaks into unfiltered joy.

"My dearest Ally!" He half chuckles, half coughs as I get

closer. Relieved to see someone familiar, I throw my arms around him, startling the old man before he chuckles warmly and pats my back.

"So, you're the girl Der's been on about?" The brother asks without breaking away from the screen.

"Luke! Where have your manners gone? Ally, I'm Margot, Derek's sister. This oaf is Luke." Margot introduces. She surprises me by embracing me sweetly. It's a pleasant surprise. I'd been worried about whether or not they would like me, her in particular. As far as I'm aware, she is the only one who knows my predicament with her brother. In her thin arms, I instantly feel my stress alleviate.

Today, Margot is wearing a mauve pantsuit. Her brown hair has so much depth to it that I can't pinpoint what shade it is—somewhere between a chestnut and Clydesdale brown. It shimmers in the light as she slides back into the booth and gestures hopefully for me to take the empty seat beside her. Once I get situated, she leans in.

"Luke's got money on Liverpool, so he's anxious about the game. He tends to forget how to be polite when that's the case."

Despite her closeness, she has to nearly yell for me to hear her. Luke scoffs at the words and takes a swig of his pint.

"Against the home team? That's a bold move." I caution.

The townsfolk are riled up enough as is. I can't imagine how they'd react to hearing there's a supporter of the opposing team in the vicinity.

"I like to play devil's advocate." He smirked, and it was shockingly similar to Derek's. Derek, who is nowhere to be seen. I scan the bar for his frame and come up empty.

"Ah, a genetic trait." I quip back, still looking around.

Luke is easily over seven feet tall. He's standing at the

end of our table to pivot his attention between our group and the TVs behind him. He shares Derek's nose but has Margot's hair. I'll have to ask Derek to see a photo of his mother later. She must have been insanely beautiful to create such stunning children. Margot should be on a runway somewhere in Paris, and Luke, well, Luke could be a stunt double for Brady.

"She's sparky. I like this one, Mags. So, what do you see in my brother? He's not even half as tall, dark, and handsome of a lad as me." He asks, giving me his full attention now.

Duke is relaxed with his arms resting on the table beside his beer. His demeanor is overly jolly, as if we were flowers that had finally bloomed in his garden. If elves really did live in trees in the forest, he'd be their king. I laugh aloud. Grey would have loved that line. I remember what Luke said, and my laugh feels appropriate.

"I'm sorry, I missed what you said. It was so dull. I must have drifted into my thoughts to entertain myself." I say, staring into the pint I've poured before looking up and holding eye contact. He stares back with mixed emotions before bursting into laughter the next. Duke has been silently shaking since we started talking, and Mags is giggling like a schoolgirl beside me.

I'm strangely at ease with these strangers. In my short time here, they've already started to feel like family. I always wanted siblings. I always begged my mother to have another, but she was unable. In the hospital, the other patients became the closest thing I had: them and my dad.

After the move, after my mother's visits had become sporadic at best, the others took it upon themselves to look after me. The nurses read to me at night when my dad was too busy. The Jazz musician a few doors down who had lost his career to cancer taught me to play my first guitar and my first piano. They had kept me contained during otherwise bleak days.

"Derek will be in before long. He's outside in Dad's car trying to get him to leave." Margot fills me in, rolling her eyes. I snap out of my thoughts and focus on Derek's mention.

"Honestly, I wish they'd stop with their little feud already. It's ripping our family apart. My father doesn't understand why Derek would rather work at a school than make over six figures working for him. It's been the conversation for months. I'm so tired of it all." She sighs.

Her pale hand lifts what appears to be scotch to her lips. She shakes a bit with the movement, telling me she often worries too much about things she can't control. A worry line appears between her brows, proving my theory. Her eyes widen as she looks out into the crowd and plasters a forced smile. I follow her gaze to where the crowd shifts to allow Derek and an older, very well-made man access through.

The older man looks exactly like Derek if I had shoved him in a time machine and aged him thirty-five years. His hair has the same effortless volume and swoops back in a posh wave of salt and pepper. He reminds me vaguely of a more angular Peirce Brosnan. His face twisted into a cross, smug grin revealing traces of Derek's smirk.

Everything about how he carries himself leads me to believe that grin never grows past a smirk, never a genuine smile. The cold set of his eyes has removed any trace of happiness from his countenance. The ego seems to wear the man.

"I'm so sorry, Ally. It looks like we'll be treating you to a proper family dinner tonight." Margot apologizes from over my shoulder. This is the quietest she's spoken. After Derek's confession, I don't know how to see his father as anything other than the villain suspected of murdering Derek's mother. All his features are sculpted in my brain to fit that narrative.

"Luca." He says once he is close enough to the group. Luke must be short for Luca, or perhaps it's what he prefers. Derek had written out Luke with a k-e in his messages about who would be in attendance for the night.

The older man coarsely lays his hand down with a thud on Luke's shoulder. Previously absorbed in the game, he hadn't noticed his father's arrival and instantly straightens in recognition of his presence. The foot that had been lifted to rest on the platform of our booth returns to the ground. All traces of the laid-back jokester vanish, replaced with a soldier at attention.

"Father, I didn't realize you were coming," Luke says formally.

"My darling, Margot." The man says as if Luke had not spoken. His face softens in a rehearsed, unnatural way.

"Daddy," Margot says, smiling amiably at the man.

"Duke." He nods at the frail elderly man across from us.

Only Duke does not appear frail anymore. Somehow, he has gained more mass since I last looked at him. Before, he appeared to have been bent, like a tree folded over after a hurricane. Now, he is upright, defiant against the winds. His expression is resilient as he acknowledges the man with a slight tilt of his head. Derek, it seems, is not the only one who shares tension in the relationship.

"And I don't believe we've had the pleasure." He says, turning to me.

"Ally," I say over the chatter of those around us. I don't

have to yell. The pub has quieted to a static murmur since he entered.

"Ally...?" He leaves in the air, waiting for my last name. *Jeez.* I feel resistant to telling him, even though I can't place my reasoning.

"Ally, as in Ally," I say with a smile. "I didn't get your name."

I might have imagined Luke's smile out the corner of my eye. When I take him in more fully, he has resumed the structured relaxed he was before. Face straight with no signs of irritation or boredom, but just as void of joy. Is he afraid? Margot seems to be the only one who positively responded to the older man's presence.

"Adeodatus Empyros. I go by Ade if you'd prefer." He offers, extending a hand. I reluctantly take it. His skin is cold despite the warmth of the room. I try to conceal the shiver that runs down my spine. He looks familiar, and it unsettles me that I can't place him. *Wait...*

"Empyros as in Empyrean?" I ask. *Say no. Say no.*

"The very same." He grins his never-smile.

Derek takes the cue to step between us. Like Luke, he is full of tension. Margot shifts over in the small seat. At the same time, a man who appears to be the pub owner appears with two chairs from the bar for the table. He is clearly aware of the importance of having Mr. Empyros as a guest. Ade takes a seat without thanking him. Derek's hand finds mine under the table, and I squeeze tightly to control my annoyance. I fail.

"Thank you so much," I say to the owner as he departs. He appears surprised by my recognition, then smiles with silent gratitude before returning behind the bar.

Ade shoots me a look more subtle than a glare, but it carries all the weight of a dagger. Derek smiles appreciatively as he leans over the table, effectively shielding me from Ade's cutting eyes while pouring himself a glass from the pitcher. I take a deep breath.

"Derek, take a seat so we can enjoy a meal together?" The man commands in the form of a question. The only open seat is across the table.

Derek's jaw tenses at the order. Maggie shifts uncomfortably. I'm sure that, growing up around the pair, she's learned the danger signs. At some point in the night, I started referring to her as Maggie instead of Margot. I suppose it's because Luke called her 'Mags,' and I like that better than sharing the name her father calls her.

I touch her arm gently and glance down at where she sits. I am thankful that she seems to understand my meaning. She sighs in relief.

"Of course." She says, answering my unspoken suggestion.

I shift out of the booth to let her pass, and she takes the seat between Ade and Duke. I slide closest to the wall, and some stress leaves Derek as he climbs into the seat beside me. I feel safer sandwiched between him and Duke.

Duke's wise eyes seem to catalog my every action and hold a great deal of praise. For what? I'm not sure, but out of all the people here, I'm happy it's *his* opinion that means the most to Derek.

I lay my hand on Derek's knee and smooth out some of the wrinkles in his jeans while Maggie catches Ade up on her wedding plans for the spring. I learned that she was marrying a corporate lawyer from Empyrean, whom she met while visiting her father one day for lunch. In typical meet-cute fashion, she spilled coffee on his jacket in the elevator exiting the building, and the romance took off from there.

When the entrées are served, Luke and Ade strike up a conversation about work. We are the only table being catered to. The rest pick up their orders from the counter. It bothers me that Ade's reputation has earned us special treatment. More so, because he seems to lack the awareness that there is anything special about it.

I loosely try to follow the conversation. It's hard not to, as no one at the table speaks around Ade. There's no separate discussion between Duke and Maggie or Derek and me. None of us seem willing to overshadow him. My admiration builds for the beautiful man beside me. I see how strong his love is for his siblings to sit through the occasion.

Luke is training to be Ade's second in command. The men discuss the latest project's performance, which beat projections. It sounds like they rolled out a new drug trial, and the patients are responding well.

Derek grows impatient at the mention of the company's dealings. His leg begins to bounce in a desire to be walking out the door. I change my tactics to distract him and begin outlining shapes on his kneecap—first a heart, then a star. Every fifteen seconds, he subtly dips his head to whisper what he thinks it is in my ear. I tap my fingers on the side of my face once if he got it wrong and repeat it. Twice, if he got it right and start something new. His leg stopped bouncing.

Maggie and Duke are paying more mind to us than the conversation at the end of the table. They keep their eyes on the men speaking but dare to dart over frequently before returning. Maggie's fixed smile becomes real the longer she steals peeks at us.

Once our plates have been cleared, the owner returns with the check. Ade hands him his card without looking at the amount. I don't like him paying for my meal, and

Derek's hardness shows that he hates it just as much. I feel obligated to thank him. He stares at me, testing my kindness.

"You shouldn't have," I say in sickly sweetness. I'm *not* thanking the man.

His smirk grows deeper into his cheeks, seemingly impressed at my response to the challenge. Derek grips my fingers, double-taping the back of my hand. *Yes!* He silently rejoices.

It wasn't all for him. Empyrean may have been my home for three years; it may have been where I got healthy, but it's also the company that destroyed my father's spirit. After we left, my father never returned to being a doctor. He never published the results that had led to my cure. I never asked why. I was too young to understand then. Once he was gone, I felt aged past the curiosity. Too phased out of that chapter for it to matter.

If Ade *had* caused Derek's mother's passing, I can only imagine how shady he was in his business dealings. Insurance fraud, corporate mirage, and any number of other factors could have influenced my father's decision to leave the practice he once loved. I owe Ade Empyros nothing.

After a few more moments of draining conversation, Ade begins to stand, and a man appears to return the chair to its home at the bar so it is out of the way. He slips his coat back on.

The pen he'd used to sign the receipt was left on the table. At first, Derek used it to mimic my patterns on napkins so he no longer had to whisper. I've since stolen it to script lyrics and limericks around his shapes. We take turns listening so the other can add to it, like we did over the summer.

Summer hopeful, something changed. I write.

Autumn aged, mulled, and spiced. He adds.

I don't want to remember life before yours intertwined. I float around a shooting star at the edge of the makeshift parchment.

Like fingers laced, always by your side. He notates in elegant script underneath my words.

I draw a heart around the addition. *The devil man sits, looking for an axe to grind.*

Don't worry, the burden's mine.

Derek flips the napkin like a sleight of hand, drawing a filled-in tic-tac-toe board on the back. At the same time, his father appears beside him and glances over, making it clear that our interactions did not escape his notice.

"Derek." Ade addresses, grabbing his shoulder the same way he grabbed Luke's. In what Derek would describe as a "microemotion," he flashes from frightened to angry to blankly acknowledging the gesture. My stomach turns. I want to scream at Ade to take his hand off of him. A satiated film possesses the older man's face as he analyzes his son. It grows more pronounced as he takes in my disdain.

"Ally, it was truly a delight to meet you." He says. "It seems my son has finally found someone who can handle his temperament."

I don't miss the poorly concealed jab at Derek's history. I feign innocence, conjuring up whatever version of the Disney princess that still lives on inside me.

"The pleasure of knowing your son has been all mine. I imagine they're your greatest achievement." I praise, glancing around the table. I compliment his children while devaluing all his other accomplishments. He smiles curtly, without agreement, before he departs for the door. We wait until he's gone, holding our breath as we listen intently for the bell above the entry. The moment the door clicks closed behind him, the pub returns to its average volume, and the table lets out a sigh of relief.

"Who are you?" Derek laughs, lighting up. "You beautiful, deranged girl. *'Ally as in Ally.'*" He mocks my earlier words gleefully. "No one has ever spoken to my father that way." He says quieter. His voice is laced with gratitude.

I lean my forehead against his cheek in an unusual display of affection. Tangling his fingers in my hair, he presses his lips to my head. I look into his eyes, and he tips them back toward the overheads. They're my favorite shade tonight.

Maggie sighs romantically from across the table. I gently put space between us, not wanting to make the others uncomfortable. Derek is having none of this. Distance has become a foreign concept to him. He loops his arm around my waist, pulling me back against his side.

"The girl's got balls, Der. That's for sure." Luke compliments, wiping the beer off his chin with the back of his hand. He's returned to the Luke he was when I walked in, more frat boy than businessman. I prefer him this way.

It unsettles me how everyone's personality seems to shift around Ade. How does he know who anyone truly is if they mold themselves to fit his preferences? It feels like a weakness, not a strength. The less you know who someone really is, the less you know their intentions. Perhaps that was my weakness today. I didn't hide behind the façade.

"I don't think Ally is capable of lying, Luca." Duke chimes in. It's enchanting to finally hear his voice's rich, worn texture in my ears. If he hadn't been so successful in his endeavors, he could have made a killing reading audiobooks. *I* would have paid to listen.

"The first night we met, I guilted her into taking a walk with me. She saw right through me, referring to my illness as leverage I used to bait her." He chuckles, and it resonates through his body. He has also returned to his former state —more willow than oak tree. Willow was always more fitting of his character.

I'm blushing at the spotlight on my mannerisms. Maggie is vibrant, observing our conversation. She lazily rests her chin in her palm. "I certainly approve." She retorts.

The scene becomes dreamy, too kind to be reality. I've survived family dinner and have been openly accepted. It's honestly more than I could have hoped for.

We shift gears, and I ask Luke about the game, which amplifies his energy. He and Duke debate which teams are doing better and stats I wouldn't have cared about if they hadn't made it so personal to the players. Surprisingly, I find myself leaning in to learn more.

Maggie and I discussed the table arrangements she'd picked for the wedding and the nightmare she had while planning it. Derek throws in that I'm excellent at decorating and tries to hide his gloating at bringing up the Riley incident. I lightly kick him under the table, earning me another round of his laughter.

I offered to help, and she tried not to look too excited as she invited me to the wedding. It's in May, which is over five months away. It breaks my two-month rule with planning. I am amazed when Derek looks at me with hope, as if he wants me to join him, as if he expects or at least is optimistic that we will still be doing whatever we are doing by then. Without thinking, I agree.

This is the part Maggie has been waiting for. She's two scotches in, starting on a third. She has decided she's comfortable enough to begin sharing Derek's embarrassing childhood stories. This topic quickly engages the rest of the group and encourages them to add their own perspectives to the stories.

She told me about the youth rugby game Derek didn't want to play. In defiance, he sat down in the middle of the field. As luck would have it, the ball landed right in his lap a few seconds later, as did another player knocking out two of Derek's front teeth. Fortunately, they had a great dentist and could fix the damage, but not in time for holiday pictures. She says those are her favorite, and she keeps one hung in the foyer of her home so she can see it every day as she leaves for work.

By the time we leave, we're all drunk and have to taxi ourselves home. I slip up and call Margot "Maggie" in our goodbye. I awkwardly explain the Luke thing, but to my surprise, she loves it, insisting I never call her anything else. Like Big Mike, Luke has delighted in making fun of my American accent and tries again to insist that he is the superior choice to Derek.

Duke catches us all off guard by pushing him light-heartedly. It's so soon, too soon, really, but I feel at home amongst the four and genuinely wish to see them again.

Duke dozes in the cab while Derek traces patterns on the back of my hand. I rest my head against his shoulder and stare at the dark shadows of the brownstones racing by as we approach my drop-off at Libby's. Outside of Ade's appearance, I had an incredible time. It's not often I feel like I fit in, but anywhere with Derek, I always seem to. His family feels like an extension of the best parts of him, and I imagine that's his mother's legacy—the spirit of her children.

"Thank you," Derek whispers when we arrive at the garden gate, him still taking me home all these months later. "For everything you are."

now, december

THE WEEKS LEADING up to Christmas pass in a blur. Derek's old bandmate, Zach Goodhart, had returned to town after the infamous tour, taking time off before recording his second solo album in London. Along with Jace, the three had met for drinks, hoping to make amends over the lingering tensions left by the fallout of Derek's actions last year. He had been skeptical to go, but Jace had asked, and Derek felt indebted.

I'd stayed up with him on the eve of their reconciliation, encouraging him and talking him through his fears. When he returned, I saw a different version of the man I loved— lighter, more cheerful, a bit more like what I imagined he'd been like before. The boys had convinced Derek he was too talented to give up his dream. I was in total agreement, thankful they had pushed him to get back in the studio.

I met Zach that same week, and I found him to be a lively character and a performer, even in his everyday persona. Zach liked to show off, liked to be the life of the party. He reminded me of Grey in that regard. Only, Grey never had to try to be the life of the party; people had gravitated towards him. Zach was loud-mouthed. He jumped into every conversation without invitation, though he was never unwelcome. He *was* incredibly likable, charming, posh. His fame made sense. Zach was flashy, and he caught on.

Despite my warmth towards the man, I worried for Derek. I worried about the timing. Derek had written every chart-topping hit Zach had, and now that he was due for a second album, I worried Zach was using him for more. Derek laughed when I finally brought up my concern.

"So, what if he is? He wouldn't have to use me, Ally. Music is what we've always done. If that's what brought us back together, I wouldn't mind. It doesn't take away from me or what I have left to create. You're so cute when you worry." He smiled at me lovingly. "But you need not, he hasn't asked. He has, however, put me in touch with his label. They want me to record my own stuff." He'd gone on excitedly, his passion flowing through his voice as he prattled on.

Duke had built Derek a small studio on the grounds as a present in early December, on his twenty-fifth birthday. Derek insisted it was too much, but Jace smacked him over the head, telling him to accept it graciously.

The boys had been getting together multiple nights during the week, creating concepts for Derek's first solo work. Derek had thought the studio was a gift for him, but truly, it was a gift for Duke.

After spending the daylight overseeing his latest construction, Duke would wander over and rest beside me on the sofa in the sound room. His eyes sparkled as he watched the boy's joke and laugh. His grandson was happier now than he had seen in a long time. It had kept Derek engaged in what he loved without missing out on time with his grandfather.

Riley had begun to join me for my sleepovers at the gardens on nights Matt was away. We'd become a group, the five of us. When we weren't writing songs in the studio or on the piano over the pool—all spirited and splashing around, we were having game nights, telling stories. Riley would pass out on the couch or in one of the rooms downstairs, and we'd ride to campus together the next day.

Riley was quite taken with Duke and Duke with him. The two chattered on through the hours, talking about their inspirations. Their unconventional personalities had bonded them instantly. Riley would leave campus between classes to bring the old man lunch as they witnessed Duke's newest build unfold. Watching my best friend treat his grandfather with such care, Derek's reservations about Riley had disappeared.

Months ago, on Halloween, Duke had announced his plan for a new room that would launch in correlation with his annual Christmas Eve party.

Duke was quiet, patient, and like his grandson—fueled by creating. He was a paradox. As much as he loved to share, he kept his projects under lock and key. Even when his plans called him to action, he remained secretive, disappearing for weeks while he brought the pieces together.

And so it was that he and Adaline evaporated after the holiday, reemerging only the day before Thanksgiving when we had met at the pub.

When he was gone, the builders arrived with a manila envelope full of Duke's hand-drawn plans. In what felt like only a weekend, the spine of a new room took shape. The crates had appeared next, stamped and mailed from Brazil, China, and Mexico. The gardeners began planting.

On December 1st, an invitation sealed-in-wax appeared under the door to our flat, inviting Riley and me to Duke's Ghosts of Christmas Eve.

now, christmas eve

FINALLY, the day had arrived. Descending the stairs from Derek's loft, I searched for my best friend in the crowd, but I found only a sea of unrecognizable faces.

The ordinarily quiet piano room has been packed with people dressed to the nines, moseying from table to table. The men wore black suits, while women adorned red silk, like blood dripping from their silhouettes. Others dressed in ghastly white gowns, like phantoms floating across the stone paths. I feel unfit, even in the maroon chiffon Libby borrowed out to me for the occasion.

I'm too on edge to feel entirely at ease. Too many factors are at play, too many particles are being forced together. I haven't surmised how the event will go: if those particles will blend organically or if they will explode.

A small sliver of my old life is coming to merge with my new, and it has my nerves entirely shot. Tonight will be Libby's first time meeting Derek. Her first time meeting everybody. I've been worrying myself sick that she will somehow find out about his involvement in my education and judge him solely on that small portion of his character.

Every night I'd awoken this past week, sweating from my nightmares, Derek held out his hand and asked me to go on an adventure with him, to live in a different kind of dream. Strolling through the labyrinth of earth and stories until dawn, we'd played hide and seek in The Woods room under the thicket of indoor trees, hidden amongst their trunks. We'd played tag up and down the corridors until I was giddy enough to forget the fears I had stirred from. The two of us enjoyed games that we should have aged out of but never did, even at 20 and 25.

It was my favorite thing about Derek: his ability to still play like a child. It made the looming date of the party dangle over us less. This was the version I hoped Libby got to know, *my* version.

The rooms seem to blur together as I wander through the masses. There is too much commotion for me to be able to appreciate the grandeur of the event. The production rivals even those of Jay Gatsby: dancers twirling through the shallow waters around the piano, cirque exhibitionists falling from the ceiling tangled in silk ribbons. It's lavish, and I'm almost angry with the turnout, as it's prohibited me from being able to appreciate it more.

I pause to catch my breath, letting the setting soak in. Hand-woven tapestries displaying family trees have been hung among the ivy walls, honoring the Rivera ancestry. The faces look more like they have been grown out of the earth below rather than sewn into the fabric. The heritage, the roots of the house, appear exposed. I pick Derek's face out of the bunch and admire his likeness. It helps to relax me.

A dainty hand rests coolly on my shoulder, bringing with it the faint smell of clay. I turn to find Libby beaming, beautiful as ever, with her strawberry hair curled into a loose bun sitting atop her head.

"Libby." I wrap my arms around her slender frame.

"Ally." She sighs happily. "You look stunning."

"I can't believe you're here." I beam, looking her over. Her dusty overalls have been replaced with a ruby garment that caters to her every curve. *She* looks stunning. "Wow. Very posh, Libs." I remark.

"Me?" She laughs. "Have you seen these ladies? What kind of crowd are you running with these days?"

I didn't get a chance to answer as she immediately dragged me through the throngs of people wanting to show me a statue she'd been marveling over for the past twenty minutes.

"My days, the detail." She gawks as we approach it. She circles the masterpiece while I observe her bewilderment. "This is the best replica of a Michael Angelo I've ever seen. Where did he find it?"

"Knowing Duke, that's not a replica." I regret to inform her. She gasps, eyeing all the reckless frames surrounding us. I wouldn't put it past her to stand guard the rest of the evening if, at that moment, Maggie hadn't stepped out of the crowd and rushed us.

"Ally! Oh, you look lovely. Have you seen my brother about recently? He's supposed to give a toast. Is this Libby? Oh, I've heard so much about you. Beautiful, just like your niece. I'm Margot, Derek's sister." Maggie regales.

I adore her, scatterbrained as ever. A man, I'm assuming her fiancé, materializes behind her and presses his lips to her cheek.

"Sebastian!" She giggles, confirming my suspicions. "Seb, this is the Ally I've been telling you so much about. She's been helping me with the wedding, love."

Libby choked on the wine she'd acquired from one of many veiled servers floating around. Tulle hides their faces and trails behind their bodies on the ground. I absently wonder if Duke's hired models to cater. Each seems to have the same phased walk. The kind performers used at theme parks as they stalked among the headstones and various props. Yet, despite their slow-phased steps, they held the elegance of a catwalk.

"*You're* planning weddings now?" Libby looks at me conspicuously, donning a stunned expression.

"I'm pinteresting flower arrangements at best, okay? You could hardly call it help. Don't go getting all shocked, Libs. I haven't lost my doom and gloom yet." I tease, nudging my skeptical aunt.

Maggie waved me off, insisting I had been a huge help already just in providing her with inspiration she could send to her florist and decorators. It was news to me that she didn't have just a single wedding planner but a whole team at her disposal. Considering the construction of the current event, it shouldn't have come as a surprise.

Luke flings his arm around my shoulder, making me jump at the sudden weight. Jesus, his arm alone is like a hundred pounds.

"No way my brother ditched you already. Not looking like that. *He's punching*, Ally." He whispers obnoxiously in my ear. I push him, having little effect against his sturdiness. His booming laugh quickly overtakes the group, drawing eyes in his direction.

"You must be Derek." Libby glows, relieved to see me lighting up now that I had found comfort among family.

"She wishes." He roars, causing Mags to cover her face in embarrassment.

"Luke!" She scolds, her cheeks taking on a rosy hue. "Do not make a bad impression in front of Ally's aunt!"

Lifting every ounce of charm he can muster, Luke reaches for Libby's hand and begins to flirt shamelessly. He reintroduces himself, claiming there was no possible way she could be *my* aunt. As he caters to her likes, delving into talks of art, the group becomes soon immersed in her latest project.

At last, I spot Derek across the room speaking at length with a man wearing a stiff suit and an even stiffer expression. Derek appears to be suffering through it with grace and a great deal of patience. Zach must have caught sight of his pained tolerance as he emerged seconds later, stealing him away. Derek cracks, the familiar relaxation resetting his jawline as they leave the man's range.

Zach leans up on his toes to whisper something in Derek's ear, peaking my curiosity. Derek searches the room frantically until Zach extends a finger in my direction, and Derek's eyes lock with my own. The same charge passes across the space dividing us.

My face morphs into whatever look it seems to reserve for Derek. Maggie searches my line of sight, finding her brother: recognition dawns, a small smile playing on her lips. My feet have already begun moving away, excusing myself from the others without breaking my gaze.

Derek is breathtaking. His maroon tie is tucked neatly into an all-black suit, stirring the brown in his eyes. As I examine him, I raise my palm to his cheek, his head tipping back in expectation.

"The verdict?" He asks after a moment, his tone rich and warm. A welcome sound. He lifts my other hand to his chin, pressing his lips to my wrist as he places it.

"Raspberry hot cocoa. Brought out by your tie." I laugh

dreamily. "Mine?" I ask, stepping back. I raise my chin goofily. He chuckled, taking it between his calloused fingers to hold me in place.

"Muddy..." He starts. I chortle, breaking his focus. "Wait, wait!" He insists. "*I've got this*. Murky, dark waters... Sexy, mysterious, like an ocean trench." Derek continues, biting the edge of his lip to keep from smiling. It doesn't work.

I love it when he jokes like this. How it lights his countenance, brighter than any of the Christmas lights wrapped around every column in the building. I press my lips to his, feeling exactly right.

"This is a public place, you absolute horndogs," Luke calls from a short distance away, coming to join us with the group I had left behind. I'd almost forgotten.

"Derek," I announce. "This gorgeous woman is the absolute best of me. This is Libby." My aunt emerges out from beside Maggie, stepping into focus.

"Derek." She sighs, her eyes twinkling as she assesses the two of us. Our closeness. "I like you already."

Duke arrives on the balcony with a glass of champagne in his hand. He clanks a silver knife against it and begins to make a toast. Standing straight, tall, and confident, he acts as a commandment to the room.

"To the newest expansion of my home and our communities' gardens. May it allow us all to reflect on our shadows. Let us never forget that even in our darkest parts, there is beauty, too."

The glass-paned walls that separate the inside from the outside lower into the floor. The dense hedge maze has been dimly lit, leading from the main conservatory to the forest at the edge of the property. Every ten feet, a person in an old doctor's mask holds a lantern to guide the way.

Leaves crunch under the feet of people marching across snow-covered trails. Like petals scattered down wedding aisles, holly berries have been scattered over the white. They leave red splotches, staining the ice as heels stomp them into the ground.

Horse-drawn carriages carry other parts of the crowd. They're lightly visible in the distance. The sound of trotting carried across the fog, over the men in their top hats, displacing the time period.

Every visual leads into the story. All are building up to the final demonstration of Duke's grand reveal.

When the doors open into Duke's newest apparatus, a building that seems to be made of the woods surrounding it, the sight is as breathtaking as I could have imagined.

Flowers that look like bats peek out from the ceiling, while flowers that look like eyeballs unsettle me from the edges of the room. Planted black moss amplifies passers-by's shadows. The entire construction evokes a strange fascination—Duke's very own cabinet of curiosities.

"What a mind" Derek says from beside me in his suit and wonder.

It was only Derek who truly understood his grandfather's brilliant thought patterns. Only he who had been in contact with Duke those weeks he was gone, receiving postcards in the mail every few days that came littered with riddles. Derek would sit, trying to decode the tidbits of information. It was an old game they had started when Derek was a boy. Duke would send clues, and Derek would attempt to figure out what he was planning next.

It still amazes me how a man as gentle yet formidable as Duke could exist. I was blessed to love Derek, who emanated this same propensity—my man who wrote songs the way Duke built rooms. I whisper my musings in his ear while we spin through the poinsettia-lined paths, the only dash of color in the otherwise dark display.

I find Riley, then, awing over the scenery while Matt and Jace speak quietly nearby. I bound over, too joyous to stop myself and tackle my best friend.

"Riles!" I chirp with my nose between his shoulder blades.

"Fucks sake, Al! All night, and this is the first I've seen of you! It's an atrocious way to treat your guest of honor." He humors. "Where's your strap on?" He asks, spinning to search for Derek while clutching me in his arms.

I looked forward to seeing him, wonderfully shocked by his suit. For what could be Duke's last big hurrah, Riley had been honorable, adhering to the dress code when I know how he despises 'stuffy clothes.'

"Libby!" He shouts, breaking free to embrace my aunt.

Riley adores Libs. They've spoken on the phone at length every time she's called. He was always around, a staple of my life now, and their conversations had taken off over FaceTime. Watching it unfold again, blooming in real time, feels so natural.

My circle had grown so large, yet it remained intimate somehow. Each of these bonds stood on its own, unique, without needing a link to chain us together. God forbid Derek and I ever break up; I still felt confident I would never lose touch with the faces around me, with the feelings that had brought us all together.

now, december

MUCH LATER, after the guests had departed and the clean-up crew had begun to tidy the mess left behind, I sat cross-legged with Libby on the couch in the lower level of Derek's apartment.

The normally open formal living room had been closed off for the event, and large panes were set up to provide privacy. I'd never hung out much in this space before. It's always seemed more for the show, another exhibition, rather than a live-in feature.

The boys were still out, enjoying drinks in the gardens, while Libs and I had changed into comfy clothes. We were ready to gossip about the evening and all the people she now had fresh in her mind to match with the names I had mentioned over the past few months.

"Well?" I asked, anxiously awaiting her feedback while she sipped from her cup.

Tonight, the room didn't feel formal at all. It had been decorated like an ad in a Christmas catalog, brought to life by the roaring fire a few paces away. I snuggled into the fur blanket, scrutinizing her scrunched nose and the tap of her finger on the ceramic mug she cradled in her hands.

"I love them." She says, at last, putting me out of my misery.

"Yeah?" I squeak.

"Truly, Al. They're all amazing. Riley is exactly what I'd expected— crude and remarkable. Margot is lovely. Duke, riveting. And Derek, Derek is yummy." She laughed, her shoulders shaking lightly.

"Libs!" My mouth fell open in disbelief as my aunt drooled over my boyfriend. I begin to throw a pillow at her but catch myself, not wanting her tea to ruin the soft leather of the Chesterfield.

She settles, then pulls her brow together, something outside the glass catching her attention and troubling her.

"What?" I pry.

"The tapestry." She muses, quieter than before.

"It's incredible, yeah? Ornate."

"Indeed, but Rivera..." She stalls. "There's something oddly familiar about that name."

Fuck me. She pulls her phone from her pocket and types something. I know the moment her face changes again, she's found it. She *knows*.

Holding the screen in my direction, I read the email sent when Derek took over the class from Anderson. It lays out how the class is graded. His model was so unique that he wanted the floor open for any concerned parents to bring forth their questions.

Damn Libby's memory! I figured this would come out, that she would discover through a slip of the tongue (most likely Riley's, if we were being honest,) but I hadn't thought of her pulling up evidence from an email sent out months ago.

The set of her lips is stern when I push back her device. Disapproving.

"Well, I suppose you had to find out one way or another." I sigh.

"Allyson Parrish! Yummy or not, you cannot seriously be screwing around with your professor! What about your reputation? What about his?" She scolds. My confidant has been replaced with my guardian, who is ready to put me in place.

"Okay, he was never my professor. He's just an advisor."

"Great, so the professor is okay with it then?" She asks knowingly.

"Well... he's out on leave," I explain.

"So, *Allyson*, would that not then make Derek your professor? However temporary a position it may be?"

"Oh, come on! You are not seriously calling me out on a technicality. You were with us all night. You think I'd be doing all this to screw around? Getting our friends and *our family* involved? I'm *in love* with him. Maybe even more than I was with Grey." I whispered the last part so quietly that I questioned whether she had heard me.

This was not the direction I'd intended to go, but I hated how quickly her demeanor changed from adoring to judging. I'd thought getting to know him would make her react differently. I'd been wrong. "Don't be cross with me, Libs."

"Don't be cross?" She laughs. "God, you even sound English."

Libby takes a moment to process a million unspoken thoughts. I watch them pass across her face. She looks older in this way, almost like a parent. I should be worried, but seeing that expression again is oddly refreshing. I *want* someone in my family to care enough about my well-being to make me think through my decisions. Even though Derek is a decision I am confident in, it's still nice to see traces of my father in her concern. I squeeze her hand reassuringly. I will love her regardless of whether she supports me in this.

"Ugh!" She flings herself back dramatically. "Your mother will have my head for being on board with this! She's always thought I was too 'alternative,' filling your head with rebellion. I detest proving her right. Why couldn't you have fallen in love with someone easier, like the boy from the summer?" She jokes, phasing quickly back to her younger self.

"Derek *is* the boy from over the summer. How did you not figure that out already, Miss Sherlock?"

"No!" She gasps.

I cherish her more than I have words for. I recount every detail, from walking in on that first day and finding him in place of the expected Mr. Anderson to now. Well, *almost* every detail.

I watch her worry fade to understanding, evaporating as I fill in the gaps. By the end, I think she's fallen slightly in love with him too.

now, december

I DREAMED OF GREY. *We were back in high school. The bell rang, and everyone packed up to leave while he sat staring anxiously at his test, his pencil flicking back and forth in his hand. He looked panicked in a way I hadn't seen before, frantically flashing from the assignment to the clock on the wall.*

"Hey, what's wrong?"

"I'm such an idiot," he said.

"Why would you say that?" I asked, genuinely concerned. It wasn't like him to talk down on himself.

"I can't finish this test. I can't concentrate."

"Grey, you'll get it." I smiled. He would. He was a straight-A student. I glanced at the sheet to see what question he was on, but all that was there was my name.

"I'm not going to pass. You're going to leave me behind." He looked so frustrated, but his eyes were sore.

"I don't want to ever leave you behind," I said truthfully.

"You already have."

Derek appeared then at the door. "Ally, ready for rehearsal?"

I headed towards him, led as always by compulsion to be near him. In the hallway, the school had transformed, the walls aging to those of the university. He let his fingers brush against mine, still too public a place for him to grab my hand the way I so desperately wanted him to. We found ourselves at the auditorium, his calloused hands holding open the door for me to enter.

"Ally?" Derek questioned.

From behind us, there was a commotion—a crash, a clatter, things being slammed into the ground—the sound of my life pulling me backward. As something else fell, I felt myself retreat. The tightening began in my chest, like a noose around my heart.

"I'm sorry. I shouldn't be here." I excused myself politely. Confused, he walked into the theater without me.

I departed in search of the noise. Back in our old classroom, Grey had thrown the desks, broken their legs, and cracked and shattered the windows. He cried as a scar formed on his chin, sitting among the shards of glass on the floor. Grey never cried.

He hadn't noticed my presence, jumping when I touched his knee. He attempted to wipe his face, to hide the tears, but it was too late. I'd already seen.

"Hey, hey." I pulled at his arm. "What is all of this about?"

"It's all falling apart." His voice caught on a sob. Tears started falling, and I pulled him to me, his arms wrapping around my waist. An immediate calm washed over me.

"I need to know I've got you, no matter what. I'll be okay if I do. We're supposed to be together. Do I have you?"

"Always, Grey. You always have me." I pushed my fingers into his curly hair, and his lips softly fell into mine. I was met with liquid warmth as his kiss spread through me all the way to my toes.

I hadn't realized I'd been cold and frozen since he'd left me as if I was the one who died. Now, his touch was thawing me into revival, replacing all my broken pieces.

I woke with a start, relieved to have not stirred Derek

for once. I could still feel Grey's mouth where I shouldn't anymore. I shook my head and stood out of bed.

The good dreams were always so much worse than the bad, and I couldn't determine which category this one fell into. It had confused me more than anything, creating a double-ended guilt. Guilt that I had left Grey behind, exactly as he had accused me of. Guilt for cheating on Derek, even if only in my subconscious.

I hadn't relived an old memory but created a new one. A fantasy, however unachievable, still felt like betrayal. I *enjoyed* kissing Grey. I had *chosen* to leave Derek in pursuit of it.

I was drenched in indecency, which coated me thicker than the layer of sweat that caused my clothes to cling to my clammy skin. Creeping to the kitchen, I searched for my habitual glass of milk, my remedy when I needed a simpler comfort.

Finding no carton in Derek's fridge, I let out a huff. I needed to cool myself and decided a walk would probably be a good start. I'd go to the main kitchen. With Adaline's holiday prep, there would surely be milk left over. I descended the stairs into the conservatory, forgoing my shoes.

It'd only been a few days since the party. Christmas had officially come and gone in a whir of golden moments. Libby had stayed, departing only this morning for her next show, a reveal for some trust fund kid in Dubai who thought it'd be "cool" to have "real art" at his New Year's Eve party. Still, Libby was proud of her latest collection, each statue embodying a resolution. I loved it, just as I had loved having her around.

I had been perfectly dreamless with all the pieces of my heart gathered around, sharing intimate moments over candlelit dinners, and proper wrapped presents. Christmas had been too good to me. So what had caused the dreams to return? What had caused me to feel as if I needed to choose between Grey and Derek? And *had* I really chosen Grey, or was there a metaphor there that I couldn't yet make sense of?

The questions plagued me as I traced my way through the heated paths, enjoying the warm air pouring out of the grounded vents. It contrasted nicely with the frost-covered glass panes, which separated me from the outside elements. The routine of walking to the main kitchen had only just begun to help me detangle the mess in my mind when I came to pause in the Wisteria Room.

Duke sat on one of the swings; his head sloped unnaturally against the swing's rope. He looked too pale, too lethargic to possibly be the same man who'd commanded a wide audience only nights before. This Duke had succumbed, finally wearing his illness as if it had appeared in the moonlight and consumed him without any of us around to take notice.

"Duke?" I called faintly, praying he wasn't already gone. It would kill Derek if he were.

"Allyson." He awoke from his slumber, wise eyes pouring into me as he regained some volume. "Would you like to sit? I'd stroll with you, but I fear I'm much too tired to be any good at it."

"Are you alright? Can I do anything?" I worry aloud, settling onto the swing beside him.

He shook his head, asking, "Is it the dreams again?" as he dismissed my concern, focusing on my woes so he could ignore the existence of his own. I played along, hoping it might help the both of us.

"Different ones, but yes. Always the dreams." I sigh.

His weathered face appeared less sickly now that he was intrigued. The lavender hue of the moonlight through the flowers cast a glow across his face, making him appear otherworldly, a God or an alien sent to harbor my confessions.

"Derek?" He asks out of the blue.

I quirk my head, bewildered that he could know the content of my dreams. But no, I realize he's simply asking where Derek is.

"Still asleep," I answer, a beat too late.

"Ah." His lips purse together tightly as he stares off in the distance, waiting me out.

"Libby does that too. Sits in silence until my secrets pour out of me. It's a brilliant trick. Effective." I snap.

I'm unsure where this anger has come from, making my tone sound bitter. The biting words coming from my tongue nip at the dulling space as if they had teeth of their own.

I feel guilty. It isn't Duke I'm upset with. Duke is the epitome of what a good man should be. Thoughtful and genuine, kind down to his bones. I turn to face him with an apology in my eyes, appalled to find him smiling warmly back at me.

"I rather enjoy the peace of the quiet. Sometimes, noise is good for the soul. Sometimes, the absence of it is better." He replies, his voice weak and full of age.

"Duke, I was out of line. I'm so sor—" I begin. The old man holds up a knotted hand to stop me.

"People share their stories in their own time. They cannot be forced, or made, to share the things closest to their hearts before they are ready in fear it will rip apart the very fabric of their identity. Have you noticed all anger spawns from fear, Allyson?

Anger is controllable, you see? Fear is not. It feels good to be in control, but be cautious of the masquerade, child. It distracts, not absolves. Often, it will lead to the same result you are afraid of. It is a genie granting your wish." He shares.

His words evoke a feeling inside of me. I sit in my guilt and fear for a while, replaying his sermon in my head—dissecting, highlighting, and defining each piece of its meaning. He was exactly right. I snapped because I was afraid, not angry.

I had started to feel that my life was becoming what it was meant to be. Every moment had led me into that bar, to Derek so I could be exactly what I am.

The dream confused me, reverted me, reminded me of the loss, and made me question: Had they not died, would I have turned out differently? I would have been happy, sure, but would I have discovered who I really was?

The thought terrified me as it was an outlook I hadn't considered. Was the war really between Grey's memory versus Derek's right now? Or was it between the Ally I was and the Ally I've become?

"So, is it more honorable to always be afraid?" I question once I've puzzled myself into oblivion.

I knew I had been wrong in snapping at Duke; there was no doubt about that. Still, I struggled to find the answers to my questions, and that same frustration, that same *fear*, rose within me. What was the right way to absolution?

"No, it isn't better to be afraid." He says, solemnly. "Fear is useful to the point of action. You must act on it, Ally. Confront yourself so you don't continue to confront others with your hurt. It's a poor way to live."

"How, though? How do I confront myself?" I demanded.

I reminded myself he was just a man, not a God. He was

not a voice of the skies. As much as I wanted to believe he knew everything, wise as he was, he was still only human. I had to be reasonable. Yet, it did not mean he had not been sent to guide me. I felt very close to religion at this moment. Confused and on the brink of an uncertain epiphany.

"Did Derek ever share why I built the gardens around this room?"

I shake my head no, explaining how Derek had wanted him to tell me himself.

"It was for my mother. To say goodbye." He tells me the story then. As he spoke, I thought of my father.

I'd never been a big believer in God, but he had. As a child, when we'd talked of the Bible, he'd said perhaps it wasn't meant to be taken literally; maybe the stories were only ever meant to teach us lessons. For some, the text spoke to them. For those it didn't, God would find other ways to communicate.

My father had recounted a time he'd been sitting in traffic struggling with a decision when a radio show came on that addressed his issue directly. He'd felt it had been God speaking to him through the only channel he could. I felt like that now, listening to Duke's story. I finally understood what it was that I needed to do.

"I need to go home. To Virginia. I need to say goodbye."

"Then you must go," Duke said.

We sat for a while, absorbing the lavender light as if we both hoped the quiet would heal us. I began thinking of Derek, asleep upstairs, his hand twitching under the blankets, searching for me. Now that my panic had waned, I missed him. I stood without thought, being called by an invisible force back to bed. I thanked Duke as I took leave.

"Allyson?" He rasped when I reached the hallway out of the Wisteria room, causing me to turn back. "Remember what I've told you. Would you—" He rarely hesitated and I listened closely as he continued with his ask. "Would you share it with Derek too? Or rather, would you share it with him when he most needs it?"

I understood very quickly what he meant. Fighting tears, I made a promise to share everything he'd told me when it became Derek's turn to say goodbye to *him*, to Duke.

now, january

DEREK HOLDS my hand tightly as we step off the plane into the RIC airport. It is small, plain, and familiar. It is nothing like the crazed neon hustle of Heathrow, and I find myself wishing for London instead, for all its comfortable chaos. I like being lost. Here, at every gate, a piece of my past that threatens to swallow me whole.

We passed the row of metal chairs where I sat with the Kingsleys as we waited for our flight to New York that year for their birthday. I can see my green travel case with the leather bindings sitting on the floor by my feet. I can hear Grey rambling about the storefront displays on 5th Avenue and which he thinks will be my favorite. I can picture the back of Charlie's blonde head bouncing impatiently as she waited for our coffee order.

I bury my nose into Derek's shoulder. I close my eyes and let him lead me as if we were walking through a haunted house and not an airport.

I admire him for his resolve. He does not question my actions. When we make it to the exit by security, he whispers, "We're through." It is a curved hall, and I know when we get to the end, there will be something new to face—something much more demanding—my mother.

I create a new mantra. I repeat it over and over: *This is not meant to be comfortable. Saying goodbye never is.*

Derek stops, pulling me against his chest. I breathe in his linen and bergamot, that addictive hint of ginger, and let myself be absorbed into him. He hums one of our songs into my hair, and some of the tension fades. I think I got it wrong. He is the one built of magic, not me.

"You are brave to be here, Ally. But you don't have to keep being brave. I am with you every step of the way." He says, shifting back.

Looking into Derek's eyes, so much like the pine trees growing in the yard of my childhood home, the home we will be visiting shortly, I regain my balance. Duke and Libby are in my head, swirling their wisdom, and I reframe my perspective.

I press my lips to Derek's and enjoy the bees that replace the chainsaws.

"They're everywhere," I whisper. "And it hurts."

"I know." He says quietly. "It was the same for me after my mom. I couldn't stand to drive past the hospital where she died. I'd take a longer route to the studio to avoid it. I'd avoid ice cream, honeysuckle, or any of her favorite things. Missing her was too painful. When I was ready, I tried again. I remembered all the things I had forced myself to forget. It felt like, in a small way, she was present in my life again."

I think this over and nod.

"Okay. Let's do it."

"I love you." He says like an oath, bracing me for what is ahead.

My mother comes into view, pacing and waving her

hands in the air as she talks to my stepfather. Michael is sitting on one of the waiting benches, appearing bored. His arms are crossed over his belly. He seems to grumble in response. Neither of them has noticed our approach.

"Mom," I announce when we are a few feet behind her. She turns, her face breaking into tears, as she hugs me.

Derek let go of my hand so I could be present, but I wish he hadn't. He is my mood stabilizer, and I feel the instability arise from being back in her arms. The maternal pull I once had to her as a child began to snap somewhere along the way when she stopped believing in me.

Now, I feel like I'm meeting her for the first time as a stranger. I need to get to know her again to let these feelings go. Abandonment is the word for it. I feel like she abandoned me when I needed her the most. She'd always sent me away when I desperately needed her to stay.

She leans back to take me in. She's crying like I've come back from war. Maybe I have.

Michael clears his throat. He's never had a problem with interrupting a moment.

"Ally." He says as she steps away. He gives me an awkward side hug. "Good to see you."

I'm as anxious as I used to feel during that week at Granny Neah's. It feels like a million tiny spiders are crawling on my skin, and I want to scream. I want to run back through the gate and beg them to put me on a plane.

I ache for the faces of the people back in England. I ache for the family I have chosen as my own. The blood and the ring that connect me to the people in front of me seem weak in comparison. Like strings that threaten to pop as the anger I feel grows in their presence.

Let yourself lose control, Al. It's okay.

We stand awkwardly for a moment before a voice breaks the tension.

"Carol. Michael. I'm Derek Rivera." Derek extends his hand to my mother, who finally acknowledges him. Her eyes drink him in appreciatively, if not a bit surprised. She flushes as if embarrassed, and I assume the worst. *"This is Derek? What is he doing with her?"* I imagine her thinking.

I focus on my man. Gratitude fills me, grounds me, and I remember what I'm doing this for. I have a life waiting for me. I don't want to go into it with guard rails. This is part of letting go. It's a battle I need to fight.

"*You're* the boyfriend?" My mother asks in awe, confirming my suspicions.

"I'm the lucky lad." He offers a show-stopping smile and pulls me to his side. I feel his heartbeat and my own begin to sync up. I admire him for not filling the silence with polite but false statements like "It's so nice to meet you." He doesn't lie to appease people, yet he remains the perfect gentleman.

"Thank you for looking after her," Michael interjects. Derek's eyes harden—jaw tenses. There's my guy.

Derek tries hard not to scoff. A pulse of air comes audibly out of his nose. He'd almost hid it. Almost.

"She's never needed me to." Derek quips, his smile turning forced. Michael shifts uncomfortably.

My mother attempts to save the conversation, but I have stopped listening. She weaves in and out of people, rambling on about town gossip that no longer interests me. She says the names of people I've forgotten the faces of.

When we make it to baggage claim, Derek collects our belongings. Michael tries to help by paying for one of those luggage carts. We only have a duffel each and our guitars. We have no need for the cart, but I thank him anyway.

"The car isn't parked too far away. We can be home in an hour or so. I'm preparing that chicken you like, Allyson, and I've got your old room all made up!" She states as if she wants to applaud herself.

"Mom, I told you we were staying in a hotel. We already rented a car. It's really sweet that you came all this way, but we already paid." I *hate* that I feel guilty.

She looks appalled as if this is the first she has heard about it. I even texted her our plans last night to avoid such an exchange.

"Now, come on, Allyson." Michael butts in. "Your mother did all of this work to prepare for your arrival. Can't you get a refund?"

Derek had excused himself to get the car and was going to meet us around the front. They must have thought he stepped away to the restroom, the way they speak like things aren't already in motion. Michael takes my silence for submission.

"Now go tell that boy you're coming home with us." He says with a huff.

I'm trying not to allow emotion to consume me. I remember now why I spent most of high school at the Kingsleys.

Fight, Ally, but fight the right way.

"No, Michael. That *man* has a name. It's Derek. And we're not staying with you." I stand my ground and turn my attention to the person who matters most.

"Mom, I love you. I know you put effort into this, and I see that, I do. It means a lot that you want me close. You saw me at my absolute worst for a year. I'm here. I want to finally confront what happened, but I can't pretend this isn't hard for me. Please don't ask so much of me because if you do, I *will* disappoint you." I take her hands in mine when I speak, and her eyes well up with tears.

She nods. When she hugs me this time, a barrier has broken between us.

"Of course, Ally." She says using my preferred name instead of the one she wrote on my birth certificate.

All I've ever wanted was for her to hear me. It seems like she finally has.

now, january

DEREK PULLS UP to the curb, our bags already loaded in the back of the SUV we rented. He gets out to open my door for me while I tell my mother goodbye. I promise we will be over for dinner tonight once we've had time to shower and rest. She looks hopeful. Michael mutters a few clipped parting words.

The moment we pull away, Derek laughs. He really laughs. The entire frame of his body is shaking.

"That was one of the most awful things I've ever been through." He chokes out. After my shock subsides at the outburst, I begin to laugh, too. His fingers entangle with mine across the console.

"You grew up with those people?" He asks once our fit dies down.

"No." I furrowed my eyebrows, pulling one side of my lip into my cheek.

Of course, I didn't grow up with Michael. From all our talks about my father, I thought he knew this.

"I mostly grew up with my dad. I lived in the hospital where he worked until I was about eight or so. I saw my mom a couple of times a week, but my dad and the staff mostly raised me."

"Wait, wait— you lived in a hospital?" He says in amazement. "How did your dad get by with that? My father would have been right cross if anyone had ever attempted. 'The scandal!'" He mocked.

"Being a patient, I suppose it was pretty easy for your father never to question mine." I laughed.

Derek pulls the vehicle over on the side of I-95 and rotates his whole body in my direction.

"You grew up in Empyrean?" He asks with unease.

My cheeks grow hot. I'm not sure why I feel ashamed like I've omitted something important from him. He knew I had been sick, just not *where* I had been sick. Being boarded in one of his father's hospitals wasn't *that* big of a secret, was it?

Suddenly, every detail he's told me about his father floods back and it *does* seem like that big of a secret.

I nod, now wary.

"I should have told you. I'm sorry. It had seemed so small, but now it doesn't feel like it. My dad took a job there when I was five or so after he published his research for Juvenile Paget's Disease in *The New England Journal of Medicine* and *The Lancet*.

Empyrean recruited him. They were offering him a grant to start his drug trial, and my care would be free. It had been costing my family a fortune, so he took it. Eighteen surgeries and too many medications later, I was cured, and we left that same year." I explain.

"God, saying it all out loud— it really doesn't seem small at all. I didn't mean to keep it from you."

Derek's sitting back in his seat with his eyes closed, looking nauseous. It's making me feel icky and deceptive.

Of all I had planned to confront in Virginia, this wasn't on the list. It hadn't occurred to me to bring it up, but now that I have, it feels explosive, like it might ruin us.

"Did you know who I was? When we met? Was it all planned to get back at my father, somehow, through me?" He puzzles out loud, finally looking at me. His eyes are piercing, like knives. It's the most he's ever resembled the man he's referring to, and it's disconcerting. Further disconcerting is the accusation.

"*What?* Derek, no. Empyrean saved my life. What would I have to get back at him for? I was shocked when I found out you had any relation to him. You don't even have his last name! I was just a patient at one of a hundred facilities. I'd never even met him before that night at the pub. Why would you think that?" I awe, stunned. I'm panicking like I've been caught and defending myself against something I can't quite understand.

"Do people use you to get back at your father?" I pose as an afterthought, bringing my hand to his knee in reassurance. It kills me to think of anyone using Derek as a pawn for his father's misdealing.

He jerks his knee away from my touch. His elbow is resting on the ledge by the window as he bites the pad of his thumb nervously. I reach for his hand, pulling it to my cheek so he will look and see *me*, not this idea he's concocting.

"Derek, talk to me. Please." I beg.

He holds my gaze, and those edges I haven't seen in so long begin to soften. Derek bows his head, letting his forehead rest against mine. His hands tangle in my hair. I hold his wrist, securing him to me like he might change his mind and pull away.

"*I love you.* This isn't a game to me." I promise.

"I didn't even know you had been sick. How did I not know this?" He asks, pained. "It's like I keep learning all these ways I could have lost you, Al. And to hear my father's involvement in your life at all, let alone from such a young age, makes my head spin. I feel like I'm going mad."

"I don't remember a lot of it," I say quietly. "It's all a blur. My life didn't really start until I got out. That's when things become clear again. I only have pieces. Holidays. Following him around the hospital, treating patients. He'd let me use the stethoscope to listen to their heartbeat." I laugh lightly.

He smiles at the sound, his fingers twisting and untangling themselves from the strands before starting over.

"It wasn't a bad childhood. It just wasn't much of a childhood at all," I admit.

It's like I'm hardwired not to talk about those days. It's such a foggy part of my memory, only coming to the surface in images of jello cups and whatever TV program kept me entertained that week.

Derek presses his lips to mine, and his mouth is so warm and inviting that I'm hungry for more. It takes away the pain, worry, and tension I had felt moments before.

"I shouldn't have reacted so poorly. I'm sorry. I fucking trust you more than anyone, and suddenly, I felt like I didn't know who you were. It honestly scared the shit out of me, Ally." He whispers, pulling back.

"I felt like I lost you for a moment," I confess. "I don't ever want to feel like that again. I had a clear lapse in judgment. I should have told you, but you know I would never lie to you, Derek.

There's this whole idea of soul mates— of two arms, two legs, and only one heart because we're always searching for our other half. I don't feel like you're my other half. I don't feel like you complete me. We're both our own people, totally whole without the other, but you're who I want, standing beside me always. I *never* meant to deceive you."

"I know." He sighs. "Fuck, I know that. I love you so Goddamn much." He says as I wrap my arms around his neck, holding him to me.

I'm oddly glad we had this conflict. We've never really fought, and if anything could break us, this seems like a good place to start. Yet, we've shown we're stronger than we thought—more capable of surviving. I feel closer to him than I ever have, and we jest about that shared sentiment as we cruise back onto the road. The stress I had been feeling about seeing my hometown feels microscopic compared to the stress I had felt over possibly losing Derek.

As we drive, our conversation shifts from heavy to light congruently. I point out landmarks of my life as we pass them. The city where Grey and I used to travel for concerts and festivals, for the good bookstores. He tells me about life on the road with Zach before Duke got sick. How favorite bands of mine had shared the stage with him. I'm so engrossed in his old life, that I don't realize when we have entered the setting of mine.

I quiet as we pass the road to my old school before asking him to turn around. We park in the student lot, which is still half full of cars, the way it always was on a Tuesday at this time. We stay in the quiet for a bit before I open the door and step out onto the pavement. The heaviness I thought we'd left on the side of the road has returned, the air thickened with memory.

Derek comes to my side and waits. He doesn't touch me, letting me do this on my own. I point out where Grey used to park his Jeep and where Charlie would park her dented-up Mercedes replacement to the KIA she had totaled when she first met me. I tell him what sports practiced on what fields during different times of the year and how we'd take our lunch breaks on the bleachers to soak up the sun and watch. We walk in that direction.

Climbing the stairs, we reach the old spot. I sit in Grey's while Derek sits in mine. I lean my head back and feel the warmth of the sun shining brighter here than it has any day in England.

I tell Derek about Grey's short stint on the field. The football team had just begun to start winning; players were getting noticed and scouted by major colleges for the first time in our school's history. We were gaining national recognition. Our no-name school was on target to compete with the nation's top schools. Then, in our homecoming game, Grey blew out his shoulder and had to quit playing. The scouts stopped coming. The media fell off.

Derek fills me in on his time playing T-ball when he lived in the States with his mom. When he went to swing, he let go of the bat, taking out his coach. This, combined with the rugby incident, caused his mother to quickly realize that sports were not going to be his passion in life.

The shadows change their angles, and I feel time moving around us. Our window to go inside is closing. The school wasn't on my list of places to visit— only my house and the Kingsleys were— but now that we're here, there's one place I want to see. I take a deep breath, feeling lighter than when we arrived.

Inside the school, we're held at security, and it's becoming increasingly apparent that I might have to remove this last-minute addition from my list after all.

"I'm sorry, ma'am. I can't let you in if you're not a

student or faculty." The officer says from behind his little glass box.

I see the stack of visitors passes in front of him and try to think of a distraction to snag one or a good enough excuse to reverse his no. I used to know the old guard and had been confident this wouldn't be an issue, but he has since retired, and the new guy is a hard ass. Derek's eyebrows bunch as he thinks through his own excuse to charm the guard into letting us in.

"Ally?" A voice stops behind us.

"Mr. Walsh?" I ask. He looks well. Happier, maybe.

He breaks into a smile. "What are you doing here? Don't tell me you're applying for a teaching position." He laughs merrily. Derek bites back a snicker, and we exchange a knowing look.

"No, actually. This is my first time being back since, well, you know, and I was hoping I could look around. Get some peace." I try for broken honesty. My explanation is not very convincing so I'm doubtful it will improve our predicament.

"Bridges, give the girl some passes. She's not going to blow the place. I'll escort them around myself." Walsh shoots at the guard, his voice dripping with forgotten satire.

Bridges does not look pleased. "Mick, you know that's not the policy." He reprimands under his breath, causally referring to Walsh by his first name.

"Well, call the Goddamn principles office and get him down here, then. We will make an exception for this no matter how high I have to go up the damn ladder!" My former English teacher steams.

Bridges—I know that name. The longer I stare at the bulky young man behind the counter, the more I see the face of the boy he was two years ago.

"Wait— you're *Clay* Bridges? Nose tackle on the football team, right?" I ask.

"Yeah?" His features transform from annoyed to worried like I might be a stalker of some kind.

"You were on the team with Grey Kingsley," I say.

The features fall, sadness taking over.

"Yeah... Yeah, I was. It's awful what happened." He says, hanging his head.

"He used to talk about you a lot. Said you were the funniest guy on the team and that was important because it kept people together." I remember out loud, smiling. It's a happy memory, and if it does nothing else, at least Bridges seems to be uplifted by it.

"You knew him?" He asks.

"She was his girlfriend, you little dipshit," Walsh says from behind me, still annoyed that the guy won't let us in.

"You're *that* Ally?" Bridges' eyes widen. "Wow. You look different. I've never heard anyone talk about anyone the way Grey talked about you. Here, take the passes. Get your peace." He quotes me from earlier, then smiles sheepishly, revealing he had been eavesdropping.

"About time." Walsh huffs. It was good to see some things hadn't changed.

"Where do you want to go?" He asks us.

"Your class is the only place on my list. The rest we'll pass on the way there." I give him my sweetest look to prevent him from scoffing.

"My class?"

I nod and start pointing out things to Derek to keep Walsh from questioning me further. I tell him about our first day at lunch, how Grey was the hot new kid catching all the attention. He'd ignored it and shocked my classmates by plopping his tray next to *mine*. I tell him how Grey would sometimes change into his gym clothes during my class, a class he was not part of, to join me in running laps around the court. Walsh laughs, remembering how the teachers had to have a meeting on how to keep attendance straight after more kids began to follow in Grey's example.

My favorite story happens when we finally make it to Walsh's classroom. He sits to grade some papers, and I take my old seat by the window. I tell Derek about the day Grey showed up outside the window and busted me out. When I tell him about the AC, Walsh jumps out of his chair.

"That was him?" He yells. I don't know who is cackling harder, Derek or myself.

"Goddamn AC was broken all year after that," Walsh grumbles.

"It wasn't broken from Grey," I confess.

"The hell do you mean it wasn't broken?"

"After Grey, Urie got... inspired. Grey had only disabled it for the day. Urie couldn't figure out how to, so he just started smacking it until it permanently broke. That's the story anyway." It's fun talking to Walsh and seeing his reactions in a new light as a peer instead of another student in his class.

"I fucking hated that kid," Walsh admits.

Before we go, Derek asks to see the auditorium. I was never in band, theater, or even a talent show. Outside of shadowing Charlie, the auditorium held no importance to me. My stage fright was so severe back then. I tell Derek this, but he insists.

Walsh sits in the front row with his bag packed full of papers he's yet to grade. He seems to deliberate doing so now to give us space but appears to decide against it. He looks happy to be our tour guide for the moment. I think, as an English teacher, he enjoys hearing the stories.

When Derek climbs the stage, he extends a hand to me.

"We came here to confront your fears, Al. Those things extend beyond Grey and Charlie. You were afraid of this stage for four years. You should perform on it at least once." He says. I had always dreamed about being brave enough to stand up here and sing. I never was.

"It's time." He assures, sensing my lingering doubt. He confidently heads for the piano on the right of the stage. I don't remember it ever being there before. It seems kismet that we're here, and it's here, even that Walsh is here. Fate twisting again. I sit beside him, regaining my confidence as I settle into the black-and-white road of keys before me. Derek starts playing the song we began to write on the plane. When he starts to sing, Walsh stops playing on his phone.

"If I could speak to you somehow,
I'd tell you you're even more beautiful now,
Than you were at sixteen.
It's okay to escape, but don't be afraid.
Of the terrible things you've seen."
He sings to me in the words we had imagined Grey would say if he could.

"You threw a pass through the sky and
I watched it fly like it had wings,
Do you think it knew, someday you'd join it up there too?
It's hard not to grieve all the spectacular things,
You'll never get to see."
I sing to Grey like he's here in the crowd.

"Truth is, I'm jealous of heaven because it gets to keep you." I belt.

"Truth is that heaven was any place I got to touch you." Derek belts back.

"Maybe our heaven was every memory we left behind, Forever mine." We harmonize together.

When the song ends, I'm sobbing. I'm laughing. The whole thing is confusing, but I feel *so much* better. Mr. Walsh is standing with five other teachers and random students who heard the commotion and came to check it out.

The after-school clubs all ended a while ago, the front doors now locked from the outside. Bridges is among the few in the room. They're all clapping. The ones who knew Grey are crying, too. This is a moment I will never forget, that I never got to have here on this stage. I will forever owe Derek for encouraging me to take it.

When we were finally ready to leave the school, Walsh pulled me aside and handed me a few pages.

"This was Grey's last essay in my class. I'm not sure why I've held onto it all this time, but your coming here today makes more sense than anything else. I think you should have it."

I throw my arms around him in a hug he didn't expect. He stumbles awkwardly before hugging me back. I thank him a million times for the paper, for the tour, for being my teacher what feels like a lifetime ago.

Derek is giddy when we get in the car. "That was— " He sighs.

"That was the best possible outcome. Thank you." I kiss him over and over before we depart for my mother's.

now, january

DINNER with my mother and Michael is somehow more excruciating than facing my memories. Derek leans in to remind me we've had worse. Michael is an opinionated stick in the mud, but he's no Ade.

My head becomes fuzzy when my mom asks about school, my friends, if I'm eating. I fight not to roll my eyes. She always hated that. I was grounded too many times for the action in middle school and even lost the door to my room for it once. I fill her in while Michael sizes Derek up across the table.

It feels surreal to see Derek sitting in the chair that Grey used to sit in. My mother had repurposed the table from a barn door she and my father had stolen. After her grandmother had passed, the property was sold quickly. Having no time to gather prized possessions from the house, they'd snuck onto the land and worked the door off its hinges— it wasn't the heirloom jewelry or the wedding dress she had wanted, but it was a memento. He spent weeks sanding and staining it, adding legs to turn it into a table.

After dinner, Derek and I climbed the evergreen trees in

the front yard. The sun had set hours ago, but once our eyes adjusted, we could see well enough to get our holds. We sat at the top for a long time, and I pointed out everything to him, including the pine trees off to the side that mirrored his eyes. I told him about this neighborhood or that and my interactions with the kids who used to live there.

I talk about things I haven't thought of in years, like the stalker I had in 7th grade who used to wait for me at my bus stop. I had to change my routine and get off at a neighbor's house until my mother could pick me up after work. That was when my mom first met Michael. He was one of the officers who had investigated. They began dating later that year and were married early into the next.

We leave a short while later, checking into the hotel. It helps to separate me from my surroundings. It's a nice break after being flooded with so many emotions today. We shower and wear our spa robes as Derek strums the chords to a new song at the desk about a beautiful girl with rainy-day eyes that brought him back to life. I lay on the bed to watch him play and wonder how I had gone so long without knowing he existed. When he finishes, I pull him into bed. His lips igniting the charge inside of me.

She's back, the insatiable girl who can never get enough of him. I'm not gentle or subtle in my teasing. I was going to be the one to stop it, to refrain this time, but he startles me by gently lifting my waist so I'm seated against his hips. All of our bare parts are touching, and I'm nothing more than a girl made of bees and sensory impulses.

"I want you." He whispers, grabbing my hair to pull my ear close. "I want all of you, Ally. Please, tell me if you don't want to, but I want to be inside of you."

Without hesitation, I raise my hips and lower myself onto him. Our moans entangle as our bodies become indistinguishable from one another. I can't tell where I end and he begins. I'd imagined it'd be amazing once we learned each other, but my vagina doesn't seem aware that this is new, that it *should* take a while to be comfortable. I immediately begin to move. His hands shoot out to stop me, holding my thighs in place.

"Stop moving." He warns. "You—that, bloody hell. That feels incredible, Al."

The rasp in his voice and the lust in his eyes have rendered me incapable of sitting still. The harder I attempt to, the more I feel myself tightening, trying to absorb him into me as if that were possible.

His cock twitches deep inside of me, and I lean forward to stifle my cries of pleasure in the pillow seated beneath his head. I'm doing all I can to keep from waking the people in the next suite over.

Leaning slightly forward, I gain friction. He curses, sitting upright to secure my place in his lap. It does the opposite of his intended effect. He bottoms out, and I become incapable of not fighting against him.

"You're a Goddamn minx. I'm not going to last long." He cautions, now working with me to guide my strokes.

"I don't care," I beg.

It's true. He could lose it right now. I have less than seconds myself. Our constant edging all these months has built me up to the shortest and most powerful orgasm of my life. It's almost blinding when I come when he locks his hands onto my ass and lets go of himself, sending the both of us careening into oblivion.

I don't remember how we cleaned up or when we separated, but I wake up from the best sleep I've ever had, and we do it all over again.

Our sex is different than anything I've had before.

Better even than it had been in my deepest fantasies. We didn't need the fingerprints or the dirty words at all. The feeling of him alone, of us connected, was unfiltered, unmade, back to basic necessity— like prose scattered across the bed.

"Why now?" I ask once we're both wasted, lying naked on dampened hotel sheets. They smell like Derek, or Derek smells like them. I can't tell anymore.

"I finally felt like I had all of you, everything you wouldn't let me see before. It felt like you *trusted* me. I didn't want to take that from you. I didn't want to be the guy that followed Grey if you weren't sure. Things shifted, Al. It wasn't just about not wanting you to regret it. I was terrified." He professes.

"Terrified of how fucked up I was?" I laugh.

"No. I was scared of the moment when you woke up, and I wasn't him. It mattered too much, and I didn't want you to leave." He explains, playing with a strand of my hair that's fallen onto his pillow. He looks so innocent, so vulnerable. I crawl between his legs, resting my head on his chest so his heartbeat thumps in my ear.

"You're everything I want. How could I ever leave you?" I ponder more to myself than him. My fingers trace pictures across his ribs before his arms tighten around my frame, securing me to him.

"I hope you never do."

now, january

AFTER OUR MORNING ROUNDS, we get our coffee from the lobby, still on a high. It isn't until the car ride over that we begin to settle, driving in silence to the Kingsleys.

This is the heavy part. My heart begins to race as we turn onto their street. I hold my breath as we pull in front of the house. Where it used to sit tall and Victorian in the distance, there is only open air now. No one has bought and built over the property. The ruins of the foundation still sit as they were, though the debris has been cleared out. Flashes of that night overtake my senses as I relive it.

I push open the door before Derek can put the vehicle in park and stumble out, holding on to the frame like I did then. He hangs back while I move forward, like a fawn gathering her footing on unstable limbs.

I sit on the porch next to where the swing used to hang. Where Grey and I would curl up in the winter while he read me his latest work. Derek comes to sit beside me, and we resonate in the silence for a bit.

When I feel ready, I share everything I can remember

about this house: where their rooms used to be, what Marilyn would fix for dinner, Grey's walls of books, and how he'd stay up late under the glow of his old green desk lamp to finish a chapter he was writing. Charlie's room, which was really just an extension of her closet, clothes strewn all about. He listens intently as I purge information.

It's a different feeling being here with him, my legs draped over his lap while his hand rests lazily on my thigh. We end up laughing over stories. The time Charlie and I dressed Gigi and let her do her own makeup, which had turned into a total train wreck, and how Marilyn's jaw had dropped when she strutted into the kitchen. Derek becomes amused as the tales shift to Grey, all his cocky self-assurance, and how he had plotted to make us a thing.

It isn't as heavy as I had thought it would be. It isn't private like I had imagined I'd *need* it to be when I came back. It's better.

* * *

On our final day, my mother saw us off. Michael had an early shift, and no one's heart broke when he couldn't make it. She hugs me tightly and sends me away with a loaf of her homemade banana nut bread and a promise to call more often.

Since I started school, our daily phone calls had dropped off. I'd blocked her, as I'd blocked the rest of the unpleasant things. It's an easy promise to make now that our relationship feels on its way to mend.

I sleep dreamlessly in the terminal, waiting for our departure and again on the flight back to London. We're exiting the plane when Derek turns on his phone to a thousand messages. We don't stop at baggage claim as we run out of the airport to hail a cab.

It's Duke. He had been rushed to the hospital overnight, as the ability to breathe on his own had diminished quickly. Upon assessment, the doctors placed him in hospice, with little hope he would make it through the day.

Derek is restless on the ride and moves briskly through the waiting room when we arrive. Maggie and Luke are already there, their faces hollow, sunken. Both sets of eyes are red-rimmed, both jaws slack, and both noses running. I know what is coming before he does. I know that Duke is gone, and we didn't make it.

"Where is he?" Derek asks. I lay my hand on his arm.

"He passed away an hour ago," Maggie tells him.

"I was here an hour ago. We had just landed, and he was still fine. I want to see him! Where is he?" Derek demands, his voice rising to a shout.

"Derek, he's gone," Luke interjects, choking on the words.

"No." Derek disagrees. "He would have said goodbye. He would have waited!" His voice starts to crack at the end. "No!" He yells. "I was here. I was *right here* in London."

Maggie breaks into sobs, and Luke wipes away his tears, rising to stand in front of his brother. Luke rests his hands on Derek's shoulders before pulling him close and hugging him tightly. I try not to let my cries escape my throat.

They held off on moving him until Derek could arrive. I don't want to go into the room. I don't want my version of Duke to be replaced with the memory of an empty shell. But it isn't about me. It's about Derek.

I hang by the door and wait for him to invite me in. I want to give him space to handle it how he needs to. As soon as he sees Duke's body and takes his cold hand, blue from the lack of oxygen—he begins to lose his composure, his shoulders shaking.

He turns to the spot beside him where I should be and searches the room frantically until his eyes land on mine in the doorway. He tilts his head, tears streaming down his face. I don't question what it means and move to his side.

"He didn't say goodbye," Derek repeats in a broken cry.

"Yes, he did." I remind him.

Duke had suggested our send-off to the States. The hotel had been his recommendation. The night before we left, the three of us had dinner, and I now see why it was so important to him. It was his goodbye dinner. He knew he wouldn't make it to see us get back. I had tapered off to bed early, and when Derek tried to accompany me, I insisted he stay longer with Duke.

"He knew," Derek whispers. I nod, kissing away the tears from his cheeks.

then, july

CHILDREN around me wept for hearts they did not know. I referred to them as children instead of classmates because I felt older than they would ever be. I had out-aged them—both the living and the dead.

The Kingsleys would never have another birthday. Gigi would never have her first kiss or be eighteen like I was at that moment. No one this young in my town had experienced loss like this. They'd lost a grandmother, a goldfish. They'd never lost their future.

Everyone wore black for the Kingsley's memorial service. We had a memorial and not a funeral because ash didn't look as good as a body inside a casket. Where there should have been a row of bodies, there were pictures instead. Charlie's yearbook photo smiled back at me. I could hear her complaining from the seat beside me.

"Ally, how could you have let this happen? There were so many better pictures they could have chosen! Didn't you get like final veto or something? I could *die* of embarrassment."

I turned to the spot from where her voice came, but of

course, it was empty. Her voice, a reproduction from my memories. I fought the urge to tell her, "It doesn't matter. You're already dead."

I detested the room, how it moved, crashing around me like an ocean of black—black pants and black dresses, all swaying, flowing together into one incomprehensible mass.

By the time the service had come to an end, I had blanketed myself in ignorance. I couldn't recall a single word that was said. I couldn't recite a single story given by our friends. They didn't seem like friends anymore. They didn't share the loss the same.

For them, it was unfortunate. It was a tragedy, no doubt, but they would move on. They'd vaguely remember the details of today or forget it entirely after a few years had passed. I would carry the weight of it forever.

The school principal and the funeral home director had asked me to stand at the front so people could pass along their condolences. This would normally be where the family stood, waiting to be graced with words of apology and faces full of support. As the entire family was dead, I stood there instead—an acting vessel for everyone else to filter out their sorrow.

I took the shape of a box so they could rid themselves of their unpleasant feelings. After the third person, I lost recognition of who was hugging me and who was crying into my shoulder. The box was full, and I no longer had room for anyone else's grief.

When I was younger, my father pulled me out of the hospital for a funeral. Someone I had never met from our family had died, and he was asked to be a pallbearer. I stayed glued to his side throughout the priest's words. I had never experienced death before that moment.

Being in a room with so many sad people scared me

worse than any horror movie ever had. There was no remote to turn it off. I felt powerless to see their sadness continue. Haunted that it would go on long after we all left the building. Long after the bodies had been lowered into the ground.

After all was spoken, my father and I retreated to a room with the other pallbearers. They went over their placement, their duty, their responsibility to the deceased. When he left the room, I was told to stay.

Minutes later, the direct family had been escorted in. Red-eyed and devastated— I felt misplaced. A trespasser among family I had never known. It wasn't long before they started asking me how I knew the man who had died, and I didn't know how to answer them.

I was never supposed to be there, invading their private moments.

I felt like that then, standing in front of the funeral home. I wasn't supposed to be there. It wasn't *me* who should have been accepting condolences from everyone at school. I was in the wrong place.

now, january

TWO YEARS AGO, it was me alone, wedged between the chapel doors of the funeral home, accepting condolences. Now, it is Derek.

I stand by his side and reach out to touch his back with every few faces that come to pass. When I left it, he still grew anxious. Now, I remove it so I can place it back when he needs it, and that seems to help alleviate some of his tensions. When the final person descends the staircase from the garden overpass above the fountains where Duke had requested his service be held, Derek pulls me tightly to him and holds on like I'm the only thing keeping him upright.

"I love you so much." He says into my neck. "Thank you. Thank you for being here." Tears are filling his eyes as he pulls away.

He flexes his jaw and rubs his hands down his face, his piano fingers taking the moisture with them. The composure floods back into him, and he reaches for my hand as we follow the procession into the Wisteria Room, where Duke's ashes are to be buried next to his mother's. I squeeze three times as we enter, a code we had developed during our dinners with Ade. One, I. Two, love. Three, you. He dips to press his lips to my cheek before standing and addressing the room.

In his last wishes, Duke had asked that Derek be the one to deliver his final eulogy as he was lowered into the ground. He gives a short speech, powerful enough to crumple the most stoic of men, and ends it by singing a song he'd written with Duke when he was little.

After his burial, Duke wanted people to stop being sad and celebrate with him one last time. The geezer had conned us all last month; *this* was his final party.

He had his favorite restaurant cater. Ballet dancers were flown in to honor that Duke was reuniting with his beloved. His early wife had been a fair woman and a talented dancer in the same company before her untimely death. I held Maggie's hand as we broke down during the performance. The piece was the very one Duke had watched when he first laid eyes on his bride.

A light show was set off in the fountains, and the open bar served cocktails named after his favorite flowers. The drinks matched the shade of the petals and were served with napkins explaining the history of the plant.

The evening was romantic and lovely. Like his gardens, he had found an intricate way to tell a story. This felt like the most special of them all because it was *his* story—the very man who brought stories to life.

Derek's absence sat with me throughout the light show. Luke was sniffling, and I held to his arm like I had held to Maggie's hand. I passed him a clean handkerchief Duke had given to me that night in the Wisteria Room. The night he finally shared its story with me.

It was where his mother would bring him as a boy for

picnics underneath the prettiest tree on all the land, the very wisteria tree we had sat under. His mother had died in his early adulthood, soon after the passing of his wife, and Duke had struggled to cope with those losses. Instead, he threw himself into the world of entrepreneurship. His dedication led to his quick success and his financial gain.

When Duke learned the property where he had so many happy memories as a boy was being condemned, he bought it. He built the whole estate around the wisteria tree. In every garden, every display, he paid tribute to her and the stories she told him. He wanted others to experience them the way he had. He left her a legacy.

As I cried over the Kingsley's deaths, over my struggle of moving on, Duke taught me how to keep them alive. He'd said my music was like his gardens. Even though they were gone, it was through me that the world would still have a chance to know them.

I recall the memory to Luke, the way I'll recall it to Derek when he most needs it, the way I had promised. It feels important that he knows how his grandfather would want to be remembered.

"Thank you, Ally." Luke hugs me tightly. "Go find my brother and remind him what a lucky bastard he is, will ya?" I laugh and push him ahead. Without Derek to flock to, Maggie has been taking the brunt of people's leftover apologies. I watch Luke glide in to offer her some relief.

I pause before going in to kiss Riley's cheek, to ruffle Matt's hair. The news of Duke's passing had hit Riley hard. By the end, he had probably spent more meals with Duke than Adaline. Riley's weekly lunches had turned daily as Duke's condition worsened. Before, they would talk for hours about music, acceptance, architecture. When Duke's cough had gotten too bad to speak, they played chess.

My dad was *my* forever teacher, but Duke was everyone's. Today is an awful day, to have to acknowledge the loss of someone so needed in the world. Today is an amazing day, to acknowledge all those left in it.

Luke, in his too-expensive suit, acting suave to cover the fact that he was just a big teddy bear. Maggie, constantly smoothing out the wrinkles in her dress and biting her cheek anxiously. She keeps glancing at the bar like she's worried the rubbish bins will overflow or the bottles will run out before the guests do. Riley, with his mohawk, who had bought another suit specially for this occasion. Libby, who flew out of Madrid to be here. Matt. Jace. Zach. Big Mike. Sonnie. There is so much love here I find it hard to be sad.

Derek is sitting in the Wisteria Room, where he has been since Duke was lowered. He had asked for time alone, and I had left him knowing he'd find me. But he hasn't moved.

"Do you want to sleep in here tonight?" I ask tenderly.

He shakes his head no and pulls me into his lap. We sit for minutes or hours in the silence— until I'm jolting upright in Derek's bed. I must have fallen asleep in his arms before he carried me upstairs.

My nightmares had been altered once again. Duke stood in the driveway of the Kingsley's, warning me not to go in. "All your pain will be wasted." He had said. I could have found meaning in it if I had stopped to ask him more, but I had to get inside.

Derek shifts beside me in bed.

"Ally, I can't do this tonight." He whispers.

"Shh. You don't have to. I'm okay."

I smooth his hair away from his face. It's started to get long again. He moves out of my reach. Trying not to let my feelings be hurt, I readjust. Derek sits up and leans against the headboard. He stares at the wall with a blank expression. There's no pain or passion, just nothingness.

"You're still having nightmares." He states emptily.

"I'm fine," I reassure him.

"You're not fine, Ally. Don't be *stupid*. We went all the way to Virginia to fix you, and it didn't work."

His words slice right through me. I fight the saltburn of my tears and beg them not to fall. I don't want to expose how much his comment stung. He's always been the person I could confide in without judgment, who saw my damage as a compliment to his own. It punctures me deeply that he's using it against me now.

"I'm sorry," Derek says, some emotion finally cracking through. "I didn't mean that. It's just hard to see you still struggle after all we sacrificed to get you closure. I rearranged my life to be there for him, and on the day he died, I wasn't there because of you." His eyes are maroon, his sentences bloodthirsty. I feel like I can't breathe. "I don't think I can do this anymore, Al. I can't even bear to look at you."

"You want me to leave?" I ask in shock. I don't understand where this is coming from. It feels like such a small thing has become so huge. I start to question if the resentment he is feeling began after Duke or if it had started before. Had I missed the signs?

"No, Ally. I want never to have met you. Break up with me." He says coldly.

Confusion swirls in my head. Only earlier today, he was telling me how much he loved me. It doesn't make sense. I make no move to leave; there's too much information circling my head. Too many moments I'm rethinking.

"Break up with me!" he yells suddenly, his face red. I

don't recognize his eyes at all. I don't recognize him. "Are you deaf, Ally? You need to GO!"

Fight kicks in, and I plead with him not to do this.

"You said you'd never leave." I choke out the words, on the verge of hyperventilating.

"I never said that." He warns coldly.

"You said you hoped I'd never go. I thought it meant the same thing."

"And you said you wanted us to be whole people, Ally! But I'm not whole anymore. I feel like I'm barely even half of anything. Hell, I'm more half of you than I am of myself, and it's fucking *suffocating* me." He pulls at his hair like I'm making him mental. It hurts, it hurts so much.

"I'm sorry." I sniffle. "I never meant to—"

"I know you never mean to, but you still do. I can't keep taking care of you, not when I need to take care of myself right now."

I nod as it sinks in that this is real, that it's really happening. He's ending it. Ending us. I thought we took care of each other, that it was a balance, and *we* balanced each other out. I thought that was the deal, but perhaps I'd been too selfish.

"You don't want me anymore," I say, wallowing in self-pity.

"Of course I want you." He softens. "You are *all* I want. That's why I have to do this. I need to get my shit together. Maybe when you're selling out shows in five years, and I can stand on my own again, we'll find ourselves back in the same pub." He smiles gently, trying to convince me of the words.

"In five years," I repeat, sounding as hollow as I feel.

"I'll give you some privacy to pack your things." He says, getting up from his spot beside me.

I crawl to the edge of the bed, catching him before he goes, and pull his hands to my face. The thought comes faintly like a whisper: if he stops to look at me, he'll see he doesn't want this. Then, somehow, we can work it out. His eyes don't meet mine before he turns away, retreating. Something about that motion solidifies his words. He doesn't want me to touch him anymore.

Stumbling to the closet, I grab my bag, gathering whatever I can fit into it while he excuses himself from the situation. He doesn't say where he's going; he just leaves. I feel numb walking out the door. The conservatory feels more like a coffin with no Duke, no Derek. Even the scent of the flowers reminds me more of a funeral home than a sanctuary.

Derek hadn't returned to walk me out, so I walked myself out, taking a seat on the steps in front of the stained-glass door. I forget I haven't called anyone to come get me, my mind too full of white noise, blinding recalls of every weak moment that pushed Derek to his breaking point. I feel pathetic, and scared, and very much alone.

Finally, I pick up my phone and dial Riley. He answers on the first ring, and when I explain what's happened, he says he'll be here in ten minutes, meaning he plans to break a lot of traffic laws.

I stare into the darkness, occasionally stealing peeks up at the light coming from Derek's room. I watch to see if he's returned, if he'll poke his head out to check on me once he realizes I'm gone, but he doesn't. The switch in his nature unsettles me. This morning, he would have killed someone for looking at me wrong, but now he seems to have discarded any care for me at all.

Before long, Riley swings into the drive and rushes over with open arms. He holds me tight for a second before ushering me out. My favorite blanket from our apartment is folded in my seat when I get in. The small act of kindness breaks my resolve. I begin to bawl halfway down the drive. As I explain what happened, Riley assures me it's not me. He says we've been around each other so much that Derek's self-sabotaging, that hurting me is like hurting himself. He swears Derek loves me. He swears he will be back.

I latch on to that hope the first two weeks we are apart. When it reaches a month, and he still hasn't called or bothered to return any of my messages, I begin to lose that hope.

It hurts to make music, so I write him letters instead. Whenever I miss him, I write another letter and add it to a box I keep hidden beneath my bed. Some are angry rants, others plead with him to come back to me, some are pure understanding of why he felt the need to end it— all are love letters. They help me make sense of things.

Derek has taken a sabbatical from teaching, and his position has been filled with another. I cheat the rest of the semester, recycling old songs for projects.

When the term ends, I move back to stay with Libby over spring break. She's as shocked as Riley was about my breakup with Derek. I hadn't been able to stomach telling her over FaceTime, though she'd sensed the change. She had startled me by suggesting there was some truth to Derek's parting words, that I should return to Virginia alone and try to process what had happened without dependence on anyone else.

I hated that it felt like he was right. As much as we had sworn to be whole people, I, too, had been split in half. I wrote my first new song in months.

"Did you know that I
Was someone's daughter when you

Sawed me in two?
I should have known better than to
Fall in love with the
Magician's son."

It was only a concept, not inspired by Derek, but by the heartbreak— the idea of being split. It feels good to know that this hasn't broken me. I may have lost Derek, but I haven't lost *me*. It's enough to feel confident with returning home. As long as there is music, I have the means to get through anything on my own.

Later that week, Libby is putting me on a flight.

now, march

BEING on the Kingsley's front porch alone is different than being with everybody else. In fact, I've never been here alone before. There was always someone in the house with me.

If I stare away from the house instead of into its ruins, I can almost pretend that time has moved backward. I sink into the heat of my puffer coat, moving from March to June. I sink until I'm sixteen again, sitting outside on an early summer's Eve, listening to the frogs and watching the lightning bugs.

When I bore of the view from the porch, I shift my perspective by moving to the backside of the house. I spy an old pool chair that's been blown to the edge of the fields. I drag it back and brush off the dirt and debris. I'm not concerned that my white jeans won't be white anymore once I sit on them. They're part of my old wardrobe, still living in my mother's house. It seems fitting that they be stained like the girl who bought them.

It's been two months, and I haven't heard from Derek once. I've stopped leaving messages. I had convinced myself he was doing this out of grief. His words didn't seem to line up with his actions. Even his actions hadn't lined up with his actions. Hours earlier, he had shown me how much he needed me. Then, I was discarded.

I'm making it about me when it isn't. It's about him, and if he feels like this is the right decision for him, I need to respect that. But it absolutely kills me that after all we shared, he hasn't missed me at all. Murders me, because I'm scared I'll never stop missing him the way I've never stopped missing the Kingsleys.

I've already written him a letter today, and it's just too sad to write him two in one day, so I call Riley instead. When he sees the state of the pool, he asks what kind of hobo hotel I'm staying at. I tell him it's the house that burned down, and now it's where the local kids hang out to tell ghost stories about the people who died when it happened.

I heard that's true, actually. It's a big party spot now. Charlie would love that. Grey would love being a scary story.

I compare myself to the girl I was when I ran in two years ago. It feels like a vast improvement, even broken-hearted. I never thought I'd fall in love again. It's unreasonable for me to be terribly sad. It was a blessing I hadn't expected to begin with. It was because of our story that I found my way back into the light.

I've grown so much since then. All the experience I've gained, the places I've been, the people I was lucky enough to meet along the way. Look at all I've accomplished in my songwriting. I've finally allowed myself to perform. To use my pain as a connector, exactly as Duke taught me. I may be hurt, but how can I not also be grateful?

I write out a single *Thank You* on a piece of parchment.

Folding it, I tuck it neatly in with the other letters in my bag. The sun is starting to set, and my mother will begin to worry if I'm not home for dinner.

I only have a few days left before my flight back to London. Thank God for all of Libby's airline miles she had saved. I start to stand and freeze when I see a man dressed in a vibrant polo tee and a tool belt circling the house with a clipboard. When he notices me, he jumps as if *I* startled *him*.

"Ma'am, you really shouldn't be here. This site isn't safe." He warns in a thick Southern accent. I relax. It looks like he's from the gas company, or maybe the county, conducting an inspection of the property. Perhaps it's finally been sold, and they're determining how safe it is for the new owners. "I'm going to have to escort you off the premises."

"Sorry," I mutter, rushing by him to my car. I slow as I pass.

His eyes are a startlingly liquid steel in the direct sun. They'd be beautiful if they weren't so chilling. He smiles in what I'm sure is supposed to be a warm gesture, but as he turns, I see the split. As if a hook had caught in his lip and stretched it upwards, the left half of his face was scarred, perpetually stuck in a smile. The mark has dragged his grin too high, sending danger signals to my brain. I flash back to images of circus clowns, the ones I've seen only in black and white photos. How even their exaggerated smiles still looked like frowns. Their makeup too void of color to be considered cheerful. He is like that, void of something vital.

He leads me to my car, now parked beside a large van with county decals on the side. The van feels like evidence of his qualifications, and I feel more secure with the designation.

I fumble with the door handle, struggling to get it open. The man has remained a few yards away. He lifts his hand in a slow wave. His uniform looks all wrong as if the polo is actually the costume and the clown suit is really his skin, hiding just beneath the collar. Buttons and ruffles lying in wait, ready to burst free in an instant.

At last, the door to the vehicle gives, allowing me access. I get in, rejoicing in the protective barrier as I peel out of the drive and down the street. When I glance at the rearview, he is there, standing in the street as he had been in the yard, still waving goodbye.

* * *

When I returned home, my mother was waiting with dinner. We ate together, enjoying each other's quiet company, before I returned to my room to sit by the window. I heard the door open down the hall and assumed it was only Michael getting home from his shift. My suspicions were confirmed when I heard his gruff voice greeting my mother. Then, her tone changed from casual to panicked.

"Michael, no! What are you doing? She's fine. *She's fine!* She's actually *healing.*"

"She's not fine, Carol! She's dragging us into her *shit* again, moping around the house all the damn time. Now she's got you manipulated enough to believe her. She needs to go back."

I hear more footsteps enter the house, and I know what's about to happen. They're sending me back to the white hospital with doors that don't lock, bathrooms that offer no privacy, women that scream in the hallways about rape and abuse. *You've got to be fucking kidding me.* I'm only here for a week, and I sure as shit am not spending it back in a psych ward. I've worked open the window and have my foot halfway out when two men burst through my door wearing the mint polos that have been branded in my memory.

My phone clatters from my pocket to the floor like the gun did last year. As it hits, it begins to buzz. Derek's photo lights up my screen with an incoming call. I look from the men to the phone, and that moment of hesitation screws me. Taking advantage, they wrangle me out of the window. I probably could have convinced my mother not to let them take me if it hadn't been for the next thing that caught my attention. If it hadn't been for the next words out of my mouth.

The man in the mint polo, leaving bruises on my arm, has a torn smile. The same torn smile that had been outside of the Kingsleys only hours ago.

"You. You were there at their house. You're not with the hospital. Why are you *here*?" I ask. The man looks at Michael with a bewildered expression. Michael shakes his head like I've proven his point.

"We see this a lot in patients when we bring them in. Their delusions grow stronger. You made the right call to get her treatment." He says to my stepdad, feigning confidence.

"Mom," I beg. "Mom, you can't let him take me. Something's not right. He was outside the Kingsley's earlier. He said he was with the gas company. Mom, please. Please." I cry.

She steps back from where she had been about to fight them on this. Shame and disappointment wreck her face, replacing the panic and outrage. My mother does not believe me.

"It's happening again, baby. Like last year, when you swore you saw Grey at the grocery store and came home trying to convince me he'd survived the fire. You're seeing things again. Ever since that boy broke up with you, you've started to lose reality again. Going back to that house and spending all that time there, I should have seen the signs. I thought I raised you to be stronger, Allyson." She says.

Then, she apologizes. I think she's saying sorry to me for doing this, but she's looking at Michael, and I realize she's apologizing for doubting his judgment. I watch all my chances of remaining free go down the drain, and I know our relationship will never heal. I'm being kidnapped and taken against my will in front of her, and she is letting it happen. I'm not sure which angle of the situation terrifies me the most.

In the van, a hand appears out of my peripheral vision before covering my mouth with a cloth. It smells sweet, too sweet. I vaguely remember the dentist's room at the hospital when I was a kid and how they'd gassed me before taking out my wisdom teeth. It's the last thing I think before I go unconscious.

now, march

WHEN I WAKE UP, I know I have been drugged. My head hurts, my brain pounding against my skull. The metal floor of the van is cold beneath my fingertips. I feel pain and extend my hand to touch the sore spot. It's wet. Sticky, like blood. I wonder if I fell once the chloroform took effect. If no one had bothered to catch me, I might have hit my head on the toolbox in the corner. It's too dark for me to make out if there is blood on it.

There is no medical equipment in the back of the van. My mom, Michael— neither had walked me out to see them load me. Had Michael been planning this since my return? I'd seen documentaries about camps where they sent off teens for rehabilitation. Was that what was happening? Was I about to be mistreated in the wilderness while they racked up money? I was twenty years old! How was this legal? It occurred to me that it probably wasn't.

I don't know what time it is or how long we've been driving. Voices chatter faintly from behind a partition separating me from the drivers. My hands have been bound in front of my body, giving me a limited range of motion.

Glancing around, I use my feet to push me toward the voices, toward the toolbox I'm hoping is loaded with makeshift weapons. A wrench could take out at least one of my abductors. I open the lid carefully and feel around. To my disappointment, it's full of items shaped like old baseball cards. Well, I can't papercut the men to death.

I try to lift the box, hoping to use *it*, but it's bolted in. There is nothing else. I test my restraints to see what kind of mobility I'll have when they finally open the door. It isn't much.

The confined air smells like animals, and it reminds me of a petting zoo. There are no other girls. In the movies, there's a shipping crate filled with girls. There's always more than one, but it's just me, and I'm alone. Perhaps this is the beginning, and I'm on my way to the crate, on my way to being trafficked. I try to stay awake, but my head is too fuzzy. My hope of fighting evaporates as I begin to fall back under the effects of the sedative.

* * *

A door opens in the distance, the metal making a nasty squeal as it rubs against something it shouldn't. Startling awake, I try to sit up again but get nowhere. Everything has succumbed to blackness, and I can't make out the details around me. It feels like fabric over my eyes, a blindfold, maybe.

With my other senses heightened, I pick up in perfect clarity the sharp snap of fingers issuing an order. Seconds later, two sets of hands tug at my arms, forcing me into a chair that splinters my thighs. Warmth pools around my upper legs. It's the feeling of blood pooling, as if the chair may have cut me.

The smell of manure infiltrates my nostrils—the smell of the farm animals from the van, but more robust and potent now that it's accompanied by the smell of mildew. When they remove the blindfold, it's the fuzzy boards I notice first. Black mold is staining and climbing all four walls of the structure, likely contributing to the smell I had recognized—the smell of rot.

The Man With the Torn Smile, I notice second. The ice of his gaze is precise and unforgiving. I realize it wasn't the sun that had made them feel so chilling before. It was something inside of him unfurling in their color. I'm uncomfortable when his stare holds mine.

"Miss Parish." The man says like he's entitled to my name and waits for me to respond. I don't. He continues. "I've waited a long time to meet you."

And it just got creepier. I scan my mind for repeat shoes, shirts, jackets— anything that indicates I may have seen the man before today. Stalkers usually don't have lackeys. CIA, then? But what the fuck would the CIA want with me? I still hadn't eliminated trafficking yet, but it seemed unlikely a trafficker would pick the words he'd chosen. I hope he takes my silence as a platform to start his bad-guy monologue.

'Bad-guy monologue' makes me want to laugh as this whole ordeal feels entirely made up, too out of a screenplay to be my reality.

"You connect them all, but as far as I can tell, you're not like them. What is it that's so interesting about you?" He studies me some more, slumping back into his chair, the only other chair in the room. *His* is finished, enviously smooth, and unsplintered.

I'm not holding my silence off principle; I just feel too weak. There's not enough energy to move the muscles in my mouth. Moving me showcased every part of my body that had been bruised. I didn't scream, but I fought like hell when they put me into that van. I was hoping I'd get to fight like hell when they took me out, too. I stop feeling angry and recall the details, committing anything to memory that could help me identify these men should I escape. The longer I remain quiet, the wider his Cheshire smile grows.

"Miss Parrish— *Ally*. Can I call you Ally?" He purrs. "I don't think you appreciate the gravity of the situation. No one knows where you are. Not your pathetic parents who *let* me come into your home and take you." He laughs as if delighting in the recollection.

"Your father was all too pleased to have you out of the way. I didn't even have to try, you know? Of course, I knew who you were, but I thought I'd have to track you down. It was my first day on this assignment, my first time going to the ruins of that house, and there you were like a fucking golden egg.

I found out your dad was part of the force, and that made him so easy to locate. There's an old cop bar down the highway from the station. Every town has one, where officers go after their shift. They'd rather drink than go home and fuck their wives." He chuckles darkly. I squirm in my chair, offended by his vulgarity.

"Again, I thought I'd have to wait for him to show up— an hour, a few days... but there he was! I walked in wearing the uniform to the rehab he had you committed to last year. I didn't even have to go over to him; he approached me! It was almost too damn easy."

I feel sick watching him cockily recount the events of my kidnapping in detail, proud of the endeavor. The feeling in the pit of my stomach turns from bad to worse. The men who committed me last time wore slacks, but this man wore dark jeans and black boots. My parents hadn't even noticed the difference. So easily, my mother had fallen into what Michael wanted her to believe. So easily, I had handed them all the proof they needed with my objections.

"Not even my bosses know you're here, Ally. Not even the Authority knows how far I've come on day fucking one. They underestimated me, but they won't make the same mistake after I break you. It's up to you how this goes, do you understand?"

How could I possibly understand? I understand this guy is an absolute psychopath, but what more is there? I don't understand anything about the Authority, how the ruins of the house tie in, or why I'm here. I open my mouth to tell him this, but words do not come out. It feels like an earthquake is shaking the room, and then I realize it isn't a fault line but my own body trembling.

He opens his mouth in an O, mocking me.

"I asked you a question. Do you understand?"

Nothing happens; I have become mute. Standing, he takes his time, removing his watch and placing it on a tray beside his chair. He rolls up his sleeves before coming closer, and the blow he delivers to my face is so swift that I don't have time to flinch before it lands.

"Now, do you understand?" He murmurs.

I nod.

"Great. Now, tell me about 4502 and 4503. Sorry, I forget." He rubs his forehead. "Tell me about the Kingsley's."

* * *

"Where are they now, Ally?" The Man With the Torn Smile questions.

Like all the previous times he has asked, and I have answered, I know he will not be satisfied because the Kingsleys are dead. If all my hopes and prayers could not bring them back, his torture surely won't.

They have been dead for over a year. It is what I have been telling The Man With the Torn Smile for hours now, but he has not been convinced regardless of how my lips have continued to echo the words "dead" and "gas leak."

"We scattered their ashes in Harper's Hope Cemetery." I choke out, hoping specificity will put an end to this.

I pray his anger has lessened since earlier. Earlier, when a pair of pliers appeared like an extension of his hand. When he built a sandcastle of my toenails in the dirt after he'd ripped them from my skin. The consequence of ten wrong answers.

My eye has swollen shut from his previous hit, but my good eye catches movement at the door. I scream a silent *Thank you!* in my mind.

"Everything we had on Allyson Parrish and everything I could find on who she was before." A short, stubby man, one of the men who had manhandled me into the chair, reappears, wobbling into the barn carrying a manila folder he hands off.

The Man With the Torn Smile has been waiting for this information, demonstrated by how he snatches the file from the short man's grasp. Stubby seems used to his temperament and quickly retreats to the door from which he entered. Whatever is going on, The Man With the Torn Smile is in charge. My hope of escape, or even survival, dwindles further. If no one is above him, there will be no one to intervene.

"Your file is thin, Songbird. They barely bothered to investigate you after the fire, did they?" He chuckles warmly.

It chills me to hear him laugh like we're old friends chatting over tea. He throws "Songbird" around casually like it wasn't stolen from the most intimate moments of my life. No one has used my dad's nickname for me since I was a kid. My file, thin or not, has already inflicted more pain than anything else he's done.

"Two years ago, we sent them to investigate you, and this is what they brought back." He throws the damning papers to the ground like they're trash. "Those amateurs bought right into the story exactly as your *Kingsleys* planned. I keep telling the Authority, 'Never send a Stolen to do a Created's work.' Maybe breaking you will be what finally digs in my point. Who knows? Anyways, I thought you'd be easy, Ally." A wicked toothy grin stretches across his face. "It pleases me that you're not. I'm a less than likable man when I have to suppress my gift." He leans forward, cracking his knuckles before standing.

His gift? Created? Stolen? His speech only gives me more questions.

The Man With the Torn Smile approaches me and slips a carabiner around the ties, binding my wrists. He uses an old pulley system rigged to the ceiling to hoist me from the chair until my feet hover above the ground and my arms fight against the weight they're being forced to carry. The cuffs slice deeper into my skin, drawing more blood. Warm lines streak down to my elbows. I imagine the scene from an outside perspective, the horror movie my life has spun into.

"They were idiots, the ones who interviewed you." he references. I think back to all the people I gave my witness testimony to. It was too many. Nurses, police officers, detectives in black suits.

"They didn't make the connection, but luckily, our research has been more thorough. I can't believe no one has caught on to it." He giggles in delight as he steps back into my personal space.

"Born with a seemingly rare degenerative bone disease. Miraculously recovered. Lived at the hospital where your very father worked as a physician. It's so startlingly obvious. To *me*, anyway. I had no idea quite how special you are, Songbird." His fingers graze my cheek, stirring my repulsion. He's learned what works and what tools he can use to break me. It's not the physical but the mental. Unfortunately for him, even broken, I won't be able to satisfy his question.

"Now, it'd be easier on both of us if you started being honest with me." He circles, grazing the bottom of my shirt before lifting it. I suck in a breath. His focus has been on causing hurt. I had never considered he would *touch* me. The idea of his body on mine makes me gag.

"There it is." He flicks the spot between my L3 and L4 vertebra. The relief I feel upon knowing he doesn't wish to touch me as I had imagined is quickly replaced by understanding what he does wish to do. He walks back to the table by his chair and takes hold of a needle I hadn't paid attention to before.

"You remember what a spinal tap feels like, yes?"

I squirm into unnatural positions to get away because I *do* remember what a spinal tap feels like.

The scar on my shoulder burns as it always does when I'm anxious. In this scenario, the burning has acted as an unusual ally. Its pain is familiar and trustworthy. I've been leaning into it when worse things threaten to overtake me.

Before today, I hated my scar. It had acted like a curse. A rune melted into my flesh; it was a constant reminder that they perished while I had lived and how, in one night, 'Parrish' had become such a fitting name for me.

I had thought nothing could be done to me that would hurt as bad as losing the Kingsleys, but the idea of this man anywhere near Derek, Riley, or Libby— has me desperate.

Part of me hopes he will just kill me and get it over with. Dead, he'd have no reason to torture the people I care about. Dead, he'd have nothing to use against me. Nothing more to gain, as he's gained nothing already but a waste of his time.

"Let's run it through again. You, a seemingly nobody seventeen-year-old girl, ran into a burning building and emerged a valiant hero. Trying and failing to save those you loved. It's truly a great cover story." He paces the floor before me, stroking his chin like a scientist trying to solve a problem. His current pose is studious. His back bent as if his bones had become flimsy and taken on the characteristics of another man. Only his cruel words remain a tell of his rotten nature.

"I mean, what kind of people would have left you there to burn while they went on to live their lives? How could they have cared so little about you to go and do a thing like that? I'm just not buying that *you* don't know. They didn't die in that house fire. So, I'm going to ask you one more time— where are they now?" The jack-o-lantern grin sneaks back across his face, and with it, I lose all hope that he'll end the inquisition quickly. He genuinely still believes I'm lying. Or he's just having fun. There is relief in neither.

The needle begins to press into my skin, and I cry out, the blackness starting to form around the edges of my vision. The pain is too much combined with all the other injuries I've sustained.

There is a commotion outside, and The Man With the Torn Smile curses under his breath. Reluctantly, he removes the needle before it gets too deep and leaves to investigate.

I'm on the brink of passing out, too exhausted to care. The world has lost its volume. I'm dizzy, the air too thick to breathe right, I'm going to lose consciousness. I feel no fear. I'm praying for the escape. My wish is granted for a few moments, and I wake up too soon wishing I hadn't woken at all. I don't want to do it anymore. The questions, the blinding pain, any of it. I'd rather die asleep in peace. If this 'Authority' he's referred to has arrived, they will be worse.

My eyes barely open, and I give up trying to force them. I let myself drift in and out of awareness. Even when I'm lowered from the suspensions and hands work at my wrists to get off my restraints, I don't open them. Let them think I'm already gone.

Someone lifts me off the ground, and I'm wrapped in warm arms. The sunlight is too bright. With my eyes closed, the red glow appears behind my lids. I bury my face into the shoulder of the muscular person carrying me. I'm not sure if I'm being rescued or relocated, but I'm sure the man holding me is not The Man With the Torn Smile. He's too gentle.

My curiosity gets the best of me, and I dare to peek out. I catch a glimpse of my torturer as we pass over his lifeless body. He's in a limp pile a few yards from the barn with a bullet hole in his forehead. They must have used a silencer, as I never heard any shots. Even in death, his eyes look the same. Cold and empty in both states. His broken smile stretches across his face as if to taunt me one last time. It works. I shiver despite the warmth of the early day and tuck my head back down. My rescuer's arms tighten around me in a gesture of reassurance.

I pretend it's Derek carrying me. That he tracked me down to wherever the hell this is and that we're going home now. The thought is a nice reprieve, and I try to disappear into it completely. I imagine ice water, flowers, and so much music. One of Derek's old piano compositions floats around in my memory and is the soundtrack to our departure. I inhale deeply, hoping for citrus and bergamot, ginger and clove, hotel sheets, and safety. I'm met with the smell of woods, earthy like the forest. It's comforting but not exactly right.

"It's all wrong." I sigh, muffled by the man's jacket. I don't have to be cautious of the slip. What does it matter now?

A door opens to a vehicle, and we climb in the back. The man doesn't situate me in my own seat. Instead, he keeps me in his lap, his arms locked around my frame. As much as I want it to be Derek, I know it's not. Still, I force myself to check.

I try again to peer out. From where my head rests on the man's shoulder, I am at eye-level with his Adam's apple. This man's skin is much too tan to be Derek's. I don't tip my head back to steal a look at his face. There's no one else I'd rather see, so there is no point.

"Drive, " he orders, and his raspy voice reverberates throughout his chest as we start to move. My hand reaches for his chin, quickly finding the familiar half-moon beneath my fingertips.

"I've got you, Al. You're safe now." He whispers into my hair.

"At least it was a quick death," I whisper back and breathe him in more deeply. I should have recognized the cedar wood. I relax, melting into his chest. This was worth it. The torture was worth it to feel this one more time.

"Quicker than he deserved." He says quietly with a sharpness I recognize from the first night he accosted me in his kitchen centuries ago. It's been so long since then. I have so much to tell him.

"I meant mine, you silly walrus." I choke out. My throat hurts from screaming. Maybe I'm not dead yet. If these are my final moments, hallucinating something even more impossible than Derek, I'm okay with it. His laugh is too low of a rumble compared to what I remember. It's dulled somehow. Maybe I can't remember it right anymore.

"Don't try to talk. You're not dying today, Ally. Get that idea out of your head." He says softly. Wait—*what?*

I force my eyes open and drop my hand. Apple eyes stare back at me. I can validate this is reality because he looks so different, yet the same. There's a hardness to him that wasn't there before. His hair is gone. His shoulders have filled out more. I couldn't have imagined him like this. Or alive. Or here.

"Grey."

acknowledgments

First and foremost, I'd like to extend the warmest thank you to my editor, Morgan Smith. Thank you for putting up with me through the many long nights spent lounging in your living room with your cats and Magni, where I rambled nonsensically about these characters when they were still just an idea in my head. Thank you for helping me work out their stories and making them come to life much more eloquently than I ever could have put together on my own.

Your support and excitement throughout this drawn-out, and at times tedious, process is what has driven me to complete it at all. Thank you. I will be forever grateful to call you my editor. I will forever be honored to call you my friend.

To my father, who very much acted as my inspiration behind so many characters. For being my guiding compass, my forever teacher, and only ever breaking one promise to me. Thank you for forgetting the Oreos and giving me so many lovely stories that I was able to pour into this book. And OH MY GOD, THANK YOU for allowing me to white out and revise your personal copy. I love you, always.

To my mother, who used to have me refer to her as her alias "Carol" when she grew tired of hearing "Mom. Mom. Mom." Thank you for your colorful personality and wild disposition, for always putting me first, for believing in me, and for not being the Carol in this book.

Thank you to all my grandparents, who have loved,

encouraged, and supported me in so many ways over the years. You gave me a home to write in and a safe place to dream.

Adelle, for being my first friend in a scary new place. For getting drunk with me on my birthday and flying me out to California to surf with the seals. You are an absolute firecracker, and I am so very lucky to know you. Jacob, for letting me use your name and making me laugh too many nights when I was down. You are such a free spirit, going wherever life takes you. Inspiring me every day to just do the damn thing and not be afraid. Thank you both for pulling Riley to life and making him my favorite.

Leslie, you were there with me through my darkest times. Without you, there might not have been me, and there definitely wouldn't have been a book. Thank you for driving to my house in the middle of the night and always being there when I needed you most.

Dee, thank you for driving twelve hours with me to Princeton just to get a sweatshirt. Thank you for being a kind and loyal light in the world, and thank you for all your bubbly brilliance.

Ci, thank you for being my escape from reality so many times, for being my inspiration behind the confessions with our balcony honesty, overlooking the lights of D.C., and for never judging me.

Carlos, thank you for being my own personal Duke, for never getting angry, and for constantly reminding me of who I am.

Dennis, thank you for always being there. You were the first person I ever spoke with freely about my idea for this story, up in my bed, in the house in the trees. Thank you for making me feel safe so often when nothing else could. Thank you for loving me more every year.

Katie, you were my very first reader back when I was carrying around a binder full of lyrics. I still have your notes in a box that you would hide between the pages, telling me all the things you loved about them. Thank you for being one of my very first readers yet again. You were *my* Charlie.

Jerell, who indulged my constant rants at work while I struggled with synonyms or wording. For often being the first person I shared each part of my creation with. And for bragging about me to too many customers who didn't care or *need* to know that I was a writer. Thank you for being my partner and buddy and always making me feel appreciated.

I sincerely appreciate all my beta readers: Renee, Kelly, Isabelle, Sarah, and Desiree. Your comments gave me so much confidence in moving forward with this. I loved your guesses, conspiracy theories, and lewd commentary. I can't wait to share the next book with you all first.

To the incredible artists who provided me with so many amazing options for my cover: AI_Lani, Sabina, and Akar.std. And to the talented Ian Janco for bringing my song to life in the video promo. You all turned my vision into reality, and I'm so grateful.

Finally, thank you to all the boys who broke my heart. Thank you for inspiring the pain and breakups in this story. Without your choices, I wouldn't be the woman I am today, and I wouldn't have this story I'm so deeply proud of.